Also by Hugh Rawson

Wicked Words

A Dictionary of Euphemisms & Other Doubletalk

A Dictionary of Quotations from Shakespeare
(with Margaret Miner)

A Dictionary of Quotations from the Bible
(with Margaret Miner)

The New International Dictionary of Quotations
(with Margaret Miner)

An Investment in Knowledge
(with Hillier Krieghbaum)

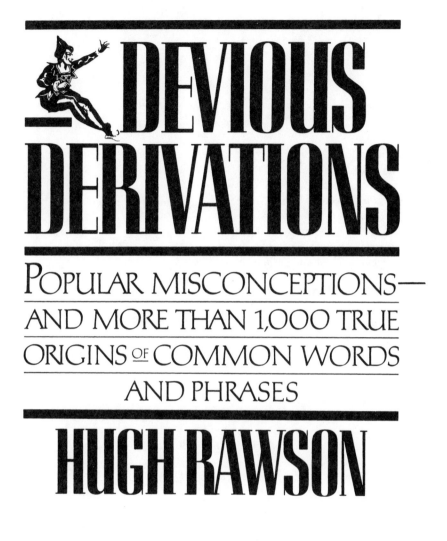

DEVIOUS DERIVATIONS

POPULAR MISCONCEPTIONS—AND MORE THAN 1,000 TRUE ORIGINS OF COMMON WORDS AND PHRASES

HUGH RAWSON

CASTLE BOOKS

This edition published in 2002 by
CASTLE BOOKS ®
A division of Book Sales, Inc.
114 Northfield Avenue, Edison, NJ 08837

Published by arrangement with and permission of
Hugh Rawson, through the author's literary representative, Multimedia
Product Development, Inc., of Chicago, Illinois.

Originally published by Crown Publishers, Inc.
Crown is a trademark of Crown Publishers, Inc.

Random House, Inc. New York, Toronto, London, Sydney, Auckland

Library of Congress Cataloging-in-Publication Data
Rawson, Hugh.
    Devious Derivations : popular misconceptions—and more than
 1,000 true origins of common words and phrases / Hugh Rawson.
    Includes bibliographical references and index.
    1. English language——Etymology—Folklore—Dictionaries.
  2. English language—Etymology—Dictionaries. I. Title
PE1584.R38   1994
422'.03—dc20
92-34135
CIP

ISBN: 0-7858-1700-X

Printed in the United States of America

To Jo, Sarah,
and Butch

O, tis a precious apothegmaticall Pedant, who will finde matter inough to dilate a whole day of the first invention of *Fy, fa, fum,* I smell the bloud of an English-man.

Thomas Nasche,
Have with you to Saffon-walden, 1596

AN INTRODUCTION TO FOLK ETYMOLOGY

The fact is, man is an etymologizing animal. He abhors the vacuum of an unmeaning word. If it seems lifeless, he reads a new soul into it, and often, like an unskillful necromancer, spirits the wrong soul into the wrong body.
The Reverend A. Smythe Palmer, Folk-Etymology, *1890*

ONE OF THE most basic of all human traits is the urge to find reasons for why things are as they are. Ancient peoples heard thunder and created gods of thunder. They witnessed the change of seasons, and devised stories to explain the coming of winter and the miraculous rebirth of spring. The tendency is universal, appearing in every aspect of human thought and endeavor. Including etymology.

People cannot resist making up explanations for the origins of words and phrases. Their theories are at once a reflection of the general reluctance to accept uncertainty and a tribute to their powers of creativity. As in the case of the thunder gods, however, the initial hypothesis—and the second and third, for that matter—may not be correct. In their effort to describe how certain words have come to be, people have devised some very curious explanations indeed—real "beauts," as Fiorello La Guardia once said of one his own mistakes.

The "beauts" are the stuff of popular, or folk, etymology, as distinguished from the rigorous linguistic detective work that scholars do, or are supposed to do. But the popular beliefs are worth studying, and not just for their own entertaining sake. Many common words and phrases have been shaped in form and meaning by mistaken notions about their origins. Collectively, these devious derivations also tell us something about the way people think.

For example, people are prone to draw false conclusions on the basis of superficial resemblances. This probably is the most common form of folk etymology. The tendency is especially evident in the case of foreign words that have been changed to sound more like familiar English terms. In the process, a new, "more logical" origin of the term emerges.

1

For example, a *belfry* is so-called because it is a bell tower, a good habitat for bats. Right? No, a belfry doesn't have anything to do with bells. The word actually comes from the French *berfroi*, a wooden siege tower. Similarly, *briar pipes* are not made from briars, but rather from the roots of white heather (*bruyère* in French). The hooped frame for a skirt, known as a *farthingale*, never cost as little as a farthing (one-fourth of a penny); the term for this fashion accessory comes from the Spanish *verdugado*, green stick, referring to the pliable cane from which early farthingales were constructed. A *lemon sole* is not a sole but a flatfish (*limande* in French). And while a *ten-gallon hat* looks as though it could hold a lot of water, the name does not allude to its carrying capacity but to its manner of decoration, deriving from the Mexican Spanish *sombrero galón*, hat with braids.

False conclusions about the origins of words also arise—and their meanings sometimes are affected—as a result of the conversion of Anglo-Saxon and other older English terms into modern parlance. Thus a *crayfish* is not a fish but a crustacean (from the Middle English *crevis*, crab). A *helpmate* may be both a help and a mate, but the word is a corruption of *help meet*, meaning a suitable helper, which is what the Lord apparently intended when He said that He would make Adam "an help meet for him" (*Genesis*, 2:18). *Hopscotch* has nothing to do intrinsically with kids in kilts; *scotch* here is a moderately antique word for a cut, incision, or scratch, perhaps deriving from the Anglo-French *escocher*, to notch or nick. (*Butterscotch* is a related term, from the cutting or scoring of the candy into squares.)

By the same token, people who eat *humble pie* may have been humbled, but only figuratively. The name of the dish comes from *umbles*, meaning the liver, heart, and other edible animal innards. *An umble pie* originally was *a numble pie*, the article and the noun having been re-divided over the years, in the same way that *a nadder, a napron*, and *a noumpere* became *an adder, an apron*, and *an umpire*. (This is a two-way street: *a newt* started out as *an ewt*, and *a nickname* is not, as might first appear, nicked or clipped from a true name, but a redivision of *an eke-name*—that is, an "also-name.")

The conversion of words from foreign languages into English and from older forms of English into newer ones frequently results in unconscious redundancies. For example, *foremost*, which looks as though it was a combination of *fore* and *most*, actually comes from the superlative of the Anglo-Saxon *forma*, first, so the oratorical cliché "first and foremost" really amounts to "first and first." Similarly, "please pass

2

the salt cellar" translates as "please pass the salt salt," since *cellar* here derives from the Latin *salaria*, pertaining to salt, and bears no real relationship to the *cellar* that is a wine cellar, root cellar, or other below-ground storage area. Then there is, or was, Ethelred the Unready, who was not so much unready as heedless, acting without proper Anglo-Saxon *rede*, counsel. Moreover, his name, Ethelred, and eke-name, Unready, constitute a contradiction in terms, for *Ethelred* means "noble counsel." Thus, *Ethelred the Unready* signifies "Noble-counsel Without Counsel."

In seeking to explain the origins of words, people tend to come up with the same kinds of answers over and over again. These themes reflect ways of thinking that are so common, so comfortable, so easy to fall into, that they should be guarded against in real life as well as etymology. Consider the following half dozen categories of word explanations:

Imaginary eponyms. This is the "great man" school of etymology. It represents the common desire to pin responsibility—whether blame or credit—for complex events on the shoulders of particular individuals. Thus, it has been hypothesized that *blanket* is named for a fourteenth-century weaver in England; that *bogus* comes from the name of a forger who operated in the American Southwest in the 1850s; that *condom* comes from a Doctor or Colonel Condom, who invented the article during the reign of Charles II; that *harlot* derives from Arlette, the unmarried mother of William the Bastard, who became William the Conqueror; and that the original *Nosey Parker* was Matthew Parker, Archbishop of Canterbury in the time of Elizabeth I.

Sometimes, it is true, the popularity of a word may have been assisted by identification with a real person. For example, *hooker* in the sense of "prostitute" does not come from General Joseph Hooker, of Civil War fame (the word pre-dates the conflict), but the general's relaxed morals—his headquarters were said to be a combination barroom and brothel—may well have given the term a boost. Meanwhile, the dissemination of *crap* probably was aided by the career of the eminent English sanitary engineer, Thomas Crapper (1837–1910), but the word itself was in use prior to 1882, when Crapper invented the Valveless Water Waste Preventer, his key contribution to toilet technology.

The detection of imaginary eponyms is complicated, of course, by the existence of many words that do derive from the names of real people. Amelia Bloomer, the Reverend William Bowdler, Captain William Boycott, Nicolas Chauvin, and Rudolf Diesel all existed. And every once in a while, just often enough to make one very cautious, it turns out that a real individual lurks behind a word that has been assumed to have another origin. For example, *flack*, meaning a publicity agent, apparently comes from the name of a real one, Gene Flack, not, as long thought, from *flak*, the World War II acronym for the German *flieger-abwehrkanone*, antiaircraft fire. Also, the evidence suggests that the *bowler* hat is named not for its shape but for its inventor, a Mr. Bowler, who had a shop in London at 15 St. Swithin's Lane in the 1880s.

Spurious acronyms. Sheer delight in wordplay has inspired many false folk etymologies. Next to breaking a code, what most people like, it seems, is to make one up. Thus, *cabal* has been interpreted as an acronym formed from the first letters of the last names of five of Charles II's ministers: Clifford, Arlington, Buckingham, Ashley, and Lauderdale; *cop* has been described as standing for Chief Of Police or Constable On Patrol; *news* as deriving from North, East, West, South; and *wop* as coming from WithOut Passport, WithOut Papers, and even Working On Pavement.

Perhaps the two most famous spurious acronyms are *posh* and *tip*. The true origin of the first is uncertain; it may derive from the earlier slang use of *posh* to mean a dandy. But it certainly does not come from *P.O.S.H.*, for Port Out Starboard Home, said to have been printed—in violet ink, yet—on tickets of the Peninsular and Oriental Steam Navigation Co. The line, which plied the route between England and India, continued in business up to 1970, but no one has yet found a ticket stub with *P.O.S.H.* upon it, nor have searches of company records uncovered any hint of the use of the abbreviation.

As for *tip*, meaning the extra money given to cabbies, waiters, and others in the so-called "service" occupations, it often is said to stand for To Insure Promptness. The letters, according to the standard folk account, were written originally on offering boxes in eighteenth-century inns and coffeehouses. Such a box would make an excellent addition to any curio collection, but alas, none have been found. More likely, the *tip* that is a gratuity is an alteration of *tap* in the sense of a light blow, a touch.

So strong is the desire to find acronyms where none exist that the Morse code distress call, *S.O.S.*, which is merely an easy-to-send series of alternating groups of three dots and three dashes, has been "explained" as meaning Stop Other Signals, Save Our Ship, and Save Our

Souls. (The last of these theories was presented in passing as fact by the British Attorney-General at the inquiry into the sinking of the *Titanic!*)

Geographic ghosts. Words that are associated falsely with place names account for another important subdivision of folk etymologies. Again, the issue is complicated by the existence of many terms that are derived legitimately from the names of cities and other places. Thus, *denim* does come from *d'Nîmes;* soft-nosed *dum-dum* bullets were manufactured first at the British arsenal at *Dum Dum,* a town near Calcutta; and *jeans* do come from *Genoa.* On the other hand . . . *diaper* derives from the Medieval Greek *diaspros,* pure white, not from the Belgian city Ypres (i.e., *d'Ypres*); *sedan* probably comes from an Italian dialect word related to *sede,* chair, rather than from the French city of that name; *tariff,* though of Arabic origin, does not derive from *Tarifa,* a port near Gibraltar, long occupied by the Moors; and *tobacco* does not emanate—linguistically at least—from the island of Tobago.

The folk also have made their fair share of mistakes by assigning place names incorrectly. For example, the *turkey* bears an Old World name though it is a New World native, while the *guinea pig,* originally from South America, has been associated mistakenly with the *Guinea* coast of West Africa. At the same time, the geographic roots of other words have been overlooked. Thus, *bridewell,* now a general term for a prison, comes from St. Bridget's well in London, while *clink,* also meaning a jail, does not refer to the shutting of cell doors in a slammer, but to a particular penal institution, The Clink, in sixteenth-century London.

Erudite errors. In etymology, as in real life, people often outwit themselves. Realizing that superficial resemblances between words frequently are misleading, learned folk sometimes strain to produce complicated explanations where simpler ones would do. Thus, *bear garden,* meaning a place where bears are kept and, by extension, a scene of strife and tumult, probably does not come from the German *biergarten,* where the uproar is alcoholic; the traditional British fondness for keeping bears, and baiting them, provides sufficient explanation for the English term. Nor is it necessary to suppose that *bloody* is a contraction of *By Our Lady, God's blood,* or some similar exclamation, considering the strong reaction that many people have to the mere sight of blood. And *sincere* is much more likely to come directly from the

Latin *sincerus*, whole, pure, untainted, than from *sine cērā*, without wax, a phrase that supposedly was used by marble dealers in ancient Rome to indicate that the fine polish on the stone had not been faked.

Great men make great mistakes, and some of the erudite "beauts" comes from grand masters of lexicography.

Samuel Johnson, arguably the greatest dictionary maker of them all, tripped occasionally on his etymologies. He asserted, for instance, that the *bon* in *bonfire* came from the French word for "good," apparently unaware that the earliest examples of the word's use show clearly that these conflagrations originally were *bone fires.*

The Reverend Richard Chenevix Trench, godfather of the monumental *Oxford English Dictionary* (he blocked out the plan for it), managed to avoid the seemingly straightforward conclusion that the *Beefeaters* who guard the Tower of London eat beef. Instead, the Reverend Trench, along with other erudite types, construed *Beefeater* as an Anglicization of the French *buffetier*, keeper of a cupboard—a theory that is rather weakened by the failure of French philologists to find any examples of *buffetier* on their side of the Channel. It apparently is a nonword.

Another distinguished philologist, the Reverend Walter W. Skeat, made a long detour into the past to find a source for *dressed to the nines*, which he explained as a redivision of the Anglo-Saxon *(dressed) to then eyne*, dressed to the eyes. The chief difficulty with this theory (and a common one when tracing word origins) is the silence of the centuries, in this case from Anglo-Saxon times to 1820, when the phrase is first recorded as appearing in print in the form of *togged out to the nines*. While the literary record of word use is admittedly and sadly incomplete (etymologists are in much the same position as paleontologists, who have to deduce the histories of species on the basis of randomly preserved fossils), ten centuries between *then eyne* and *the nines* suggests that the phrase arose in another way. *Dressed to the nines* may be an offshoot of *up to the nines*, used earlier to mean "excellent" or "to perfection."

False refinement. A great many words have low origins, and etymologists, amateur and professional alike, often go out of their way to avoid any hint of indelicacy. For example, determined efforts have been made to relate *ball up* to the tendency of new-fallen snow to clump up beneath snowshoes and horses' hooves, and to connect the *-skite* in the talkative *blatherskite* to a fish, the skate, in preference to *skite* or *skyte*, Scottish variants of a well-known word for excrement. Even so great a jurist as

Sir William Blackstone shielded his eyes from the anatomical *bum* in *bumbailiff*, deriving the term instead from *bound bailiff*, although this minion of the law, who serves warrants and makes arrests, typically nabs his man by the seat of his pants.

The list of nervous-nellie etymologies is long. For instance:

The *grass widow*, divorced or otherwise separated from her husband, is not termed a widow by French *grâce*, as if this were a courtesy title. Rather, the *grass* harks back to the expression's earlier meanings, when it referred to unmarried mothers and discarded mistresses. The original implication, then, was that the woman had roamed, like a horse turned out to grass, or had made her bed upon it.

Pumpernickel does not come from a remark attributed to Napoleon, *pain pour Nicol*, bread for Nicol, supposedly uttered when the Emperor, regarding the dark bread as unfit for human consumption, gave a loaf to his horse instead of eating it himself. Actually, the *pumper-* is from the German *pumpern*, to break wind, and the name of the bread refers to its common physiological effect.

Shyster frequently is said to come from the name of a real person, a notably sleazy lawyer named Scheuster, who supposedly practiced in New York City in the 1840s. It has been established that no such person existed, however. The word is basically German, deriving from *scheisser*, an incompetent fellow, particularly one who cannot control his bodily functions. The root is *scheisse*, shit.

More examples can easily be added. *Clinchpoop*, an old epithet for a boor or lout, probably does not have anything to do with clinching nails on the poops of vessels. *Spitting image* as a metaphor for physical identity almost certainly has more to do with saliva than—the cleaned-up explanation of the phrase's origin—*spirit and image*. *Tinker's dam* and the folk etymology offered for it—a temporary wall of dough used by tinkers when repairing pots and pans—has the earmarks of a euphemism for the profane *tinker's damn*. And so it goes in the Department of False Refinement.

The love of storytelling. The "vacuum of an unmeaning word," as the Reverend A. Smythe Palmer put it in his pioneering work in the field, *Folk-Etymology* (1890), often evokes stories that have been embellished with considerable detail to give them an air of authenticity. For example:

A poetic tale relates *gringo* to Spanish speakers hearing Yankee soldiers singing "Green grow the rashes [rushes], O," as they marched into Mexico during the war of 1846–48. But *gringo* has been dated to 1787 and most likely comes from the Spanish *griego*, Greek, the reference being to English and other foreigners whose efforts to speak Spanish were as incomprehensible to the Spanish as if they were speaking Greek.

Marmalade is reported popularly but on no good authority to come from *Marie malade*, referring to Mary, Queen of Scots, who supposedly developed a craving for this fruit concoction whenever she was *malade*, ill. In truth, however, the word derives from the French *marmelade*, quince jam, and ultimately from the Greek *melimēlon*, honey apple, originally meaning an apple grafted upon a quince tree.

Quiz is said to have sprung full-blown from the brow of James Daley, a theater manager in Dublin who made a bet in 1791 that he could introduce a new word into the language within twenty-four hours, then won the wager by hiring street arabs to write "quiz" on walls all over town. "What's a 'quiz'?" everybody is said to have asked the next day. Perhaps Mr. Daley, like General Hooker, helped popularize the term. It has been dated in writing to before 1791, however.

Then there is that famous knight of the table, *Sir Loin*. The cut of meat was dubbed a knight by—depending on which version of the story one prefers to believe—Henry VIII, James I, or Charles II. The story is practically as old as the word itself. The poet John Taylor referred to "Sir Loyne of Beefe" back in 1630. The oft-told tale stems from the confusion that occurs when foreign words are assimilated into English (as in the case of *belfry*, *briar pipe*, etc.). In this instance, the English associated the French *sur*, above (as in *surlonge*, above the loin), with the "Sir" of knighthood.

A number of the stories about word origins began as jokes, which then took on lives of their own. Thus, the original suggestion that *jingo* (probably a euphemistic deformation of "Jesus") derives from St. Gengulphus was made with tongue firmly fixed in cheek. The same applies to some of the many guesses about the origin of *Yankee*, such as the assertions that it comes from the name of an Indian tribe, the *Yankoos* (i.e., Invincible Ones), or from the Persian *janghe* or *jenghe*, as in Jenghis (i.e., Yankee!) Khan. Nevertheless, these and other equally improbable etymologies have been accepted by some as gospel.

A good story that explains a mystery is irresistible. The folk do not like to live in doubt, and only the rare individual will admit so candidly to lack of knowledge as did Samuel Johnson, when queried about a mistake in his *Dictionary of the English Language* (1755): the fault, he confessed, was due to "ignorance, pure ignorance." See PESTER for details.

8

A

adultery. You have to be *adult* to commit *adultery*, but that is about the only thing the two words have in common, despite the perhaps apocryphal story of the au pair girl who told a friend that she worked in a household that included two children, one adult, and an adulteress. *Adultery* stems from the Latin *adulterāre*, to corrupt, to pollute, to commit adultery, while *adult* comes from the Latin *adultus*, which is the past participle of *adolescere*, to grow up, to mature, that is, to become *adolescent*. The Latin ancestor of *adultery* also produced *adulterate*, now used most often as a verb to refer to the debasing of materials or elements by mixing them with inferior substances, but which once enjoyed a sexier meaning. Thus, in Shakespeare's *King John* (1594–97?), Constance, Countess of Brittany, tells her son Arthur that fickle fortune—also termed "that strumpet Fortune"—"is corrupted, changed, and won from thee; Sh' adulterates hourly with thine uncle John."

agita. This is a relatively new word in English (from ca. 1985), but already the folk etymologists have mangled it almost beyond recognition. The term does not mean "agitated," as one might well assume when encountering it in such a context as a *New York Times* column by Anna Quindlen about New York Governor Mario Cuomo: "He communicates the agita of the immigrant child who simultaneously sees the dream gone wrong and believes it can come true" (8/17/91).

The erroneous impression of the word's meaning stems from a spelling mistake, made when attempting to render into American English the Italian *AH-jah-da*, which is the southern pronunciation of the Tuscan *acido*, pronounced *AH-chee-doe*. The trail now becomes a lot clearer. *Acido* is acid—stomach acid in this case. In a letter to the *Times* (9/11/91), Peter D'Epiro explained that *agita* could be used in three senses:

(1) acid indigestion or heartburn, as in "No, thanks—health food gives me agita"; (2) the gastrointestinal afflictions we experience while fretting over an outcome that means a lot to us, such as whether the Internal Revenue Service will notice that $13,000 deduction for work-related expenses; (3) the plunge in stomach pH

caused by having to deal with an exasperating or otherwise unpleasant person, as in "You know what? You give me agita!"

To avoid confusion, Mr. D'Epiro suggested that the *Times* and other setters of style steer clear of *agita*, rendering the word as *acida* to reflect the southern Italian pronunciation and always italicizing it as a foreign term. He is probably fighting a losing battle, however, considering how quickly English absorbs foreign words and how often spellings and meanings have been changed in the past to make strange terms seem more like native ones. For example, see BOOTS AND SADDLES, FURBELOW, and WISEACRE.

albatross. The name of the bird often is associated with its color, as though the word came from Latin *albus*, white. The term actually is of Arabic origin, however, coming into English via Portuguese. The original Arabic word was *al-ghaṭṭis*, sea eagle, in turn from *al-qādūs*, a bucket or other vessel for raising water. The bird's name stemmed from the belief that adult pelicans carried water in their huge bills to their children in the desert. The Portuguese converted the bird's Arabic name into *alcatraz* (hence the name of the island in San Francisco Bay, once the site of a famous prison and home to many pelicans as well as to jailbirds). English voyagers then proceeded to render the Portuguese word in various ways, as *alcatras, algatross, albetross,* and *albitross,* and to apply it by mistake to other sea birds, especially the frigate bird, which is smaller than the albatross and black. The present spelling of the word, dating from the late seventeenth century, and the shift in its meaning to denote the present family of large white birds, almost certainly is due to the influence of the Latin *albus*.

anadama bread. A number of stories have been created to explain the name of the yeast-raised bread featuring cornmeal and molasses. All of them revolve around a Yankee housewife named Anna. In one version, she was the wife of a fisherman who always served her husband cornmeal mush and molasses for dinner. Getting tired of this, one night he added some flour and yeast and baked the concoction, all the time muttering "Anna, damn her." In another version, Anna walked out on her farmer husband in the middle of preparing a meal. Left with a batch of cornmeal mush, he finished making the bread himself, while grumbling "Anna, damn her; Anna, damn her." Then there was the sea captain's wife, who is said to have baked numerous loaves of this bread before her husband went on a voyage because it kept for a long time without molding or spoiling. The captain, according to this account, habitually referred to his wife as "Anna, damn'er," with the result that his crews began calling the staple "Anna damn'er's bread."

The stories about Anna and her fisherman–farmer–sea captain husband reek of folk etymology, but they persist and have become enshrined in various cookbooks if only because the real story of the origin of the name of the bread isn't known. Even the age of the recipe is something of a mystery. From the ingredients, it would appear to date to colonial times. Yet the earliest known written reference to it in the *Dictionary of American Regional English* comes from as recently as 1915 in the form of a recipe for "Ammy Dammy bread" at the Old Salem Tavern in Massachusetts.

anchorite (anchoret). Similarity to the marine *anchor* has caused confusion from an early date about the origin of this term for a religious recluse or hermit. Thus, the *Ancren Riwle* (Rule of the Nuns), composed about 1225, holds that an *anchoress* (a female *anchorite*) was so called because she served as an anchor for the church: "Even so all holy church, which is called a ship, shall anchoresses, or the anchor, so hold, that the devil's puffs, which are temptations, may not overthrow it." A pretty metaphor, but the word actually comes from the Greek *anakhōrein*, to withdraw (as from the world).

andiron. The name of the one of a pair of stands for holding logs in a fireplace has nothing to do with *iron*, though the objects usually are made of that metal (or brass). The word comes from the Old French *andier*, whose ending sounded to the English like their word for the metal, with the result that they transmuted the borrowed term into *aundyrne, aundiren*, and, by the middle of the fifteenth century, *andiron*.

The origin of *andier* itself is uncertain. Because early andirons often were ornamented with the heads of animals, a Gaulish root, *andero-*, bullock, has been proposed. The hypothetical Gaulish term would be akin to such known words as the Breton *annoer*, heifer, and the Old Irish *ainder*, young woman. Which is something to think about next time you toss a log on the fire. See also GRIDIRON.

angel. Reaching far back into history, some have suggested that *angel* in the sense of a person who backs a play or other theatrical production is an eponym, honoring Luis de Santangel, who raised the funds that enabled Christopher Columbus to make his great voyage of discovery in 1492. The *angel* with deep pockets doesn't appear in the written record, however, until almost four hundred years after Columbus set sail. The term is American slang, not Spanish, with the earliest example in *The Oxford English Dictionary* coming from 1891. It is almost certainly an extension of the idea of the older (from the eighteenth century, at least) *guardian angel*. As for Santangel, a confidante of Queen Isabella and keeper of King Ferdinand's privy purse, he helped convince the Queen to authorize Columbus's expedition. Isabella did offer to pledge her crown jewels against the expenses, but—something history books tend to leave out—Santangel told her that wouldn't be necessary, so the jewels were never actually in hock for the mariner's sake. See also FARTHINGALE.

antelope. The deerlike animal is famous for running with long, easy strides, but its name has nothing to do with how it *lopes* along. *Antelope* comes from *antalops*, the name of a fierce but mythical creature that supposedly lived near the River Euphrates. The antalops figured in medieval bestiaries and heraldry. Thus, from a translation by T. H. White of a twelfth-century manuscript: "The Antalops is an animal of incomparable celerity, so much so that no hunter can ever get near it. It has long horns shaped like a saw, with the result that it can cut down even very large trees and fell them to the ground" (*The Bestiary*, 1954). Unfortunately, the antalops also liked to play with a shrub that had "subtile, long twigs," sometimes entangling its horns so thoroughly that it could not get free. Then the animal would bellow, hunters would hear it, and they would come and kill it. White suggests that the antalops probably was an elk, eland, or reindeer. The original author of the medieval bestiary converted the natural history into a religious fable: The animal's horns were the two testaments with which the man of God could saw off fleshly vices, the entangling shrubs were alcohol and lust, the hunter was the devil, and the moral was the standard one that "Wine and Women are great turners-away from God."

The oldest example of the animal name in the *OED* comes from a poem that was written about 1430. All the early references are to the mythical animal, with *antelope* in the modern sense not appearing until 1607. The ultimate source of the word is a mystery. The medieval *antalops* stems from the Late Greek *anthólops* (from ca. 336), itself a word of unknown origin. Whatever, it is most definitely not related to *lope*, which comes from the Old Norse *hlaupa*, to leap. See also ELOPE.

apple-pie order. Apple pie is a classic American dish, but *apple-pie order*, meaning to have everything neat and in perfect condition, is a British phrase of mysterious origin. *Apple pie* here probably is a mispronunciation of a foreign phrase, and has no true connection with the dessert, apple pies not being any more orderly than, say, cherry pies, pumpkin pies, or whatever.

The presumed antecedent is uncertain, however. The earliest example of the phrase in *The Oxford English Dictionary* comes from 1780: "Their Persons Clean and in apple-Pie order on Sundays." One suggestion is that *apple pie* in this context is a corruption of the fractured French *cap-a-pie*, from head to foot, as in, describing the ghost in *Hamlet* (1601–2): "...a figure like your father,/Armed at points exactly, cap-a-pie,/Appears before them." Arguing against this theory is the fact that no examples of the presumed ancestral phrase, *cap-a-pie order* in full, have been found either in English or in French. The closest standard French expression is *de pied en cap*, originally referring to a man wearing a full suit of armor, from top to toe, or, more precisely, from foot to head.

Another guess is that the phrase stems from the French *nappes pliées*, folded linen, with the *n* having migrated to the preceding article, just as it did in the case of *a napron, a nauger,* and *a nuncle,* which became *an apron, an auger,* and *an uncle.* (For more about such transformations, see EAT HUMBLE PIE.) In the absence of any examples of *nappes pliées* in otherwise English texts, this theory seems at least as farfetched as the *cap-a-pie* hypothesis except for one thing: the appearance of a similar phrase, *apple-pie bed,* at almost the same time as *apple-pie order.*

An *apple-pie bed* (also called an *apple-pie turnover*) may look neat, but it is definitely not in perfect order, one sheet having been doubled back in the middle and tucked in so that the would-be slumberer's feet can go only halfway to the end of the bed. The practical joke has been traced (under this name, at least) to 1781: "Had but an indifferent night of Sleep, Mrs. Davie and Nancy made me up an Apple Pye Bed last night" (James Woodforde, *The Diary of a Country Parson,* J. Beresford, ed., 1924–31). Not the kind of treatment generally dished out to visiting clergymen today—and the folded bedsheet could be described as *nappes pliées.*

apricot. The name of the fruit has been dated in English to the mid-sixteenth century as *abrecock.* The *b* in the first syllable apparently was changed to a *p* in the mistaken belief that the word came from the Latin *apricus,* sunny. Thus, toward the start of the seventeenth century, John Minsheu derived the word from *in aprico coctus,* ripened in a sunny place (*Guide into the Tongues*, 1617). Actually, *apricot*'s history is considerably more complicated. It comes from the Latin *praecoquum*, early-ripening (plum), via the late Greek *praikokion* and the Arabic *al-birqūq*. The English probably did not learn the word directly from the Arabs, however, but took it from the Spanish (*albaricoque*), Portuguese (*albricoque*), or Catalan (*albercoc* or *abercoc*).

Meanwhile, the last syllable of the word has changed from *-cock* to *-cot*, and here, too, hangs a tale. The *-cot* form has been dated to 1601, but *apricock* and, in the plural, *apricocks* or *apricox*, seem to have been used more frequently in the sixteenth and seventeenth centuries. Starting around the middle of the eighteenth century, however, English speakers began to get nervous about articulating words that sounded like other words having anatomical meanings. Thus, the strutting barnyard *cock* metamorphosed into the modern *rooster*, *haycocks* blossomed into *haystacks*, *weathercocks* became *weathervanes*, and Amos Bronson *Alcox* changed his surname, so that we know his daughter, the author of *Little Women* and other classics, as Louisa May *Alcott*. Given this proto-Victorian prudery, it seems inevitable that today's fruit stands should display *apricots*, not those other, unmentionable things. See also COCKROACH, DONKEY, and KEEP YOUR PECKER UP.

artichoke. The sound of the vegetable's name has spawned a variety of spellings and associated theories of the word's origin, including *hortichoke* (it chokes the garden) and *hartichoak* (it chokes the heart). The term actually comes from the Arabic name for the plant, *al-harshūf*, via the Italian *articiocco*. The word has been dated in English to 1530. Still, many twentieth-century children take it as an article of faith that just one small bite from the choke will cause instant death. Of course, this also makes a good excuse for avoiding an exceedingly strange-looking vegetable. See also JERUSALEM ARTICHOKE.

asparagus. The plant name comes from the Greek *aspáragos*, but from the middle of the seventeenth century to the early nineteenth century, professional botanists were about the only people who called it *asparagus*. Ordinary people thought this was entirely too affected and used the corrupt *sparrow-grass* and *sparagrass*, which they took to be the plant's true name. For example, Samuel Pepys noted in his diary on April 21, 1667, "Brought home with me from Fenchurch St. a hundred of sparrowgrass, cost 18*d*." The corrupt forms entered the language in a process called aphesis, a term that was coined in 1880 by Sir James

Murray, editor of *The Oxford English Dictionary*, to describe the gradual dropping of the short, unaccented vowel at the beginning of such words as *esquire* (reduced to *squire*) and *adown* (*down*). Thus, *asparagus* progressed to *'sparagus*, and then, through popular etymology based purely on the similarity in sound, to *sparrow-grass*. Times do change, however. To the Victorians, *sparrow-grass* seemed entirely too common, and so they returned to the affected but correct *asparagus*. By the second half of the nineteenth century, some cookbooks still called for *grass*, but by and large, the corrupt forms were used only by the illiterate. (An exception is the grocery business, where even today, *grass* is British tradesman's jargon for the vegetable.) As Edward Bradley, who wrote under the name Cuthbert Bede, noted in *The Rook's Garden* (1865): "I have heard the word sparrowgrass from the lips of a real Lady—but then she was in her seventies." Bradley was a sensitive observer of language; see also the *blank* in BLANKET.

B

babble. The term for meaningless chatter is associated with the biblical Babel, so called, according to *Genesis,* 11:9, "because the Lord did there confound the language of all the earth." No longer able to understand each other, the town's inhabitants had to stop work on the Tower of Babel, which offended the Lord by reaching so far toward heaven. *Babel,* however, comes from the Hebrew name for Babylon, *Bābhel,* which the Hebrews probably derived from an Assyrian word, *bāb-ilu,* gate of God, or the pantheistic *bāb-ili,* gate of the Gods. *Babble,* meanwhile, is of onomatopoeic origin. It imitates the inarticulate sounds of a baby. Cognates in other languages include the Old Norse *babbla,* the Dutch *babbelen,* and the German *pappelen.* All share the Indo-European root *baba-,* which also has produced such words as *baby, baboon* (baboons seem to babble), and *barbarous.* See also *barbarian* in GRINGO.

Baby Ruth. The name of the candy bar does not come from George Herman "Babe" Ruth, a.k.a. the Sultan of Swat. Nor does it derive from, as alternately suggested, President Grover Cleveland's daughter, Ruth, born in the White House in 1891. Rather, the name honors the granddaughter of a candy manufacturer, George Williamson, president of the Williamson Candy Co., original producer of the sweet treat. The names of the candy bar and the great Yankee hitter are so close, however, that when the ball player endorsed a new product called Babe Ruth's Home Run Candy, the manufacturer of Baby Ruth, then Curtiss Candy Corp., appealed to the U.S. Patent Office, claiming infringement upon its trade name. The Patent Office agreed, and the Babe got out of the candy business. See also MARS BAR.

bad egg. This epithet for a dishonest or otherwise unappetizing person sometimes is said to come from Thomas Egg, a nineteenth-century American criminal, which seems most unlikely, considering that Mr. Egg is not otherwise remembered in the annals of crime. *Bad egg* has been dated only to 1855, but the expression flows naturally from long-established usage, e.g., "What, you egg! Young fry of treachery!" (William Shakespeare, *Macbeth,* 1606). *Bad egg's* opposite, *good egg,* did not come into vogue until the early twentieth century (1903, *OED*). It seems to have been popularized at Oxford University, which prior to World War I was divided into "Bad Men" and "Good Eggs." See also BOGUS and LAY AN EGG.

badlands. The expression caught on because the original *Bad Lands*, the barren, deeply eroded region of southwestern South Dakota and northwestern Nebraska, are not good for farming, though the soil between the buttes and mesas is fertile and makes fine pasture for cattle. The name, however, comes from the French of the voyageurs, *les mauvais terres a tràverser*, bad (rough) lands to cross, in its turn probably based on a Native American phrase with the same meaning.

The original French was badly mangled, however, when Jules Verne's *Twenty Thousand Leagues Under the Sea* was hastily translated for the American audience in the early 1870s. Thus, Chapter 2 of most current editions opens with Professor Aronnax's remark that he "had just returned from a scientific research in the disagreeable territories of Nebraska." As Walter James Miller pointed out in *The Annotated Jules Verne: Twenty Thousand Leagues Under the Sea* (1976), the region was far from disagreeable to the professor, since the deeply eroded land formations are ideal for fossil hunting, which was the purpose of his expedition. For Professor Aronnax, the "disagreeable territories" actually constituted a paradise.

ball. The *ball* that is dance has been confused with the *ball* that is a globular object, the supposition being that social dances originally featured a ball that was thrown back and forth among the dancers. One writer has even attempted to connect the English word with an Italian liturgical celebration. " . . . our 'ball' developed from the curious ancient ball-play in church by the Dean and choir-boys of Naples, Italy, during the Feast of Fools, at Easter time. The boys danced round the Dean, singing as they caught a ball thrown by him to them" (Edwin Radford, *Unusual Words*, 1946).

Maybe the Dean and choirboys once danced this way, as early Christian ceremonies did include dancing. Religious dancing faded away, however, along with the agape, or love feast, and most likely for the same reason, i.e., the sacred spiritual euphoria often led to profane physical euphoria after strictly religious devotions were over. It also is true that early social dances had gamelike qualities. Catches generally were made with kisses, not balls, however. In Tudor times, when country dances first became popular at the English court, all the dances required partners to kiss one another. The same was true in France, where, as *The Encyclopædia Britannica* dryly notes: "In the *Pavane* and *Branle*, and in nearly all the dances of the 17th and 18th centuries, the practice of kissing formed a not unimportant part, and seems to have added greatly to the popularity of the pastime" (13th edition, 1926).

In fact, the *ball* that is a dance comes from the French *baller*, to dance, in turn from the Late Latin *ballāre*, and the Greek *ballezein*. The word is a comparative newcomer in English, first recorded in 1632. Its relatives include *ballade*, originally a song for dancing, and *ballet*. The *ball* that is thrown is a much older word. Of Scandinavian origin, it has been dated in English to the early thirteenth century. It is related to, among other words, *balloon* (from a game played with a leather ball), *ballot* (from the use of small balls in secret voting), and the Anglo-Saxon *bealluc*, testicle. See also BALL UP and THREE GOLDEN BALLS.

ball up. The polite explanation of the origin of this expression for fouling up or otherwise making a mess of things is that it referred originally to the tendency of soft, newly fallen snow to ball up beneath horse's hooves or people's snowshoes. The expression has been dated only to 1856, however, with the earliest example collected at Middlebury College, where students used it to refer to failing at an examination or recitation. Mark Twain employed the phrase in a more general sense in an 1885 letter: "It will 'ball up' the binderies again."

In practice, however, when our forefathers and foremothers talked about traveling through snow, they usually spoke of *balling*, not *balling up*, e.g., "Apprehension of the Horses balling with the Snow that had fallen . . . induced me to relinquish the journey" (George Washington, *Diaries*, 1788). More likely, the nineteenth-century *ball up* comes from *ballock* or *bollock*, a little ball, or testicle. This is a very old word, recorded first in the plural form, *beallucas*, around 1000, and it is responsible for such analogous expressions as *to make a balls [of something]*, which is British English for making a mess [of something], and *bollix* (or *bollux*) *up*, where *bollix* is another plural form of *bollock*. In no case is snow involved. See also BALL.

ballyhoo. The American slang term for an extravagant sales pitch commonly is said to derive from *Ballyhooly*, a village in County Cork, Ireland. This is logical enough on the face of it, given the well-deserved reputation of the Irish for blarney, but other possibilities exist, including, in more or less ascending order of likelihood, the following:

1. That it is a portmanteau word, combining *ballet* and *whoop*, produced first by some unusually exuberant barker on a carnival or circus lot. And the earliest examples of the word (1901) in *The Oxford English Dictionary* do refer to the spiel of a sideshow pitchman.

2. That it imitates the cry of Muslim dervishes, *B'Allah hoo*, meaning "Through God it is," but which sounded like gibberish, or blarney, to Americans who watched the dervishes whirl at the Columbia Exposition of 1893 in Chicago.

3. That it is a shortening of *ballyhoo of blazes*, a disparaging term for a ship, used by sailors in the nineteenth century. Melville and Kipling, among others, knew the expression in this sense. This form of *ballyhoo* probably comes from the *ballahou*, a two-masted West Indian vessel (in turn from the Spanish *balahu*, schooner). Though fast-sailing, the *ballahou* presents an ungainly appearance, with the foremast raked forward and the mainmast raked toward the stern. This probably accounts for the contempt with which sailors in conventional vessels looked upon it. And dismissal with contempt is but a short step from dismissal as nonsense, which *ballyhoo* often is.

In the end, however, despite the best efforts of etymologists, no convincing connections have been drawn between the *ballyhoo* of the circus lot (and Madison Avenue) and any of the sources proposed. The term must be labeled "origin unknown," which lets the Irish off the hook—for the time being, at least.

batty. The desire to pin words on people has led to the belief that crazy or eccentric people are *batty*, thanks to *Fitzherbert Batty*, a barrister of Spanish Town, Jamaica, who attracted much attention in the London newspapers when he was certified insane in 1839. And going back into the previous century, efforts also have been made to attribute the meaning of the word to William Battie (1704–76), author of the *Treatise on Madness*.

Arguing against both theories is the fact that *batty* in the eccentric sense has been dated only to 1903, with the earliest examples coming from the United States, not Great Britain. (The related *bats in the belfry*, from ca. 1901, also is an Americanism.) In prior centuries, when people were compared to bats, it was because they were *blind as bats* (though bats actually can see quite well); *bat-eyed*, another way of saying they were blind; or *bat-minded*, i.e., mentally blind. The modern sense of craziness probably derives from the animal's seemingly erratic flight as it uses its sonar system to dodge obstacles in its path, perhaps influenced by the *bat* that is a (usually alcoholic) spree or binge, from 1848. See also BELFRY.

bear garden. In the mistaken assumption that all English words come from other languages, it has been suggested on occasion that this term for a place where bears are kept—and figuratively, for any scene of strife and tumult—comes from the German *biergarten*. The lunge into German is hardly necessary, however, since, as noted by John Moore, "we English baited bears in our parks, and roughs and toughs frequented the places set aside for them, long before the Germans were drinking beer in theirs" (*You English Words*, 1962). The *OED*'s oldest example of *bear garden* conveys the flavor of such a place: "And go to the . . . bear-gardens . . . where they lose their time . . . and offend the laws . . . of her majesty" (John Norden, *A Progresse of Pietie*, 1596).

Beefeater. A number of nineteenth-century philologists, including none other than the Reverend Richard Chenevix Trench, the man who laid the groundwork for the great *Oxford English Dictionary*, dodged the obvious etymology for the popular name of the Warders of the Tower of London (officially known as the Yeoman Extraordinary of the Guard), contending instead that *Beefeater* was an Anglicization of the French *buffetier*, one who tends the *buffet*, here meaning not a buffet of food but a cupboard in which dishes and other valuables are kept (the crown jewels and coronation plate in this case).

The chief trouble with the proposed French origin is that *buffetier* is a nonword, no examples of it ever having been discovered. Meanwhile, *beaufet*, proposed as the missing link between *buffet* and *beefeater*, is merely an eighteenth-century misspelling of the former and not nearly as old as the latter, which dates from the seventeenth century. The underlying idea in the case of *beefeater* is the same as in the Anglo-Saxon *hláfoetā*, loaf eater, the change in nomenclature illustrating the improvement in dietary standards over half a millennium.

English soldiers did like to eat beef and were famous for the quantities they consumed. In Shakespeare's words: "Give them great meals of beef, and iron and steel; they will eat like wolves and fight like devils" (*Henry V*, 1599). Doubts about eating too much beef were expressed early on, however, with Shakespeare also suggesting that eating too much beef could make one into a dullard: "I am a great eater of beef and I believe that does harm to my wit" (*Twelfth Night*, 1600–2).

From the start of the seventeenth century, *beefeater* and the plain *eater* were used to refer contemptuously to household servants, especially overfed ones. Thus, a character in Ben Johson's *Silent Woman* (1609) calls for his servants: "Where are all my eaters? My mouths, now? Bar up my doors you varlets!" The earliest example in the *OED* of a *Beefeater* that is a Yeoman of the Guard comes from 1671—and, again, the context is not entirely flattering: "You Beef-eater, you saucy cur" (John Crowne, *Juliana, or the Princess of Poland*).

belfry. Appearance to the contrary, *belfry* has nothing to do with *bells*, at least not linguistically. In twelfth-century France, a *berfroi* or *belfroi* was a wooden siege tower that could be moved up against the walls of a castle or fortified city when it was being attacked. Subsequently, the term was applied to ordinary towers, especially watch towers (in which alarm bells were hung), and then to bell towers and steeples of churches. In English, paralleling French, both *berfrey* and *belfrey* were used into the fourteenth century, with the *l* form of the word eventually winning out. The phonetic shift from *r* to *l* form is fairly common. Similar examples are *pilgrim*, from the Latin *peregrīnus*, a foreigner, one from abroad, and *purple*, from the Old English *purpure* and the Latin *purpura*. In each instance, one of the *r*'s in the base word changed as speakers gradually differentiated that sound from the neighboring *r* sound. Linguists call the process "dissimulation," but in the case of *belfry* the phonetic change almost certainly was reinforced by popular association with *bell*. See also BATTY.

bite the bullet. The expression obviously is of military origin, but the exact reference is unclear. Usually, it is explained by saying that soldiers were given bullets to bite on while undergoing surgery without anesthetic. For example: "When President Johnson asked Congress today to 'bite the bullet' and pass a tax increase, he was referring to an old practice used . . . to perform painful operations on soldiers in the field. . . . The wounded man would be given a bullet to hold between his teeth and asked to bite it and take his mind off the pain" (*New York Times*, 3/4/68).

Another theory links the expression to the development in 1849 of the Minié ball, or bullet, which was packaged in a paper cartridge, along with the gunpowder needed to propel it. John Ciardi opted for this one: "The new Enfield rifle issued by the British in the 1850s took a cartridge with a paper tube. In loading his piece, the rifleman had to bite off the end of the tube to expose the powder charge to the spark. Thus the root sense 'to stand and reload calmly when under attack' " (*A Browser's Dictionary*, 1980). And to avoid conscription, some men knocked out their front teeth so they couldn't bite the bullet.

The association of the phrase with Minié balls also ties in nicely with the great Indian Mutiny, or Sepoy Rebellion, of 1857. This began when the British introduced the new cartridges, which were greased to facilitate ramming them down rifle barrels, without taking into account the religious taboos of the native troops. Hindu sepoys believed that they would be defiled if the grease came from the fat of cows; Muslim soldiers regarded pig fat with equal horror. Though there were other, more profound causes for the revolt, the mutiny began when the sepoys refused to accept the new cartridges. In other words, they declined to bite the bullet.

Unfortunately for the Minié theory, no one has found an actual example of the use of *bite the bullet* in connection with paper cartridges, either in India or elsewhere. (The paper cartridges were adopted quickly by most Western armies.) Nor are there any known references from an early date to soldiers biting on bullets to alleviate pain during surgical operations. In fact, the oldest example of the phrase in the *OED* comes only from 1891: "Bite on the bullet, old man, and don't let them think you're afraid" (Rudyard Kipling, *The Light That Failed*). This raises the possibility that *bite the bullet* may be a variant of an older phrase, used when a soldier underwent another kind of operation. Thus, from Captain Francis Grose's *A Classical Dictionary of the Vulgar Tongue* (3rd edition, 1796):

NIGHTINGALE. A soldier who, as the term is, sings out at the halberts. It is a point of honour in some regiments, among the grenadiers, never to cry out, or become nightingales, whilst under the discipline of the cat of nine tails; to avoid which, they chew a bullet.

bitter end. It may leave a bad taste in one's mouth to be pushed to the last extremity, but the origin of *bitter end* does not involve the flavor of food or anything else. Actually, this is a sailors' term, deriving from the *bitts*, the pairs of strong posts on a vessel's deck to which ropes and cables are attached. Thanks to Pocahontas, Captain John Smith lived to explain that: "A *Bitter* is but the turn of a Cable about the Bits. . . . And the *Bitter's end* is that part of the Cable doth stay within board" (*A Sea Grammar, with the Plaine Exposition of Smiths Accidence for Young Sea-Men, Enlarged*, 1627). To have reached the *bitter end*, then, is to have reached—by extension, so to speak—the end of one's rope.

black art. There is black magic, which is the work of the devil, and white magic, which is good magic, but the *black art* that is witchcraft actually is a linguistic mistake—a product of folk etymology that has nothing to do with color. The English *black art* is a straight translation of the Old French *nigromancie*, in turn from the Medieval Latin *nigromantia*. The medieval scribes had erred, however, substituting the Latin *niger*, black, for the *necro-* of the Greco-Latin *necromantia*. The Greco-Latin word really was compounded from the Greek *nekrós*, dead body, and *manteía*, divination. The Greek root also is preserved in such words as *necrology*, a list of people who have died; *necrophilia*, an erotic attraction to dead bodies; *necrophobia*, an abnormal fear of dead bodies or death itself; *necropolis*, a large cemetery, a city of the dead; and *necropsy*, an autopsy. As for the original *necromancers*, we know from their name that they foretold the future by examining corpses, a *black art*, perhaps, but not a color-related one.

blanket. A false eponym when attributed to a real person, Thomas Blanket, a weaver in Bristol, said to have produced the first blankets in England, around 1340. The trouble with this theory is that *blanket* was used earlier to describe white or undyed woolen material, and it is much more likely that Mr. Blanket took his name from the cloth than the other way around. *Blanket* comes from the French *blanc*, white, plus the diminutive suffix *-ette*. The sense of whiteness, absence of color, and hence, emptiness or vacancy, also is the source of the *blank* in *blank cartridge, blank check, blank look, blank verse*, and similar phrases in English as well as in French. (See CARTE BLANCHE.) This goes, too, for the *blank* that dashes out words or letters that might offend the eye, as in *d——d*, or, from *The Further Adventures of Verdant Green* (1854), by Edward Bradley (see ASPARAGUS), who seems to have introduced the spelled-out word in its euphemistic sense: "I wouldn't give a blank for such a blank blank. I'm blank if he doesn't look like he'd swallowed a blank codfish."

blatherskite. Tracing the *blather* part is easy enough; it is a variant of *blither* and *blether*, with all forms denoting voluable, nonsensical talk. The *skite*, meanwhile, alternates with *skate*, as in *bladderskate*, *blatherskate*, or *bletherskate*, meaning one who runs off at the mouth in this fashion. Attempts have been made to connect the *skite/skate* to the broad, flat fish, considered a delicacy in many parts of the world. This is not altogether unreasonable, considering the frequent use of piscine labels to derogate human beings, as in, "That crabby shrimp Frank is a cold fish, and I wish he'd stop sponging off me." A simpler explanation, however, is that the last syllable comes from the Scottish *skite* or *skyte*, used as both noun and verb to refer to one who voids excrement and the act thereof, as in, from *The Paston Letters* (1449): "I cam abord the Admirall, and bade them stryke in the Kyngys name . . . , and they bade me skyte in the Kyngs name." The notion that *skite* and *skate* are Scottish, not fishy, is reinforced by the early use of *bletherskate* in the song "Maggie Lauder," as recorded ca. 1650: "Jog on your gait, ye bletherskate." Thus, *blatherskite* probably can be translated more accurately as "one who talks a lot of shit." A near cousin is the equally contemptible *cheapskate*.

blindfold. The name of the folded piece of cloth that covers the eyes when playing pin the tail on the donkey or blindman's bluff has only a coincidental resemblance to the way the material is doubled over. *Blindfold* actually comes from *blindfeld*, in turn from the Middle English *blindfellen*, to strike blind, that is, to fell [one] with blindness. The confusion of the felling with the folding occurred in the sixteenth century. Walter Tyndale used "blyndfolded" in the first translation of the Bible into English (1526), and if he was not the first to make the mistake, his example was certainly the most influential.

    Blindman's bluff, by the way, is a corruption, due to the guessing element in the game, of *blindman's buff*, in turn, apparently, from *blindman's buck*, referring to a male animal, probably a deer or goat. This would be in accord with the name of the game in other languages, e.g., *gatta orba*, blind cat, in Italian; *gallina ciega*, blind hen, in Spanish; and *cabra ciega*, blind goat, in Portuguese.

bloody. Many theories of the origin of this word have been offered to justify the strength of the traditional British taboo against it. The taboo flowered from about 1750 to 1920. Its onset is marked by Dr. Samuel Johnson's note, *"This is very vulgar,"* (his italics) in *A Dictionary of the*

English Language (1755); its end by Eliza's line in George Bernard Shaw's *Pygmalion* (1914): "Walk! Not bloody likely. [*Sensation.*] I'm going in a taxi." In the intervening years, though heard often enough in common speech, the word hardly ever graced the printed page. Instead, writers evaded it with *b——y* and such euphemisms as *bally, bleeding, blinking, blooming, ensanguined, rose-coloured, ruddy,* and *sanguinary.*

Since the word is relatively innocuous compared with some of the other intensives that people commonly use when they are angry, bored, disgusted, etc., philologists, amateur and professional, had to make some fairly long reaches in trying to explain why the term was so *bloody* shocking.

Probably the most popular theory—still held by many—is that the word derives from an oath, *By Our Lady,* via *by'r lady.* Alas, there is no proof of this, and the fact that the English have not worried a great deal about blasphemy since Puritan times argues against it. This reasoning also applies to the speculation that the term comes from *God's blood,* via another contraction, *'s blood.* Sir James Murray, the great editor of *The Oxford English Dictionary,* suggested in his entry on *bloody* that the word might memorialize the rowdy lordlings of the Restoration period—*young bloods,* who were often described as getting *bloody drunk.* But this, too, seems farfetched, considering that Swift, Fielding, Richardson, and other writers used the word freely in the intervening years, from about 1700 to 1750, e.g., Swift's remark in a letter to Stella: "It was bloody hot walking to-day" (5/28/1711). And Stella (her real name was Esther Johnson) was no rowdy. In his account of her life, Swift noted that "It was not safe, nor prudent, in her presence, to offend in the least word against modesty" (1/1728).

Most likely, in this case as in so many others, the simplest explanation for avoidance of the word is best: Many people fear blood. It has long been a symbol of violence and death, of murder and mayhem. Even when the taboo was at its strongest, British schoolchildren learned about Bloody Queen Mary.

Significantly, the onset of the taboo on *bloody* coincides with the beginning of what frequently is characterized as "Victorian" prudery, but which actually began in the middle years of the eighteenth century. *Bosom, limb, darn, donkey* (to avoid saying *ass*), and *rooster* (to avoid *cock*) are among the typical "Victorian" euphemisms that were popularized—in the United States as well as England—prior to Victoria's ascent to the throne in 1837. See also BUMBAILIFF and DONKEY in this connection.

While the Victorians (and proto-Victorians) were embarrassed to speak openly of practically all parts of their bodies and bodily functions, this particular taboo may well have been reinforced, at least in the minds of some, by association with the unspeakable subject of menstruation. Literally "unspeakable": For example, at the trial of Lizzie Borden in 1892, the prosecution and defense agreed for the sake of delicacy not to mention that she was menstruating at the time her parents were hacked to death. She said that she had been in the cellar, washing out the rags that women usually used in the pre-tampon era, during part of the morning on which the crime was committed. The prosecutor accepted the statement, apparently believing that no woman would dream of bringing up this subject unless the excuse was true. Even with this part of her alibi suppressed, however, the prosecution's case was so weak that it took the jury only about an hour to acquit Miss Borden—a minor detail that has somehow slipped from popular memory of the case. (The maid may have done it.)

The strength of the taboo against menstruation in former times also is indicated by the large number of euphemisms that survive for this natural phenomenon, e.g., *female complaint, flagging, illness, indisposition, monthlies, period, that time,* and *tummy ache.* The very word *menstruation* is a generalized Latinate euphemism, dated only to the proto-Victorian period (1776–84) in *The Oxford English Dictionary.* Its literal meaning is "monthly" (from the Latin *mēnsis,* month).

In an age in which supermarket shelves are crowded with hygiene products, the taboo against menstruation has pretty much withered away (though attitudes associated with it are quite resilient, e.g., that women cannot perform certain tasks, or hold leadership positions, because they are subject to raging hormonal tides). And hardly anyone worries about *bloody* anymore, though it is within living memory (1962) that the British Post Office refused to allow the Crime Club to advertise a book entitled *Bloody Instructions* on its envelopes because, according to Her Majesty's Moral Minions of the Mail, "The words . . . may offend quite a number of people."

bogus. This term for whatever is fraudulent or counterfeit was thought for many years to be an eponym, a corruption of *Borghese,* said to be a swindler who in 1837 or thereabouts flooded the western and southwestern states with forged checks, notes, bills of exchange, and similar securities. According to the *Boston Daily Courier* of June 12, 1857, the surname *Borghese* was converted by word of mouth to *borges* and then to *bogus,* and at the same time was extended because of this individual's notoriety to apply to fraudulent practices and counterfeit objects of all kinds, as *bogus* diamonds, *bogus* accusations, and so on.

The principal difficulty with the *Courier*'s explanation—aside from lack of any other records of this particular gentleman—is that *bogus* appeared in a closely related context a decade prior to Borghese's reputed activities. *The Oxford English Dictionary* includes two citations from the *Painsville* (Ohio) *Telegraph* of July 6 and November 2, 1827, both describing a *bogus* as a machine for stamping out counterfeit coins. Most likely, the generalized applications of *bogus* stemmed from *bogus* money, which was produced on a *bogus*.

And where did the name of the machine come from? The editor of the *Painsville Telegraph*, Eber D. Howe, later said in his *Autobiography* (1878) that the newspaper picked up the word from someone in the crowd of onlookers who termed the odd-looking contrivance a *bogus* when it was found in May of 1827 in the hands of a gang of coin counterfeiters in town. Dr. Samuel Willard, of Chicago, who supplied the *Telegraph* citations to Sir James Murray, editor of the *OED*, speculated that the name was short for *tantrabogus*, a word that he had heard in his own childhood and which in his father's time was commonly applied in Vermont to any ill-looking object. Dr. Willard went on to suggest that *tantrabogus* was related to *tantrabobs*, a name for the devil in Devonshire. (*Tantrabobus* and *tantarabobus*, with the same devilish meaning, are also recorded in Joseph Wright's *English Dialect Dictionary*, 1898–1905.) If Willard was correct—and Murray and later lexicographers have tended to agree—then *bogus* probably derives from the Welsh *bwg*, ghost, making it cousin to *bugbear*, *bogle*, *bogy*, and *bugaboo*. Another suggestion is that *bogus* comes from the French *bagasse*, rubbish. Just how the fraudulent *bogus* is related to the mixture of rum and molasses that also is called *bogus* remains an open question. Perhaps the combination, like *bwg* and its descendants, has fearsome qualities, or perhaps, like *bagasse*, it is not fit to drink. More research is indicated.

See also BAD EGG and CONDOM.

bombast. Because the German-Swiss physician and alchemist Paracelsus (1490–1541) wrote in a notably boastful and exaggerated manner, it has been supposed by some that *bombast* is an eponym, deriving from his real name, Theophrastus Bombastus von Hohenheim. (His sobriquet, a compound of *para-*, above, and *Celsus*, demonstrates what an exaggerated opinion Theophrastus Bombastus had of himself, since Aulus Cornelius Celsus was recognized as one of the greatest anatomists of classical times.) Actually, *bombast* comes from the French *bombace*, cotton padding or wadding, the cloth stuffing serving as a metaphor for the overblown language. *Bombace*, in turn, probably came from the Middle Persian *pambak*, cotton, with the *bom-* part influenced by the Latin *bombȳx*, silk. Thus, *bombast* closely parallels *fustian*, another term for pretentious language, which originally denoted a kind of coarse cloth made of cotton and flax. The name of the cloth, in turn, comes from the Medieval Latin *fustāneus*, most likely from *Fostat*, a town near Cairo that was a center for manufacturing the material. See also GIBBERISH.

bonfire. Sitting around a bonfire on a summer evening can be exceedingly pleasurable, and perhaps Samuel Johnson had such a happy reminiscence in mind when he explained in *A Dictionary of the English Language* (1755) that this word for "a fire made for some publick cause of triumph or exaltation" was composed of the French *bon*, good, and the Anglo-Saxon *fire*. People still write letters to Merriam-Webster backing this etymology. But, alas, this was one of the times that the great Dr. Johnson stubbed his toe. (See also CURMUDGEON.) The word actually comes from *bone* plus *fire*. It has been dated in *The Oxford English Dictionary* to 1483 as *banefyre*, where *bane* is a Scottish variant of *bone*, and to 1493 as *bone fyre*. In both cases, the meaning is clear. The *banefyre* is defined in Latin as an *ignis ossium*, that is, a fire of bones, while the second reference reads: "One [of the fires] was clene bones and noo woode, and that is called a bone fyre."

The original *bonfires*, made of the bones of oxen, sheep, and other animals, were lit to celebrate midsummer anniversaries, especially the eves of St. John and St. Peter. The custom almost certainly dated to pre-Christian times. Later, *bonfires* of trash, brushwood, leaves, etc., were lit on such occasions of public celebration as victories, anniversaries, births, and marriages. Toward the end of the sixteenth century (1581, *OED*), people also began making *bonfires* out of heretics as well as Bibles, books, and other proscribed articles. Nowadays, of course, *bonfires* themselves are proscribed in most well-regulated communities, which is good for the atmosphere but a pity otherwise.

boo. The loud sound (also rendered *bo*, as in Little Bo-peep, and *boh*) intended to frighten or startle is a natural one to make, its force coming from the sudden expulsion of air through pursed lips. If one searches hard enough, however, weird explanations can always be found for natural phenomena, e.g., "The word *boh!* used to frighten children, was the name of Boh, a great general, the son of Odin, whose very appellation struck immediate panic in his enemies" (M. A. Thomas, *Pulleyn's Etymological Compendium*, 3rd edition, 1853).

Lewis Carroll, by the way, did not name the mysteriously dreadful *Boojum* in "The Hunting of the Snark" (1874) after the *boojum tree* that grows in the desert of Baja California. The real etymology is vice versa. The *boojum* (also called the *boogum* or, more formally, *Idria columnaris*) is one of the strangest-looking trees in the whole of North America. It resembles nothing so much as an upside-down carrot, except that it may be sixty feet tall, narrowing upward from a base of eighteen to twenty inches in diameter, and covered all over with short, spinelike branches. The tree was given its common name in 1922 by Godfrey Sykes, a British ecologist. Spotting one through a telescope, he studied the bizarre apparition for a few moments, then exclaimed, "Ho, ho, a boojum, definitely a boojum."

boondoggle. The origin of this term for unnecessary work (typically performed at public expense) is a minor mystery, but it seems clear that the word does *not* come from, as has been suggested: (1) Daniel Boone's dog or a toy that he made for it; (2) the hypothetical Scottish *boondoggle*, meaning a marble, or *doggle* in dialect, that one receives as a gift, or *boon*; or (3) the presumed idleness of people in the *boondocks*, in turn from the Tagalog *bundok*, mountain.

Boondoggle was popularized in 1935 during an investigation of New Deal relief programs in New York City. As an example of wastefulness, a Mr. Robert Marshall testified to a committee of aldermen on April 3 that he had gone so far as to teach "boon doggles" (spelled as two words by the *New York Times* on the following day). Asked just what these were, the witness explained: "Boon doggles is simply a term applied back in pioneer days to what we call gadgets today—to things that men and boys do that are useful in their everyday operations or recreations about their home."

Subsequent sleuthing revealed that the word was (and still is) used widely by Boy Scouts to describe the braided leather lanyards for holding keys, etc. that they wear about their necks. Weaving these lanyards is a mindless task, often saved for rainy days when there is nothing else to do. Thus, among Scouts the word also combines the senses of "gadget" and "make-work." Employed as early as 1925 by Robert H. Link, a Scoutmaster in Rochester, N.Y., first as a nickname for his son and then as a name for the plaited leather thongs, *boondoggle* was disseminated among Scouts attending an international jamboree in England in 1929. Attempts have been made to trace the term to the Ozarks, a rich repository of similar-sounding words, and to the Wild West, where cowboys are said to have *boondoggled* by making saddle trappings from odds and ends of leather when there was no other work to do on the ranch. Actual examples of earlier uses have not been found, however, and many dictionaries now credit Mr. Link with having coined it. See also LANYARD.

boots and saddles. The traditional order or trumpet call for the cavalry to mount doesn't have anything to do with footgear. It is a perversion of the French command *boute-selle*, place (or put) saddle. The correct *boute-selle* appeared in English toward the beginning of the seventeenth century (1628, *OED*). It took several generations (to 1697) for cavalrymen to convert the foreign phrase into English words that sounded about the same and seemed to make sense to those who wore boots every day but didn't know French. See also AGITA.

booze. Harder to spike than Dracula in his coffin is the rumor that this word comes from the name of a distiller, E. C. (or E. S. or E. G.—take your pick) Booz, who flourished in Philadelphia around 1840, peddling whisky in bottles shaped like a log cabin. *Booze*, however, is dated in the *OED* to 1732 as a noun and to 1768 as a verb meaning "to drink heavily." And other sources have older examples. Thus, Thomas Harman glossed the cant of vagabonds this way in *A Caveat for Common Cursitors* (3rd edition, 1568):

> *This booze is as beneship as Rome-booze.*
> This drink is as good as wine. . . .
> *Now we have well boozed, let us strike some cheat.*
> Now we have well drunk, let us steal something.

At about the same time, John Awdeley, presumed author of *The Fraternity of Vagabonds* (1561), described the tinkard, or tinker, in these terms: "A tinkard leaveth his bag a-sweating at the ale-house, which they call their boozing inn, and in the mean season goeth abroad a-begging." See also TINKER'S DAM (or DAMN), NOT WORTH A.

All forms of *booze* derive from a variant pronunciation of the Middle English (ca. 1300) *bouse*, itself a derivative of the Middle Dutch *būsen,* to drink heavily. Thus, this basic element in the drinker's vocabulary was well established long before anyone set up a distillery in the City of Brotherly Love, and the word, though popularized by the underclass, is not really slang but sufficiently venerable to qualify as Standard English.

See also CANT and CONDOM.

bowler. The name of the hat, known as a derby in the United States (and as a *melon* in France), often is said to come from its shape: it looks like an overturned bowl, and if caught in the wind, the round, stiff hat may be bowled along for a considerable distance before being retrieved. Which is logical enough, except that a Mr. Bowler, a nineteenth-century hatter, seems to have been involved—contrary to the opinions of *The Random House Dictionary* (2nd edition, unabridged, 1987), which derives the word from *bowl* + *er*, and the otherwise perspicacious William E. Kruck (see the final paragraph of CONDOM).

The best evidence that *bowler* actually is an eponym comes from a squib in the London *Daily News* of August 8, 1868: "Mr. Bowler, of 15 St. Swithin's Lane, has, by a very simple contrivance, invented a hat that is completely ventilated, whilst, at the same time, the head is relieved of the pressure experienced in wearing hats of the ordinary description." Different sources give Mr. Bowler's first name as John, Thomas, and William, the confusion probably stemming from the fact that this was a family business.

It may be, too, that credit for the hat really should have gone to another person, since it also was called, from ca. 1850, a *billycock*. This appears to come from the name of a Norfolk landowner and avid sportsman, William "Billy" Coke, who arranged to have a domed, shellac-hardened hat—better gear for hunting or shooting than a traditional topper—made up for him in London at James Lock & Co., where such a hat is still known as a *Coke*. (See also TWEED.) The use of *billycock* might have been aided, however, by the eighteenth-century use of *bully-cocked*, to refer to a hat worn, or cocked, in the swashbuckling style of a bully.

The *bowler* is called a *derby* in the United States because this type of hat was so popular in the nineteenth century among those attending the Kentucky Derby, which is named after the English Derby, which is run at Epsom Downs, not Derby, the name of the race coming from the title of the original (1780) sponsor, Edward Stanley, twelfth Earl of Derby.

In the end, then, the same piece of headgear has three names, all of them eponyms. In ice hockey, this would be called a HAT TRICK.

bozo. Popularity of Bozo the Clown has stimulated interest in the origin of this word for a fellow, a guy, especially a big, stupid, or obnoxious one. Most appealing is the idea that it's an eponym, deriving from Boso, abbot of the Norman monastery at Bec from 1124 to 1136. According to this theory, as set forth in a letter to the *New York Times* (8/16/91), Boso became a figure of fun for medieval scholars because he appears as St. Anselm's foil in the latter's *Cur Deus Homo* ("Why God Became Man"). St. Anselm, who preceded Boso as abbot at Bec, and who went on to become Archbishop of Canterbury, cast this work in the form of a dialogue in which the seemingly obtuse Boso played the straight man, asking the questions, while Anselm himself supplied all the answers.

Unfortunately for the *Boso* theory, the earliest example of *bozo* in the *OED* comes from an article in *Collier's* magazine in December of 1920—leaving a gap of some eight hundred years between the monk and his presumed intellectual heirs. Thus, *bozo* appears to be a twentieth-century Americanism, not a twelfth-century Normanism. Various etymologies have been suggested, all deriving the term in one way or another from Spanish—either *bozo* (in the sense of "down growing on the cheeks of youths"), *bozal* (stupid, inexperienced), or *boso* (a variant of *vosotros*, you people).

The clownish sense of the word is still newer, coming from the children's program *The Bozo Show*, syndicated since the 1950s, and used before that (from 1940) by Capitol Records as the name of the narrator on a series of story-telling albums for children. Another late development is the feminine *bozette*. This person is more likely to be found in a bar than in a circus ring: a bozette is a broad, babe, or bimbo—that is, a female bozo in the masculine term's primary sense.

brazilwood. The red wood used in cabinetwork and for making red or purple dye comes from trees that grow in Brazil and other tropical locales, but the name of the wood does not come from the country. Things are the other way around. Long before the discovery of the New World, similar wood from the East Indies was used in Europe for making red dyes. The English called the dyestuff *brasil*, their word coming from the Old French *bresil*, red-dye wood. Other languages had related terms for the material. After the Portuguese found trees of this type in

South America, they named the territory where they grew *terra de brasil,* red-dye-wood land, which later was abbreviated to the modern form of the nation's name. See also CANARY ISLANDS, CONDOM, and TOBACCO.

briar pipe. The pipes are not made from thorny briars but from the roots of white heather, and they take their name from the French word for the plant, *bruyère.* The pipes began to be imported into England, principally from Corsica, about 1859. They were initally called *bruyer* pipes. By 1868, *bruyer* and *brier* were being used interchangeably in advertisements. The native word completely superseded the foreign one soon thereafter.

bridegroom. It is pleasant to think of the new husband or husband-to-be grooming his princess bride, but this would be a mistake, linguistically if not actually. *Bridegroom* began as a compound of the Anglo-Saxon *brȳd,* bride, and *guma,* man. In the sixteenth century, after the older word for "man" had become obsolete, *bridegome* metamorphosed into *bridegrome,* thanks to the influence of another Anglo-Saxon word, *grome,* meaning a boy, youth, or attendant. Itself of obscure origin, *grome* or, as we say today, *groom,* may be related to the Anglo-Saxon *grōwan,* grow.

The earliest example of *groom* in the sense of one who leads a bride to an altar as opposed to a horse to a stable comes from Shakespeare's *Othello* (1604). The *bridal* ceremony, meanwhile, derives from the aforementioned *brȳd* plus *ealu,* ale, which tells us how nuptials were celebrated in Anglo-Saxon times. As late as 1577, a good Puritan lamented the "heathenish rioting at bride-ales" (William Harrison, *A Description of England*). It is all quite different today, of course, now that people drink champagne. See also BRIDEWELL.

bridewell. Chances are that in the course of human affairs some poor bride has been tossed into a well, but *bridewell,* meaning a prison, comes from *St. Bridget's well* in London, as contracted to *Bride's Well,* near which Henry VIII constructed a mansion for visiting royalty. In 1553 Edward VI gave the building to the city, which converted it to a jail for vagabonds and prostitutes, and before the century was out, *bridewell* was being used generically for similar structures in other towns. See also BRIDEGROOM, CLINK, and STIR.

bumbailiff. Some jurists, including none other than Sir William Blackstone (1723–80), have construed the name of this officer—a bailiff or sheriff's deputy who serves warrants, makes arrests, and so on—as a corruption of *bound bailiff*. From our present vantage point in time, however, it seems clear that this strained effort to avoid the common meaning of the British *bum* is merely an example of proto-Victorianism at work. (And for more on that subject, see BLOODY.) No evidence of a *bound bailiff* has ever come to light, and it seems more than coincidental that the French have employed an equivalent expression, *pousse-cul*, or simply *cul*, referring to a person's hindermost part, since at least the seventeenth century. In fact, then, and contrary to Blackstone, *bumbailiff* alludes to the way the officer of the law chases after his man, nabbing him by the seat of the pants.

Bumbailiff has always been a disparaging term, probably because it was popularized by the people who were being nabbed, usually debtors. An early report on prison life accurately conveys the word's connotations: "The very offscum of the rascall multitudes, as . . . Decoyes, Bum-bayliffes, disgraced Pursivants . . . and a rabble of such stinkardly companions" (Geffray Mynshul, *Essayes and Characters of a Prison and Prisoners, by G. M.*, 1638).

By the bye: *Dun*, meaning to persistently demand payment, may be an eponym, from Joe Dun, a sixteenth-century bailiff of Lincoln, who was famous for successfully pursuing debtors. His name is said to have become proverbial as a result of the rhetorical question to anyone who complained about late payment: "Why do you not *Dun* him?" (Captain Francis Grose, *A Classical Dictionary of the Vulgar Tongue*, 1796). While surnames should be looked at askance when proposed as the sources of words (see BLANKET, CONDOM, and CRAP, for instance), in the case of *dun* no other explanation comes readily to hand.

buttery. Students in colleges and other residential schools may repair to the *buttery* for sandwiches, but unlike *larder* (which does come from the French *lard*, bacon, kept there) and *pantry* (from the Latin *panis*, bread), the *buttery* has nothing to do with butter. Originally, going back to the fourteenth century, a *buttery* was a place for storing liquor in bottles, butts, or casks, from the Middle English *botterie*, bottle, and the Old French *botellierie*. (*Butler*, the fellow who brings the bottle to the table, is a related term.) The transition in *buttery*'s meaning, however, from a storeroom for liquor to a storeroom for food, which took place in the second half of the seventeenth century, seems to have been assisted by the fallacious association with the spread for bread.

B.V.D.'s The inherent fascination of underwear has combined with the strong acronymic impulse of folk etymologists (see TIP) to produce many ingenious explanations for the initials by which this once-popular brand of men's one-piece underclothing was known, e.g., *Back Vented Drawers, Boys' Ventilated Drawers, Baby's Ventilated Diapers,* and *Body Vest Doodads.*

When H. L. Mencken pursued this matter, he ran up against a blank wall, with the manufacturer informing him in a letter on May 29, 1935: "From the standpoint of business psychology and because of the great public curiosity as to the meaning of our trademark, we would not care to have you publish any information regarding its origin, but for your personal use, if you request it, we will be glad to tell you the history of *B.V.D.*" Mr. Mencken did not bother to so request, but it was subsequently revealed in *Time* (11/9/62) that the initials stand for the surnames of the three men who founded the company in 1876—Bradley, Voorhees, and Day. See also UNION SUIT.

C

cabal. The desire to explain the origins of words as acronyms of other words is nowhere more evident than in the supposition that *cabal* derives from the names of five ministers who formed an inner circle in the government of Charles II—Clifford, Arlington, Buckingham, Ashley, and Lauderdale. The word actually comes from the Hebrew *cabala*, the complex body of occult lore developed by medieval rabbis, and it was used in English prior to the Restoration (1660) to characterize a plot or intrigue of a sinister character developed by a small group of people.

During the first ten years of Charles II's reign, the term *cabal* also was applied without any particularly negative connotations to the Committee for Foreign Affairs of the Privy Council, a precursor of the modern cabinet, which managed most of the business government. The ministers in this *cabal* included others besides the infamous five. It was merely happenstance that these particular names formed the word in acrostic fashion. Their political opponents were quick trade on *cabal*'s older, sinister associations, however, and applied the label to the entire group.

The *cabal*'s policies, as it turned out, were extremely unpopular. After closing the exchequer in 1670 (the functional equivalent of declaring national bankruptcy, this ruined many people who had lent to the government), the *cabal* started a war in 1672 with a Protestant nation, Holland, then entered into an alliance in 1673 with a Catholic one, France. As a result, *cabal* survives today only in a negative sense. See also TIP.

call girl. The modern *call girl* may use the telephone to make appointments with her *dates* (as they are called), but she got her name from association with the older *call house,* or assignation house, an establishment in which women did not live, but to which they were called, not necessarily by means of Mr. Bell's invention, as occasion demanded. *Call girl* has been dated to ca. 1935, and *call house* to ca. 1920, though both terms certainly are older. Thus, Herbert Asbury described the modus operandi of a brothel that was set up on Mason Street in San Francisco's Uptown Tenderloin district shortly after the earthquake and fire of 1906: "The active management of the establishment was entirely in the hands of an old Negro woman known as Aunt Josie, who operated it as a call house; that is, the members of the—well, staff—were not actually resident upon the premises, but were chosen from photographs, and from charts which furnished all needful information as to color of the eyes and other physical details. Once selected, the [staffer] was summoned by telephone or messenger" (*The Barbary Coast*, 1933).

The particular distinction of this establishment, by the way, was that it catered to women, the staff being composed of a dozen handsome, stalwart young men. The fee for their services was $10, half of which went to the management. (Rumor had it that some staffers refused to exact a fee, believing themselves to be sufficiently compensated by the experience itself.) Though designed to service an upscale clientele (patronesses were furnished with silk masks, so that their partners would not know who they were), the house apparently attracted only a few female prostitutes, intrigued by the novelty of paying for what they themselves were paid. The establishment closed within a few months, sad to say, partly because of slow trade and partly because of threats from local pimps, who claimed to be upset at seeing their women spend hard-earned dollars so frivolously.

See also PHONY.

Cambridge. One could easily be forgiven for assuming, as many have, that *Cambridge* means "the bridge over the river Cam." The town's name comes from the Anglo-Saxon *Grantabrigge*, which evolved into *Gantabrigge*, *Cantabrigge*, and, finally, *Cambridge*. The Cam River, then, actually was named after the town, not the other way around. Upstream, the river still is known by its older name, the *Granta*.

The river that flows through another—"the other," as some would say—university town, Oxford, is known locally as the Isis, which is a corruption of *Tamesis*, the Latin name of what people downstream call the Thames.

Canary Islands. The little bird—greenish in the wild and usually yellow in domesticated varieties—was found first in the Canary Islands, but the name of the islands (and thus the bird) comes from the Latin word for dog, *canis*. The Romans knew the archipelago in the Atlantic, to the southwest of Spain, as the *Canariae Insulae*, Dog Islands. The islands got this name on account of the large number of wild dogs, *canes*, that were discovered to be living on them by an early visitor, Juba II (ca. 50 B.C.–ca. A.D. 24), King of Numidia and Mauretania. See also BRAZILWOOD.

cant. Sir Richard Steele may have been writing with tongue in cheek when he reported that this term for the jargon of a particular group or social class comes from a real person's name, but his explanation is so typical of the eponymous school of folk etymology (see BOOZE, CONDOM, CRAP, and TRAM, for example) that it is worth preserving here in full. From *The Spectator*, No. 47, of August 18, 1711:

> "Cant" is, by some people, derived from one Andrew Cant, who, they say, was a Presbyterian minister in some illiterate part of Scotland, who by exercise and use had obtained the faculty, alias gift, of talking in the pulpit in such a dialect, that it is said he was understood by none but his own Congregation, and not by all of them. Since master Cant's time, it has been understood in a larger sense, and signifies all exclamations, whinings, unusual tones, and in fine all prayer and preaching, like the unlearned of the Presbyterians.

Just as the best lies are always partly true, so the fiction here leans on fact. Andrew Cant (1590?–1663) was a well-known Presbyterian minister in Scotland, but his parishioners were by no means illiterate; a staunch royalist, he was forced to resign his post in Aberdeen in 1660 because of his frequent attacks on members of his own congregation. Steele's credibility also was enhanced by the different senses of *cant* that were current when he wrote. For example, the word was used to refer to a whining manner of speaking (from 1567, *OED*); to the jargon of professional beggars, pickpockets, gypsies, and other groups on the fringes of conventional society (from 1609); and to the phraseology of particular religious sects (from 1681).

The key to the term's actual origin is the oldest sense of singsong whining. *Cant* comes from the Norman French *canter*, to sing, to chant, in turn from the Latin *canere*, to sing, and *cantāre*, the verbal form for conveying a sense of repetitive action, which was used to refer contemptuously to church services prior to 1200. See also PATTER and SLANG.

cardinal. This prince of the Roman Catholic Church wears a bright red robe, but his title comes from the Latin *cardo*, hinge, not from the bright red songbird. He is, literally and etymologically, one of the hinges on which the church turns. The ecclesiastic *cardinal* has been dated in English to 1125. The bird that is named after him—the *cardinal grosbeak,* in full—has not been sighted prior to 1800.

carte blanche. *Blanche* is the feminine form of *blanc,* white, in French, but the phrase doesn't really mean "white card" or "white charter." *Blanche* is translated here more accurately as absence of color, emptiness, blankness, or, figuratively, without effect. Thus, the *carte* that is *blanche* has no writing on it; the bearer has the power to fill it in any way he wants. The sense of emptiness or ineffectiveness rather than whiteness also appears in such expressions as *guerre blanche,* war without hostilities, and *mariage blanche,* one that has not been consummated. English has a number of similar phrases; see BLANKET.

Cat and the Fiddle. The source of the image of the musical feline, who appears in the nursery rhyme "High Diddle, Diddle, The Cat and the Fiddle," is of much dispute. As the name of a British inn, the phrase has been derived from *Caterine la Fidèle,* sobriquet of Henry VIII's first wife, Catherine of Aragon. However, Bill Byson reports in *The Mother Tongue* (1990) that the inn was listed as *Caterine la Fidèle* in the Domesday Book, and this work was compiled in 1085–86, almost exactly four hundred years prior to the birth of the queen whose marriage was annulled despite her fidelity. Thus, the origin may be linguistically correct, but the reference has to be to some other Catherine, the saint perhaps. (Picturesque pub names tend to evoke farfetched explanations. The attribution of this one to Catherine of Aragon is on a par with the suggestion that *Elephant and Castle* comes from *Infanta de Castille* and no wilder than the theory that *Goats and Compasses* stems from *God Encompasseth Us,* even though the commercial attraction of the latter name for a pub is not at all clear. Something to do with God's looking after drunks?)

Inevitably, *Caterine la Fidèle* has been linked to the nursery rhyme as well as to the inn name. This is only one of a number of origins that have been proposed for the phrase *Cat and the Fiddle,* however. Others include: (1) that it honors either of two Empresses of Russia who were "Cats"—Catherine I (1684–1727), wife of Peter the Great, or Catherine II (1729–96), better known as Catherine the Great; (2) that it derives from the name of Caton, a supposed governor of Calais, who was called *Caton le fidèle;* (3) that it refers to a ball game called *cat* that was often played in inns where fiddlers also held forth; (4) that it comes from the name of a fifteenth-century forest warden named Caterling (see also GRIN LIKE A CHESHIRE CAT); and (5) that it alludes to England's Queen Elizabeth I (1533–1603), said be be called *The Cat* because she toyed with her ministers as though they were mice, and who also is supposed to have enjoyed dancing to fiddle music.

And this only begins the scholarly analysis of the nursery rhyme, which continues (for the benefit of those who have blocked out childhood memories): "The Cow Jump'd over the Moon; The Little Dog Laugh'd To see such Sport, And the Dish ran away with the Spoon." For example, it has been proposed that the line about the Cow and the Moon refers to (1) elaborate charades enacted at the court of Elizabeth I; (2) worship of Hathor, Egyptian goddess of love, who is sometimes depicted as having a cow's head; and (3) the periodic flights of ancient Egyptians from the flooding Nile.

Others have said that the Cow and the Dog are astronomical allusions to the constellations *Taurus*—though *Taurus* is the Bull, not the Cow—and *Canis Minor*, the Little Dog. Then there is the theory that the Little Dog stands for Robert Dudley, Earl of Leicester (1532?–88), upon whom Queen Elizabeth doted as if he were a lap dog. For those who wish to pursue this subject further, additional "explanations" of the origin of the line about the Dish and the Spoon are included in *The Annotated Mother Goose* (William S. Baring-Gould and Ceil Baring-Gould, 1962).

This kind of etymologizing can go on practically forever, the only limit being the etymologizer's imagination. As Iona and Peter Opie, the leading authorities on children's games and rhymes have pointed out, "High Diddle, Diddle" is "probably the best-known nonsense verse in the language," and "a considerable amount of nonsense has been written about it" (*The Oxford Dictionary of Nursery Rhymes*, 1951).

One thing is certain: The song has been around for quite a while. It was first printed in *Mother Goose's Melody: or Sonnets for the Cradle*, published by John Newbery, ca. 1765, and very possibly edited by Oliver Goldsmith, who is known to have done a lot of hack work for Newbury. Most likely, the song was old at the time, but just how old it is impossible to say. It seems significant that *diddle-diddle* was used to imitate the sound of a fiddle from at least the early sixteenth century, as in "What blunderar is yonder, that playth didle diddle He fyndith fals mesuris out of his fonde fiddil" (John Skelton, "A Garland of Laurel," ca. 1523). Thus, we know that that the *diddle-fiddle* relationship at least was established prior to the birth of Queen Elizabeth and the two Russian Catherines.

Explanations of the origins of children's rhymes constitute a rich subdivision in the field of folk etymology. See also RING AROUND THE ROSY.

cat's-cradle. The origin of the name of the game that children play by weaving a string in complicated patterns between the hands of the players is uncertain—except that it is unlikely to involve a *cat*. Best guess is that the game began as *cratch* or *cratch-cradle* (*scratch-cradle* is another early variant), where *cratch* is an old word for a rack, crib, or manger for holding fodder for farm animals. See also KITTY-CORNER.

cesarean. The name of the operation—*cesarean section*, in full—has been associated with Julius Caesar (100–44 B.C.) since classical times, the supposition being that he was cut from his mother's womb. Even Pliny the Elder (A.D. 23–79) thought that the operation's name came from the Emperor's surname. However, the belief is almost certainly wrong for two reasons: first, the family name, from *caesus*, the cut one, was established long before Caesar's birth; second, Caesar's mother survived his birth for many years. (The operation was hardly ever performed on living women in classical times, and if it was, they rarely survived more than a couple of days.)

Another suggestion is that the name of the procedure (*caesarian*, *caeserean*, and *ceserian* are also acceptable spellings) comes from a Roman law requiring that the belly of any woman who died near term be cut open in order to rescue her infant. The law was supposedly codified as *lex regia* during the reign of Numa Pompilius (ca. 750 B.C.) and renamed *lex caesara* in Julius's time, but the authenticity of this law is highly suspect, considering the early date at which it is said to have been enacted. Most likely, the name of the operation derives simply from *caesus*, past participle of *cadere*, to cut, which was confused almost immediately with *Caesar*.

The earliest example of *Caesarean section* in the *OED* comes from 1615, though a detailed report exists of the performance of the operation on a living woman in Germany in 1610. Shakespeare also alluded earlier to the operation, but not by name, in *Macbeth* (1606). The witches told Macbeth that he could not be killed by "one of woman born," leading him to think himself invulnerable, a fatal mistake, as he learns too late that his final opponent, Macduff, was not born in the natural way, "but from his mother's womb untimely ripped." Shakespeare took this eleventh-century story from Raphael Holinshed's *Chronicles of England, Scotland and Ireland* (2nd edition, 1587). Assuming the incident is based on fact, it is likely that Macduff's mother died before anyone risked cutting her open. Which is not to say that successful cesareans have not been done under primitive conditions. An illustration of one, performed in Uganda in 1879, with the wound closed by iron spikes and thread, is included in Guido Mano's *The Healing Hand: Man and Wound in the Ancient World* (1975). Banana wine was used for anesthesia. Only a few examples of this sort are known, however, and they may not be truly native or have prehistoric equivalents.

charlatan. This term for an impostor or mountebank has been attributed to a nineteenth-century quack dentist in Paris by the name of A. M. Latan. This gentleman, tricked out in a long robe and brass helmet or other fancy headgear, such as a feathered hat, did business in a traveling dispensary—a magnificent carriage, or *char*, whose progress through the city streets was announced by a man blowing a horn. When citizens heard the herald, they would cry out *"Voilà, le char de Latan."* E. Cobham Brewer (1810–97), author of the valuable and entertaining *Brewer's Dictionary of Phrase & Fable*, said that he himself had often seen M. Latan and his famous carriage while living in Paris in the 1840s and '50s.

Possibly, this quack—or Dr. Brewer's account of him—helped popularize the term. But *charlatan* is a considerably older word in both French and English. It comes from the Italian *ciarlatano*, a mountebank, a babbler, in turn from *Cerreto*, a village near Spoleto. The connection between the village and the charlatan who purveys fake remedies is that the inhabitants of the town apparently got a bad name for themselves by specializing in the sale of papal indulgences of doubtful provenance.

Ben Jonson, in *Volpone* (1605), referred to *ciarlitani* who "spred their Clokes on the Pavement," and the word was converted to the present English spelling by 1618 (*OED*), more than two centuries before the appearance of *le char de Latan* in the streets of Paris.

cheap John. This term for inexpensive goods, or a person who sells them, is sometimes said to have been inspired by John Wanamaker, whose department stores in Philadelphia and New York once were among the largest in the United States. Wanamaker made many contributions to merchandising, not least of which was his lament "Half the money I spend on advertising is wasted, and the trouble is, I don't know which half." He was by no means the first *cheap John*, however. *The Oxford English Dictionary* includes an example of a *cheap John* (also called *cheap Jack*) from 1826. This *cheap John* was a British peddler who offered inferior goods at high prices, which he lowered until he found a buyer. By the 1850s, the term was being used in a more general sense as far away as California: "Notwithstanding all its Peter Funk and Cheap John establishments, it sustains a better character than any other city in the state" (H. R. Helper, *The Land of Gold*, 1855). The expression, then, was quite common prior to the founding of John Wanamaker and Co. in 1869.

Cheap, by the way, was once a neutral word, originally referring simply to buying and selling or a place where bargaining was done. Thus, London's *Cheapside* and *Eastcheap* were so called because of their many shops, not because of the prices charged. The word's negative connotations, revolving around low cost and worthlessness, date from the early sixteenth century, when the phrase *good cheap*, meaning a good bargain, was shortened to *cheap*. *John* and *Jack*, meanwhile, have been used generically for all males from at least Chaucer's time, as in *John Doe* and *jack-of-all-trades*.

cheerio. The parting exclamation has been derived from "Chair-oh," as supposedly uttered by departing guests when hailing sedan chairs, much as people today call out "Taxi." This etymology gets high marks for imagination but seems most unlikely, considering that sedan chairs were not seen much on London streets after 1800, while the earliest recorded *cheerio* has been dated only to 1915. It was preceded slightly by *cheeryo* (1914) and *cheero* (1910), from which it probably is descended. The sense of the expression certainly is more similar to *cheer up* (1597) or *cheers* as shouts of encouragement (1751) than to the hypothetical *chair-oh*. See also SEDAN.

chippy (chippie). Now applied to young girls generally, especially fast ones, and sometimes to professionals who play for pay, *chippy* is of comparatively recent (late nineteenth century) but indecently obscure origin. Some of the guesses that have been made of the word's formation are quite picturesque, however. For example, the unabridged *Random House Dictionary* (2nd edition, 1987) suggests that the female sense of the term may derive from *chipping sparrow*, apparently on the theory that the original *chippies* attracted customers by lining up along the street and uttering "cheep, cheep" as though they were birds. But while it is true that women commonly are disparaged as *chicks, geese, quail,* and so on, and that "cheep, cheep" is a variant of "chirp, chirp," one does wonder if—assuming the prostitutes made sounds of this sort—they weren't really saying "cheap, cheap."

A completely different explanation for this word is offered in *A Second Browser's Dictionary* (1983) by John Ciardi, who concluded that the original *chippies* worked in Mexican brothels. The connection here is that the women were paid in poker chips, which they turned back to the management for cash, much as the services of taxi dancers in dance halls used to be procured with paper tickets. The assumption in this case is that *chippy* is a translation from the Spanish, deriving from *una ficha,* a poker chip, via *fichera,* a woman who works for *fichas.* Unfortunately, as Ciardi noted, he himself was unable to find any examples to attest to the existence of the intermediate term, *fichera.*

Which leaves us with the more likely possibility that *chippy* is a spin-off from the French *chipie,* a bad-tempered woman. Arguing in favor of this last theory is that the earliest example of *chippy* in print comes from that center of French culture in America, New Orleans: "This class of females are known by the gang as 'Chippies,' and most of them come from the slums, and work in the cigar and cigarette factories" (*Lantern,* 10/27/1886).

chow. The *chow* that one eats does not come from *chowder,* logical as that assumption might seem, but from the pidgin-English *chow-chow,* used in the nineteenth-century China trade to describe mixtures of different foods, especially a relish of mixed pickles or fruit preserves.

The next question, of course, is the origin of *chow-chow*—a matter of some gastronomic as well as semantic interest. The most palatable theory (to Western tastes) is that it stems from the Mandarin *ch'ao,* to stir, fry, cook. On the other hand, it is difficult to forget the note that the eminent statesman Li Hung Chang addressed to the family of General Charles George "Chinese" Gordon, who had presented him with a prize pedigreed dog upon his visit to England in 1896: "As I am advanced in age, I usually take little food. Therefore, I have been able to take a very small portion of your delicious meat, which, indeed has given me great gratification." With this in mind, and remembering, too, that the Chinese fondness for dog, also called *fragrant meat,* dates to ancient times (recipes for dog flank and liver were found in the tomb of the Marquis of Tai, who died ca. 160 B.C.), it seems more than possible that *chow*, the food, has the same root as *chow*, the dog, deriving from either the Cantonese *kao* or the Mandarin *kou*. And in the latter case, one wonders if the original pidgin-English *chow-chow* did not include something besides pickles and relish. A hair of the dog, so to speak.

clinchpoop. An obsolete term for one who lacks gentlemanly breeding, i.e., a boor or lout, but well worth reviving if only because of its piquant etymology. The august *Oxford English Dictionary* speculates that the term originally meant *clincher*, in the sense of "one who clinches or clenches the poops of vessels." The *clincher* here was a shipyard worker, who clinched, or pounded down, the bolts that fastened *clincher-* or *clinker-built* boats together. We still speak of *clinch* nails and *clinching* arguments. All these *clinches* are variants of the older *clench*, as in *clenched* teeth.

Still, it seems a long stretch from shipwrights—a rough-and-ready sort, no doubt—to the ungentlemanly *clinchpoops*. With all due respect to the monumental *OED*, it is more likely that the *poop* that is *clinched* so tightly by a boor or lout is not the back end of a vessel but the stern of a person (see also FANNY). Consider the sense of the term in the following verse, which happens to be the second item in the earliest known collection of Mother Goose rhymes, *Tommy Thumb's Pretty Song Book*, published in 1744, when children were less sheltered than they are today:

> Little Robin red breast
> Sitting on a pole,
> Niddle Noddle,
> Went his head,
> And Poop went his Hole.

Where *poop* is defined in Nathan Bailey's *English Dictionary* of this period as "to break Wind backwards softly." In this interpretation, then, a *clinchpoop* is practically bursting with what might be called hot air.

clink. The doors of cells in old-time jails may have gone "clink" when they were shut, but *clink* as a generic term for a *hoosegow, lockup, slammer,* or—the newer, softer term—*correctional facility* comes from The Clink, the name of a prison in London's Southwark borough. The prison, in turn, seems to have been so called because it was located on a part of the former Manor of Southwark that bore the name *Clink*. People were being sent to The Clink as early as 1525; by the eighteenth century the term was being used in a general sense for places of confinement, especially small, dismal ones. The prison is long gone, but Clink Street on the south bank of the Thames, just to the west of London Bridge, still exists. See also BRIDEWELL and STIR.

cockroach. The name of the omnipresent insect has nothing to do with either the *cock* that is a male fowl (or any other kind of *cock*, for that matter) or with the *roach* that is a freshwater fish (or any other kind of *roach*, such as the butt of a marijuana cigarette, the upward curve at the foot of a square sail, or an upwardly curved coiffure). Rather, *cockroach* is the product of folk etymology, English speakers having converted the Spanish *cucaracha* into animal names with which they were familiar.

The modern form of the insect's name probably was influenced by an early observer, Captain John Smith, who lived (thanks to Pocahontas) to render the Spanish term as *cacarootch*. Smith, however, was using *caca* in the familiar vulgar sense. (The term comes from the Latin *cacare*, to defecate.) As the Captain reported: "A certaine India Bug, called by the Spaniards a Cacarootch, the which creeping into Chests they eat and defile with their ill-sented dung" (*General Historie of Viginia, New England, and the Summer Isles,* 1624).

Not until the nineteenth century did nervous nellies shorten *cockroach* to *roach* in order to avoid uttering the first syllable. *Rooster roach* also was proposed, but it never caught on, which is surprising, considering that at about this time the *cockchafer* beetle had its name shortened to *chafer*, children's *cockhorses* became *rocking horses,* and the *turkey cock* metamorphosed into the *gentleman turkey*. See also APRICOT.

comptroller. This is a common misspelling, repeatedly made for five centuries by corporations and governments, as in Comptroller General of the United States and the Comptroller of the Currency. The correct spelling is *controller*, reflecting the official's original function, i.e., keeping copies of the official rolls so as to check the treasurer or other person in charge of accounts. The word comes from the Old French *contre*, against + *rolle*, roll. As early as the thirteenth century, however, people began to mix up the *contre-* part with *count*, leading to *counterrollour* and *countrollour*. The next step, accomplished by about 1500, was for highfalutin official scribes to dignify themselves by Frenchifying their job titles. They did this by translating *count* into *compte,* thus producing *comptroller.*

Comptroller's origins, while relatively humble, are not nearly as lowly as those of some other offices. For example, a *constable* (from the Late Latin *comes stabuli,* count of the stable) originally was a head groom; a *marshal* (from the Old High German, *marah,* horse, equivalent to *mare,* and *scalh,* servant) also was a stable hand, and a *steward* (or *sty-ward*) was the man who looked after milord's pigs. These are also the sources of the well-known surnames Constable, Marshall, and, a further distancing from their lowly past, the royal Stewart-Stuart-Steuart clan. It was Walter, the sixth steward, or stewart, of Scotland, who married Marjory, daughter of Robert the Bruce, thereby establishing the line that inherited the Scottish and then the English thrones. See also EQUERRY.

condom. The name of the penile sheath often is ascribed to its presumed inventor, a Doctor or Colonel Condom or Cundum, said to have lived in the time of Charles II. This supposition is nearly as old as the article itself, but the trail of the doctor (or colonel) has proven singularly elusive to modern students of etymology. The search is complicated, moreover, by variability in the spelling of early references to the device—when it was mentioned at all. C—— and c——m were among the early evasions, while Samuel Johnson, Noah Webster, and other compilers of dictionaries for general readers excluded from their works any mention at all of this article of personal apparel.

The first known mention of this item in writing is in connection with the visit of John Campbell, second Duke of Argyll, to Edinburgh on March 6, 1705. Argyll had been appointed by Queen Anne as High Commissioner to the Scottish Parliament, which was then considering union with England. He was only twenty-four, however, and the union of England and Scotland was not the only kind of union he had in mind as he set forth on his journey north from London. As reported in a letter of the time:

He brought along with him a certaine instrument called a Quondam, q$^{ch.}$ occasioned ye debauching of a great number of Ladies of qualitie, and oy$^{r.}$ young gentlewomen.

This example of the word's use, contained in *The Letters from and to Charles Kirkpatrick Sharpe, Esq.* (1888), was supplied to James A. H.

Murray, editor of the *OED*, in a letter on December 6, 1888, from James Main Dixon, who said he supposed the word to be a "curiosity" that would be considered "too utterly obscene for the Dictionary." Dr. Murray apparently agreed, as there is no entry for *condom* either in the first edition of this, the greatest of English dictionaries, or in its initial supplement, published in 1933. *Condom* did not gain admittance to the *OED* until 1972.

As early as 1708, according to William E. Kruck's entertaining and instructive "Looking for Dr. Condom" (Publication of the American Dialect Society, No. 66), the word was attributed to an otherwise unknown *Condon*, in an anonymous poem, "Almonds for Parrots: or, A Soft Answer to a Scurrilous Satyr, Call'd, St. James's Park. With a Word or two in Praise of Condons. Inscrib'd to the Worthy Gentlemen at Wills." Additional evidence of the familiarity of the worthy gentlemen who patronized Wills Coffee-house with this device comes from an item in *The Tatler*, No. 15 (5/14/1709): "A Gentleman of this House . . . observ'd by the Surgeons with much Envy; for he has invented an Engine for the Protection of Harms by Love-Adventures, and has . . . by giving his Engine his own Name, made it obscene to speak of him more."

The trail continues: In 1724, a medical man, Dr. Daniel Turner, described "Dr. C——*n*" as one of the principal candidates for "the Glory of the Invention" (*Syphilis. A Practical Dissertation on the Venereal Disease*, 4th edition), while four years later, "a certain Colonel" was said to be the inventor in a footnote to a poem, "Allusion to the Splendid Shilling," attributed to a Reverend (!) White Kennett. A later edition of this poem (1741) expanded the footnote, saying "Colonel Condom was the Inventor of what is vulgarly called a *c——m*, alias ARMOUR, by the Girls of the Town, and who generally carry this *Defence* about them, at 1 *s*, each."

All the evidence for the existence of the eponymous doctor or colonel is secondhand, however. No independent confirmation of his existence has been discovered, and not for lack of trying. Intensive searches have been conducted of military rosters, directories of London physicians and surgeons, and a wide range of other sources—including the diaries of Samuel Pepys and John Evelyn; the rolls of the Royal Society; the uninhibited poems of the Earl of Rochester; and newspapers, letters, and other records of the time—all without turning up any trace of a Doctor or Colonel Condom or Cundum (not British names, in any event). The same goes for similar surnames that have been suggested, including Compton, Conden, Condon, Conten, and even Gondom.

Nor have any convincing connections been made between the word and any of the other sources that have been proposed for it, including the Latin *condus*, that which preserves; the Medieval Latin *conduma*, house; the Persian *kondū* or *kendū*, an earthen vessel for storing corn or grain; *conundrum*, a riddle without a satisfactory solution and also an old slang term for a woman's genitals; and *Condom*, a town in southern France.

All of these are fairly wild guesses, and some are demonstrably false. For example, the French pronunciation of *Condom*, the town, is like a nasalized "hobo" in English. This is so different from the English pronunciation of the name of the device that the French themselves make no association between the two terms, despite their identity in spelling. Thus, the French have adopted the English word for the article, *le condom*, with essentially the English pronunciation. Of course, the desire to connect words and place names is very strong; see also BRAZILWOOD, CANARY ISLANDS, DIAPER, and SEDAN. Note also that this item, often called *a French letter* by English speakers, is to the French *une capote anglaise*, an English cloak, or—Casanova's term—*une redingote d'Angleterre*, an English overcoat.

And where does this leave us? Mr. Kruck, with the help of a distinguished poet, sums up admirably:

> I believe that Dr. Condom will continue to appear in dictionaries and textbooks for some time to come. And why not? Hundreds of people—Captain Charles C. Boycott, Nicolas Chauvin, the Reverend William A. Spooner, Rudolf Diesel, the Cherokee named Sequoya, Étienne de Silhouette, Thomas Bowdler, Dr. F. A. Mesmer, General Henry Shrapnel, and all the others—have given their names, willingly or not, to our language. These are people, though, who are known to have existed. It is at the edge of their light that the etymologist perceives, at a distance too great for certainty, and in a chiaroscuro too dim for confirmation, a sailor of unusual whittling ability named Scrimshaw . . . a London plumber named Thomas Crapper . . . a wife-killer named Bluebeard . . . an American distiller named Booz or Booze . . . an innovative London hatter named Bowler . . . a printer of bogus U.S. currency named Borghese . . . an eighteenth-century British physician . . .
>
> "for who is not certain that he was meant to be?"
>
> —W. H. Auden

See also, in the order just named, SCRIMSHAW, CRAP, BOOZE, BOWLER, and BOGUS.

cook [someone's] goose. Fable has it that this expression for ruining or spoiling someone's plans or chances arose in medieval times when the inhabitants of a besieged town displayed a goose upon their walls as a sign of contempt for the surrounding army. The exact motive for showing the goose remains under discussion. Perhaps the townsmen meant to imply either that the besiegers were extremely stupid (silly as geese) or that the town was so well stocked with provisions that it could withstand a siege of any length. In any event, so the story goes, the walls were breached despite the townsmen's bravado, and the conquerors avenged the insult by cooking the goose.

The trouble with this explanation is that the phrase *to cook [someone's] goose* doesn't crop up in writing until the middle of the nineteenth century (1851, *OED*), while the variant, *to do [someone's] goose*, has been dated only to 1849, at which time it was characterized as "a vulgar phrase." While words and phrases often are used for many years before they happen to be set down in writing so that makers of dictionaries can record them, the long period of dormancy in this case is—together with fuzziness about the actual time and place of the supposed siege— highly suspect.

On a related culinary question, accountants and others may be interested to learn that *cook* in the sense of falsifying, doctoring, or *cooking the books* has been dated to 1636. In our time, books that have been extremely well cooked are sometimes said to have been *stewed*.

cop. This is not, as sometimes stated, an acronym for Constable On Patrol or for Constabulary Of Police or even for the more elevated Chief Of Police, nor does the term come from *copper*, referring to the buttons on a police officer's coat (made of brass today). *The Oxford English Dictionary* dates the *copper* that walks a beat to 1846, but the noun (abbreviated to the modern *cop* by 1859) was formed from the verb *to cop*, meaning to capture, catch, or nab. A *copper*, then, was "one who cops," or catches, thieves. What happened was that the same terminology was applied to the police as to their closest associates, the criminals. Just as the thief was said *to cop* merchandise, so the lawman was said *to cop*, or catch, the thief.

The origin of the verb (dated to 1704) is matter of some debate. *The American Heritage Dictionary* traces the English word to the Dutch *kapen*, in turn from the Old Frisian *cāpia*, to buy, which also was used as a euphemism for "to practice piracy." The *OED* and *The Random House Dictionary*, meanwhile, suggest that *cop* represents a broad pronuncation of the Scottish *cap*, to seize or arrest, in turn from the Old French *caper*, to take, and ultimately the Latin *capere*. This last would make *cop* cousin to *capture*. Other possibilities are that the verb comes from the Gypsy *cop*, to steal, or the Hebrew *cop*, a hand or palm, used by the thief when *copping* something. Whatever the truth here, it is certain the *cop* is based neither on the metal nor on one of the acronyms of which folk etymologizers are so fond. See also TIP.

coward. This epithet for a timorous person has nothing to do with the *cow* that gives milk, or with the similar-sounding *cowherd*, who runs away when rustlers appear because he is *cow-hearted*, or with *cower*, even though that is what *cowards* do (*cower* probably comes from a Scandinavian word meaning to sleep or lie in wait). Rather, the term of reproach derives from the Old French *coart*, coward, in turn from *coue*, tail (hence, also, the tail-like *queue*, and the *cue* that is used in playing billards or pool). The Latin root is *cauda*, also denoting the anatomical appendage (and also the source of the musical *coda*).

The exact association between tails and cowardice is lost in the mists of the thirteenth century, when the word appeared in English, but the basic image seems to be of the frightened animal that slinks away, tail drooping between its hind legs, or perhaps to the one that actually turns tail and flees as fast as it can. It seems significant that the name of the timid hare in the medieval fable *Reynard the Fox* is *Couart*. The *-ard* part of *coward*, meanwhile, frequently appears as a pejorative suffix indicating that someone is doing something in an excessive or conspicuous way, as in *bastard, buzzard, dastard, drunkard, laggard, sluggard,* and *stinkard*.

cowslip. Illustrating the lengths to which our more refined ancestors would go to avoid the obvious are some of the etymologies that have been proposed for this common name for the Old World primrose (or marsh marigold in the United States). Among them: (1) that it comes from the Anglo-Saxon cow, *cū* + *slyppe*, with the *slyppe*, in turn, deriving from *slupan*, to paralyze, the name referring to the plant's use as a sedative; (2) that it derives from the basic cow, but in the possessive form, *cūs*, cow's + *lippe*, lip, i.e., cow's lip; and (3) that it is a corruption of the Anglo-Saxon *ceselib*, the dried stomach of a calf, which the plant supposedly resembles. These are all "nice" explanations. Actually, the earthy Anglo-Saxons had another image in mind, based on the afore-mentioned *cū* + *slyppe*, a sticky substance or slime, the bright yellow flower's name translating as "cow dung." A relative of *cowslip* is *oxlip*, which has nothing to do with the animal's lip and is somewhat larger.

See also PRIMROSE.

crap. Yes, Virginia, there really was a Thomas Crapper. An English sanitary engineer, he was born in 1837 and died in 1910, and he did make an important contribution to toilet technology. In 1882, Crapper invented a Valveless Water Waste Preventer (Patent No. 4,990). This siphon-and-ball device, a direct ancestor of the modern john, produced an efficient flush with as little as two gallons, then automatically shut off the flow of water to the holding tank after it was refilled. This saved large quantities of what already was becoming a precious commodity.

The virtues of Patent No. 4,990 were recognized immediately by public authorities, private householders, and Royalty, with Thomas Crapper & Co. receiving a series of warrants over a period of fifty years that enabled the firm to proclaim in advertisements that it served "By Appointment" to Edward VII, while Prince of Wales as well as King, and then to George V, also as Prince and King. (An ingenious fellow, Crapper deserves to be remembered, too, for such related inventions as his system for automatically flushing public urinals and, Patent No. 11,604, a Self-Rising Closet Seat.)

Folklore and folk etymology have it that the various forms of *crap* encountered today—whether as noun, verb, or exclamation; or in the extended senses of nonsense, rubbish, insincere talk, and so on—derive from the inventor's name. But this is inconsistent with the use of *crapping-casa, -case, -castle,* and *-ken* to refer to a privy or water closet some years before Mr. Crapper began to market his device. The term first appears in the written record in 1676 as *croppin-ken,* where *ken* is an old slang word for a house, especially one frequented by thieves or other low characters. *Crapping ken,* meanwhile, has been dated to 1846 (when Thomas Crapper was but a lad of nine).

The difference between *crop* and *crap* here and in other instances has caused some debate about the origin of the term. The initial allusion might have been to the *crop* that is harvested, in which case "I have to go to the cropping ken" was a euphemistic expression on a par with "I have to go to the garden to water some petunias." Or the reference might have been to that which is cropped, as in Captain Francis Grose's definition of *croppen:* "The tail. The croppen of the rotan; the tail of the cart. Croppen ken; the necessary house" (*A Classical Dictionary of the Vulgar Tongue,* 1796). More likely, however, the *crop* spelling merely represents the southern English pronunciation of *crap* (from the Middle English *crap* or *crappe,* chaff), in use from the fifteenth century to refer to discarded husks of grain and other scraps, leftovers, sediments, and residues.

The two spellings were used interchangeably throughout much of the eighteenth and nineteenth centuries. Thus, in the eighteenth century, a man who was hanged might be said to be *crapped* or *cropped* (i.e., harvested, or cut down), and Grose listed both *crap* and *crop* for money. (The fiscal sense may have arisen from the earlier characterization of money as a residue, *dust,* from ca. 1600, and perhaps from *gold dust.*) Meanwhile, in the United States, from Revolutionary times onward, *crop* was (and still is, to some extent) pronounced and even spelled *crap* in the Southeast, e.g., "North Carolina is notorious for a peculiar flatness of pronunciation in such words as *crap* for 'crop' " (S. A. Hammett, *A Stray Yankee in Texas,* 1853). Mark Twain, who had an excellent ear for dialect, also rendered *crop* as *crap* when imitating the speech of East Tennessee in *The Gilded Age:* " 'Ole Drake Higgins he's been down to Shelby las' week. Tuck his crap down . . . hit warn't no time to sell, he says, so he fotched it back again . . . ' " (1873, with Charles Dudley Warner).

The *a* form of the word, as a verb meaning "to defecate," is dated to 1874 in *The Oxford English Dictionary,* the citation coming from the second edition of John Camden Hotten's *Slang Dictionary.* The verb also was listed in *Slang and Its Analogues* (1890–1904) by J. S. Farmer and W. E. Henley. (Henley is better remembered as the author of "Invictus," with its oft-recited "I am the master of of my fate . . . the captain of my soul.") Farmer and Henley included it in their first volume in a list of synonyms for "To bury a Quaker," an expression that they defined as meaning "To evacuate; to ease oneself." Among the synonyms: "To go to the crapping castle, casa, or ken . . . ; to [go to] the bog-house, rear, dunnock, coffee-shop; to see one's aunt; to crap; to go and sing 'sweet violets'; to go where the Queen always goes on foot."

Hotten's reference predates Thomas Crapper's great invention by eight years. The absence of other early citations is not too surprising, since low words such as this were not ordinarily committed to writing during the Victorian period. Nevertheless, it is hard to believe that the short form of the word was not in use long before Crapper's time, considering the older examples of *crapping ken*, the seventeenth-century *croppin* and *croppen ken*, the interchangeability of *crap* and *crop*, and the widespread circulation of the verb. Thus, in Volume II of *Slang and Its Analogues* (C to Fizzle, 1891), the verb is characterized as "common," while in Joseph Wright's six-volume *English Dialect Dictionary* (1898–1905), the short form is recorded both as a noun meaning "ordure" and in extended use "as a term of gross insult, south Nottingham. What crap's that y'er talkin?"

Which does not mean that Thomas Crapper loses all honor. If he was not the progenitor of the word, the confluence of his surname with the term almost certainly helped popularize it. Otherwise, people today might be using the name of one of his competitors, announcing that they have "to pay a visit to the Twyford" or that such and such "is a load of Sharpe."

Judging from the frequency with which *crap* began, er, cropping up in the works of Hemingway, Dos Passos, and other Americans following World War I, it appears likely that the members of the American Expeditionary Force (many of whom were country boys, unfamiliar with the wonders of indoor plumbing) were especially impressed by seeing Crapper's name on porcelain fixtures when they went, as the saying goes, to wash their hands in the little boys' room. In return, Crapper himself has gained through association with the word a measure of immortality. It seems a petty injustice, therefore, that the nonentities who made up the Greater London Council in 1979 should have decided against marking his former residence at 12 Thornsett Road with a commemorative plaque. He deserves better, though he does not really need it.

See also CANT, CONDOM, JOHN, and LOO.

craps. The name of the dice game has nothing to do with the preceding entry, despite that word's use as an exclamation of disgust by disappointed players. Nor does it come, as various writers have suggested, from *crapaud*, toad, a traditional term of disparagement for a Frenchman. (The coat of arms of the City of Paris features three toads in the act of jumping, but the epithet may reflect some confusion with another amphibian, and another insult for the French, i.e., *frog eater*.) According to the *crapaud* school, Bernard de Marigny, a notorious gambler in New Orleans around 1800, was known as *Johnny Crapaud* to Americans, who subsequently shortened the name of his favorite game to *crapo* and then *craps*. The story has a couple of large holes in it, however.

First, de Marigny named a street Rue de Craps about 1804—an unlikely choice if the term was based on an insult to himself. Second, the game that de Marigny played was not craps as we now know it but hazard, an English predecessor of craps, which had emigrated to France, where it was known as *krabs*. (The French name, used in 1792 in the *Encyclopédie Méthodique*, came from *crabs*, the English term for a throw of two or three, in which case the shooter lost his stakes and was said to have *crabbed* or *come off crabs*.) Third, the French themselves, not the Americans, corrupted *krabs* to *creps* and then *craps*, the last appearing in 1818 in an article on Parisian gambling houses in the *Bibliothèque Historique*.

The root word, then, is *crabs*, not *crapaud*, and de Marigny is not responsible for the name of the game. Just why the English called a low throw *crabs* is not known, but crabs commonly are regarded as cross, ill-dispositioned critters, as are losing gamblers.

See also MAIN CHANCE.

crayfish/crawfish. The fishiest thing about the creature (also known as a *crawdad* in the United States) is its name, since it is a crustacean, not a fish. The term is a product of folk etymology, the folk gradually converting the last syllable of the Middle English *crevis*, crab, into a word that sounded and looked more familiar to them. The process seems to have been largely accomplished during the sixteenth century, which witnessed the appearance of *crefysshes* (1555), *crefishe* (1571), and *crayfish* (1597), although careful writers kept using the correct term for many years thereafter, e.g., from the *Works* of Thomas Brown (1663–1704): "Crustaceous animals, as crevises, crabs, and lobsters." The original English term came from the Old French *crevice*, whence the modern French word for crayfish, *écrevisse*.

curmudgeon. All writers are thieves, always stealing to some extent from each other, but the etymological history of this term for a grouchy, miserly person provides an object lesson of the dangers of automatically taking without thinking.

When Samuel Johnson began preparing the entry for *curmudgeon* in his monumental *Dictionary of the English Language* (1755), he found that he had mislaid a note with the name of his source for the word's etymology (an occupational hazard for lexicographers, who swim in seas of slips of paper). Accordingly, he passed along the information that the term arose as a faulty way "of pronouncing *coeur mechant*, Fr.

an unknown correspondent." The unknown correspondent was making a fairly wild guess—*coeur mechant* translates as "evil heart"—but etymology was not Johnson's strong point; see also BONFIRE, INTERNECINE, and SEDAN.

Unfortunately, the next great English dictionary maker, John Ash, not only swallowed Johnson's explanation hook, line, and sinker, but sought to improve upon it. Misinterpreting the "Fr." in Johnson's entry as an abbreviation for "French" instead of "From," and apparently not knowing any French himself, Ash informed readers of his *New and Complete Dictionary of the English Language* (1775) that *curmudgeon* derived "from Fr. *coeur*, unknown, *mechant*, correspondent"!

With advances in etymology, Ash's mistake was recognized. Both the Reverend Walter Skeat, in the first edition of *Concise Etymological Dictionary* (1882) and the Reverend A. Smythe Palmer, in *Folk-Etymology* (1890), explained that *curmudgeon* actually derived from *cornmudgin*, i.e., corn hoarder, the *mudgin* part being associated with the Anglo-Saxon *much* or *mich*, to hide, or the Old French *mucier*, also to conceal or hide away. Their basis for this was Philemon Holland's rendering of the Latin *frumentarius*, corn dealer, in his translation of Livy's history of Rome (1600). In Holland's version, "certain cornmudgins" were said to have paid fines "for hourding up and keeping in their graine." It also seemed to Skeat and Palmer that the disparaging use of *curmudgeon/cornmudgin* fit logically with the bad press traditionally given to those stingy fellows who sit on stocks of food in time of public need, e.g., "He that withholdeth corn, the people shall curse him" (*Proverbs*, 11:26).

Alas, this explanation, too, had to be abandoned after it was realized that *curmudgeon* (1577, *OED*) appears in the written record nearly a quarter of a century before *cornmudgin* and, the clincher, that the latter does not seem to have been used by any writer except Holland. The *cornmudgin*, then, was just a joke—Holland's pun upon the preexisting word.

With this, students of language are left in disarray. Skeat retracted his earlier opinion in the fourth edition of his work (1910), marking *curmudgeon* as "origin unknown." He speculated that the *cur* part came from the *cur* that is dog and that the *mudgeon* was somehow connected with the Lowland Scottish *murgeon*, to mock, to grumble, or *mudgeon*, a grimace. Other lexicographers have seen resemblances between *mudgeon* and the dialectical *mudgel* as in *mudgel-hole*, a dunghill midden, and between the *-eon* endings of *curmudgeon*, *bludgeon*, and *dudgeon* (the last two also being of unknown origin). But no one has been able to make any firm connections between the word and any of the sources suggested. The uncertainty is enough to make a curmudgeon weep.

curry favor. In the beginning, it was a horse that was being curried, not a favor. This expression derives from the Old French *estriller fauvel*, to curry the fallow horse, used by the old French themselves as a metaphor for insincere flattery. (*Fallow* here does not refer to that which is unseeded, as fallow land; rather, it is an old word for a brownish or reddish yellow, not often used today except when referring to the *fallow deer* of Eurasia.) The phrase entered English about the year 1400 as *curry favel* and began to be transformed within the next hundred years into *curry favor*, as in "Flatter not as do some, With none curry favour" (Alexander Barclay, *The Mirrour of Good Manners*, ca. 1510). Thus, the original image of grooming was lost as the English connected *favel* with a more familiar word, *favor*, that seemed to be in accord with the sense of the expression.

The original Old French *estriller fauvel* comes from an allegory, the *Roman de Fauvel* (ca. 1310), in which the *fauvel* horse stands for fraud, cunning, and duplicity. The bad opinion that the medieval French had of such horses (because of their indefinite color?) also is indicated by an anagram that was devised to explain the word's origin from the initial letters of the vices of *Flatterie*, *Avarice*, *Vilenie*, *Variété*, *Envie*, and *Lâcheté* (corruption). As explanations go, however, this one is in the same class as that for CABAL or TIP.

cutlet. Not a "little cut," as often presented in restaurants, but a "little rib," from the French *cotellete*. The Latin root is *costa*, side, rib, which means that *cutlet* has more in common, etymologically speaking, with the seashore or *coast* than it does with the butcher's *cut*.

D

dark horse. The idea of a horse whose capabilities are unknown is so picturesque that a myth inevitably was created to explain it. Thus, it is said that a Tennessean named Sam Flynn (or Flyn) went from town to town, entering a dark horse named Dusty (or Dusky) Pete in local races. The horse looked like a lame plug until each race began, when it would suddenly stop limping, begin sprinting, and make its owner a lot of money. This is such a good story that one yearns to believe it. Alas, the expression began as British slang, not American. Benjamin Disraeli helped popularize it, the oldest known example of the phrase coming from his novel *The Young Duke* (1831): "All the ten-to-oners were in the rear, and a dark horse, which had never been thought of, and which the careless St. James had never even observed, rushed past the grand stand in sweeping triumph."

Nowadays, the phrase is heard more often in political circles than around the race track. The extension in meaning from little-known, long-shot horses to little-known, long-shot political candidates seems to have taken place in the United States in the 1840s or '50s. James K. Polk, who came out of nowhere to win the Democratic presidential nomination on the ninth ballot at the party's convention in 1844, usually is described as the first *dark horse* candidate, but it is not known if the term was applied to him at the time. He is referred to as a "dark horse" in S. M. Welch's *Home History. Recollections of Buffalo During the Decade from 1830 to 1840,* but this memoir was not published until 1891, after the political sense of the expression was well established. The oldest known specific reference to a political *dark horse* comes from a tub-thumping speech by New York's Hamilton Fish in 1860 in support of Abraham Lincoln: "We want a log-splitter, not a hair-splitter; a flat-boatman, not a flat statesman; a log cabin, coonskin, hard cider, old Abe and dark horse—hurrah!" (Hans Sperber and Travis Trittschuh, *American Political Terms,* 1962). Which is not the kind of oratory that one expects from staid and dignified Republicans today.

Davy Jones's locker. Various explanations have been offered for this nautical expression denoting the bottom of the sea, especially with reference to sailors' graves or the place where ships or goods are lost forever. Some say there was a real Davy Jones, perhaps the owner of a British pub, commemorated in a sixteenth-century song, "Jones Ale Is Newe." This Jones kept his ale in a locker, which became an object of dread to seamen. Just why hard-drinking sailors should fear the locker is not known. Maybe one or more of them met the same fate as the Duke of Clarence, executed in 1478, reportedly by being drowned in a butt of malmsey wine. Others say that the real Davy Jones was a pirate, presumably a ferocious fellow, who caused many poor souls to walk the plank.

The *Jones* of *Davy Jones* also has been construed as a corruption of *Jonah* (or a variant of the name, *Jonas*). This interpretation makes sense to the extent that the expression arose among sailors and that the Hebrew prophet is a symbol of bad luck. Mariners, especially, have cause to remember the biblical story of the boat bound for Tarshish that was caught in a terrible storm, raised by the Lord, because Jonah was aboard.

The *Davy* part, meanwhile, has been explained both as a reference to St. David, patron saint of Wales (the idea being that the expression was coined by Welsh sailors), and as a corruption of the West Indian *duffy* or *duppy*, meaning "devil."

The last of these theories seems to hold the most water, so to speak, in large part because of the testimony of Tobias Smollett, an early user of the expression. (Smollett often is credited with having been the first to employ *Davy Jones's locker* in print in 1751, but Ernest Weekley includes a citation from 1726 in *An Etymological Dictionary of Modern English*.) Smollett's explanation of the expression fits well with the "devil" theory, and he was in a good position to know what he was talking about, since before embarking on a career as a novelist, he had served in the Navy as a surgeon's mate and lived long enough in the West Indies to meet and marry the daughter of a Jamaican planter. Thus, Smollett tells in *The Adventures of Peregrine Pickle* how his hero and two friends created an apparition that frightened Peregrine's uncle, Commodore Hawser Trunnion, practically out of his wits:

> "By the Lord! Jack, you may say what you wool; but I'll be damned if it was not Davy Jones himself. I know him by his saucer eyes, his three rows of teeth, and tail, and the blue smoke that came out of his nostrils. . . ."

This same Davy Jones [Smollett explains], according to the mythology of sailors, is the fiend that presides over all the evil spirits of the deep, and is often seen in various shapes, perching among the rigging on the eve of hurricanes, ship-wrecks, and other disasters to which the sea-faring life is exposed, warning the devoted wretch of death and woe.

Smollet's portrait, then, is of a devil that brings bad luck—a *duppy Jonah*, perhaps, that has metamorphosed into *Davy Jones*.

dead as a doornail. A popular explanation of this phrase is that the knockers on doors used to be placed so that they would strike against one of the large-headed nails with which doors formerly were studded. The theory is that people thought of this nail as being dead because it was rapped on the head so often. This conjecture was put forward as far back as 1818 by Henry J. Todd, who put out an edition of Johnson's dictionary "with numerous corrections and additions." But his conjecture is just that—an inference without any real evidence to back it up.

A better guess was made much more recently by Robert Claiborne, who pointed out in *Loose Cannons and Red Herrings* (1988) that until fairly recent times ships, houses, and articles of furniture usually were constructed with wooden pegs, or treenails, rather than with metal nails, which were produced by hand and accordingly expensive. But for making doors, which are under repeated stress from opening and closing, metal nails often were used. The doornails were driven all the way through the boards, then clinched by hammering down the points. Hence, Claiborne concluded, the doornails were "dead" because they could never be reused.

About *dead as a doornail* only one thing is really certain, and that is that the expression is extremely old. It has been dated to 1350 in *The Oxford English Dictionary* and probably was in use for quite some time before being committed to writing. Variations on the theme include *deaf as a doornail*, *dour as a doornail*, *dumb as a doornail*, and *dead as a herring*. Some of these are of considerable antiquity, too. "As doumbe as a dore" appears in William Langland's *Piers Plowman* (1362), while "Dom as a dore-nayle & defe was he bathe" crops up in the anonymous *Wars of Alexander* (ca. 1400–50). Thus, this metaphor has shown remarkable staying power even though the original image is hazy, to say the least.

debt. This is an example of misguided scholarship by medieval monks for which modern grade schoolers still pay a price. The word entered English in the thirteenth century as *dette*, a direct transferral from the

Old French *dette*, also referring to a liability or other obligation. The more learned monks realized, however, that the French word derived from the Latin *dēbitum*, and so they began "correcting" *dette* by inserting a *b* into it. By the sixteenth century, the standard spelling had become *debt*. Most people kept on pronouncing the term in the same old way, however, with the result that students now have to remember to add the silent *b* when spelling it. Similarly, the existence of Latin forms led to the insertion of silent *b*'s in the Middle English *dout, plummer,* and *sutel* to form *doubt, plumber,* and *subtle.* See also ISLAND.

demijohn. This term for a large, narrow-necked bottle, often encased in wickerwork and holding five gallons or more, underwent a sex change while crossing the Channel from France to England in the eighteenth century. The French call this bottle a *Dame Jeanne,* or Lady Jane, which the English misheard as *demi-john,* perhaps because they were in their cups at the time.

For more about personal names for containers, see JUG, IN THE.

devil and the deep blue sea, between the. The *devil* in this old saying often is construed as referring to a seam between the planks of a wooden ship rather than to His Satanic Majesty. According to this interpretation, a sailor caulking this seam would be perched in a precarious position—in what a landlubber might describe as between a rock and a hard place. There are difficulties with this theory, however, the first being disagreement among authorities over the exact position on a vessel of the *devil* seam. *Funk & Wagnalls Standard Dictionary* (1893–95) defines the nautical *devil* as the long seam on the bottom of a ship's hull, between the keel and the adjoining plank, or (technically speaking) the garboard strake—which doesn't fit at all with the sense of the saying. For anyone to be between this *devil* and the deep blue sea, the ship would have to be turned upside down. Other authorities have suggested that the *devil* is either the longest seam on a ship's deck, nearest the side; or the seam at, or just above, the water line; or any seam at all that is difficult to caulk ("the devil to caulk"?).

Beyond all this, there is a chronological problem with the theory of a marine origin for the *devil* in *between the devil and the deep blue sea.* While the term has been dated in the sense of a vessel's seam only to 1865 (in Admiral William Henry Smyth's *The Sailor's Word-Book; An Alphabetical Digest of Nautical Terms*), much earlier examples have been found of the phrase (and a variant, *between the devil and the Dead Sea*).

The oldest citation in the *OED* is from the memoir of a Scottish soldier who used the expression when telling how he was caught between friendly and enemy fire while serving with the Swedish Army of Gustavus Adolphus: "I, with my partie, did lie on our poste, as betwixt devill and the deep sea" (Colonel Robert Monro, *His Expedition with the worthy Scots Regiment called Mac-Keyes Regiment*, 1637).

Though it is a truism that words may be bruited about for many years prior to the earliest written examples recorded by dictionary makers, the lag of more than two hundred years in this case seems very odd, considering that caulking is a routine operation in wooden vessels and that *devil*, if it existed in the marine sense, must have been used frequently. Given the absence of earlier nautical examples, and the profusion of analogous devilish phrases, such as *give the devil his due*, *go to the devil*, *play the devil*, and *speak of the devil*, all of which have been dated to the seventeenth century or before, it appears likely that Satan himself originally was meant in *between the devil and the deep blue sea*. The sense of the expression probably had more to do with being caught between fire and water than with the perils of caulking a boat. See also DEVIL TO PAY, THE.

devil to pay, the. In the search for a complicated explanation of the apparently obvious, it is often stated quite confidently that this proverbial saying arose as a nautical expression. The *devil*, according to this interpretation, originally referred to a seam that was awkward to caulk. *Pay*, meanwhile, is a standard marine term meaning "to smear or cover with pitch or other waterproof material." This kind of *pay* has nothing to do with one's salary; it derives from the Old French *peier* and the Latin *picāre*, to smear with pitch, and ultimately the Latin word for the substance itself, *pix*. The supposition, then, is that *the devil to pay*, in the sense of trouble to be faced, began as a reference to a particularly difficult caulking job, a notion that is reinforced by the common extension of the phrase to "There'll be the devil to pay and no pitch hot."

The principal difficulties with the notion of a marine origin for this saying are doubt as to which of the many seams on a wooden vessel was the *devil* and the fact that this sense of the word has been dated only to 1865. Meanwhile, the phrase itself is known to be some four hundred years older. Thus, from the *Reliquiae Antiqua: Scraps from Ancient Manuscripts*, T. Wright and J. O. Halliwell, eds., 1841–43): "Better wer be at tome for ay than her to serue, the devil to pay," which translates (assuming "tome" is some scribe's mistake for "home") as

"Better were it to be at home forever than here to serve, the devil to pay."

The same two difficulties are encountered in the case of DEVIL AND THE DEEP BLUE SEA, and for the same reasons cited there, this appears to a good time to get out Ockham's razor. According to this principle, formulated by William of Ockham in the fourteenth century, one should not assume more causes for any phenomenon than are absolutely necessary to explain it. Following this rule, it is more probable that *devil* and *pay* should be taken at face value in their dominant senses than construed in their specialized marine meanings. If so, *the devil to pay* originally referred to the traditional, somewhat optimistic belief that those who gain advantage by dealing with Satan eventually will have to pay for what they have obtained.

diaper. Attempts have been made to connect this word for a kind of cloth and a baby's undergarment to the Belgian city of Ypres, a historic center of the cloth trade. But *diaper* actually derives from the Medieval Greek *diaspros,* pure white. The geographic theory is, as *The Oxford English Dictionary* puts it, "a gratuitous guess," with "no etymological or historical basis." The guess may have been inspired by the common British mispronunciation of the town name as "wipers," as in the World War I saying "We were wiped out at Wipers." See also SEDAN, TWEED, and VALANCE.

dickens. The exclamation "What the dickens!" or "Go to the dickens!" may conjure up the name of the great novelist (1812–70), but it is much older, as in "I cannot tell what the dickens his name is" (William Shakespeare, *Merry Wives of Windsor,* 1597). The origin of the term is in doubt. Among the possibilities suggested: that it is an elision of *devilkins,* little devil; a fanciful use of the personal name *Dicken,* a pet form of *Richard;* or a euphemistic deformation of *Nick,* meaning Old Nick, who is Satan.

In practice, the exclamation certainly is a minced oath. "What the dickens!" is on a par with "What the deuce!" as a euphemism for "What the devil!" (speak of the devil and he may appear), while "Go to the dickens!" is another, marginally nicer, way of telling someone to "Go to hell!" See also HARLEQUIN, JINGO, and OLD NICK.

Dixie. The nickname for the Southern states that formed the Confederacy is of obscure origin. It appeared just before the Civil War (or War Between the States, if you come from Dixie) in "Dixie's Land," a song composed in 1859 for Byrant's Minstrels in New York City by Daniel Decator Emmett, himself a famous minstrel. Written in dialect ("In Dixie Lann where I was bawn in, Arly on one frosty mawnin"), the song was popular with Northern as well as Southern audiences. Southerners made it their own in 1861, however, playing it at the inauguration of Jefferson Davis as President of the Confederate States of America on February 18. Thereafter it became the unofficial national anthem of the Confederacy. Given the importance of *Dixie* in our national history, it is not surprising that a number of theories have been proposed to explain its origin. (Word lovers abhor linguistic vacuums.) The three principal ones, in ascending order of probability, are:

1. *Dixie* comes from the name of a kindly slave owner, Johan Dixie, or Dixy, who had a farm on the island of Manhattan in the late eighteenth or nineteenth century. His slaves, so this story goes, either were sold or sent south, either because Mr. Dixie (or Dixy) died or because of the rising tide of abolitionist sentiment in the North. (By 1804, all the Northern states had either abolished slavery outright or enacted measures that would lead to its abolition.) The transported slaves then looked back longingly upon their former home, *Dixie's Land*, which became a symbol for them of comfort and contentment. If all this is so, the original *Dixie Land* was in New York City and Emmett got it all wrong when he wrote, "I wish I was in de land ob cotton, Old times dar am not forgotten, Look away . . . Dixie Land!"

2. *Dixie* is a modification—a Creole pronunciation—of the last name of Jeremiah Dixon, who, with Charles Mason, settled a dispute between Pennsylvania and Maryland by surveying the boundary between them in 1763–67. The border, commonly referred to as *Mason and Dixon's line* (from 1779 in *A Dictionary of American English*), was regarded prior to the Civil War as the boundary between the free states of the North and the slave states of the South. It is not clear why, considering the neutrality of the line itself, *Dixie Land* should have been applied to the South rather than the North or, for that matter, why it was the *Dixie* that caught on, not *Mason Land*. Lending some credence to this theory, however, is the fact that the *Dixon* and *Dixie* apparently were confused from an early date, e.g., "Suffysit to say I got across Mason & Dixie's line safe at last" (*Vanity Fair*, 5/25/1861).

3. *Dixie* comes from the French *dix*, ten, which appeared on bilingual bank notes issued by the Citizens Bank of Louisiana prior to the Civil War. According to this theory, the ten-dollar bills, with English on one

side and French on the other, were called *dixies*, with *land of dixies* referring to the area where the bills circulated, first just New Orleans, then Louisiana, and finally the entire South. The catch here is that an example of the plural *dixies* has not yet been recorded. On the other hand, the assumed *dixies*, as in *land of*, is very close to the original title of Emmett's song, "Dixie's Land."

donkey. The name of the barnyard critter is of uncertain origin though surprisingly new. Captain Francis Grose, who was the first to record the word, made a pass at its etymology: "DONKEY, DONKEY DICK. A he, or jack ass; called donkey, perhaps, from the Spanish or don-like gravity of that animal, intitled also the King of Spain's trumpeter" (*A Classical Dictionary of the Vulgar Tongue*, 1785). This is a fairly wild guess, revealing more about traditional British prejudices against the Spanish than about the origin of the term. More likely, it comes from *dun*, the animal's color, or from *Duncan* (Celtic for "brown head"), which is one of the pet names often given by farmers to this animal. Other familiar names for Mr. Long Ears include Dicky, Jenny, Neddy, and—in Scotland—Cuddy, perhaps from Cuthbert. (*Donkey's years*, meaning a long time, is just a play, by the way, on *donkey's ears*.)

A new name was needed for the animal, hitherto known as an *ass*, because of the shift that had taken place in the preceding hundred years or so in the pronunciation of the anatomical *arse*, with the *r* dropping out, so that the four-letter word sounded like the three-letter one. As a result, refined people became nervous about saying the animal's name. Thus, Captain Grose noted in a later entry in his dictionary on another term for the same creature: "JOHNNY BUM. A he or jack ass; so called by a lady that affected to be extremely polite and modest, who would not say jack because it was vulgar, nor ass because it was indecent."

The change in this animal's name was part of a general proto-Victorian movement to clean up the English language. See also APRICOT, BLOODY, EASEL, and HAVE [ONE'S] ASS IN A SLING.

dormouse. Not a mouse that lives in or near a door, but a small, Old World rodent that nests in trees or bushes. Looking more like a squirrel than a mouse, and intermediate in size, the animal is both nocturnal and hibernatory. As a result, dormice (or sometimes *dormouses*, back in the sixteenth and seventeenth centuries) usually are asleep, or dormant, when stumbled upon by people. The first part of the animal's name probably derives from the French *dormir*, to sleep, also the ancestor of *dormant*.

The world's most famous dormouse is the one that Alice met when having tea with the March Hare and the Mad Hatter. It was fast asleep, naturally, when Alice appeared. The other two animals used the dormouse as a cushion for their elbows, but when they wanted it to tell them a story, they woke it up by pinching it. As Alice left the party, the Hare and the Hatter were trying to stuff the dormouse into the teapot.

Dormice do become quite plump before hibernating—especially the Continental species, which are somewhat larger than their British cousins—and the French, particularly, think they are quite tasty. They are not usually taken with tea, however. See also GRIN LIKE A CHESHIRE CAT; MAD AS A HATTER; and TITMOUSE.

doughboy. George Armstrong Custer's widow explained in her memoir of life as a soldier's wife that "A 'doughboy' is a small, round doughnut served to sailors on shipboard, generally with hash. Early in the Civil War the term was applied to the large globular brass buttons on the infantry uniform, from which it passed by natural transition to the infantrymen themselves" (Elizabeth Bacon Custer, *Tenting on the Plains,* 1887).

Well, perhaps. Mrs. Custer is certainly wrong about when the term arose, and she may be wrong about the source, too. The word has been traced back to the decade prior to the Civil War, and it may well go back to the time of the Mexican War of 1846–48. Thus, from a reminiscence of that conflict, written about 1859 though not published until much later: "If twenty Dragoons can't whip a hundred greasers with the Sabre, I'll join the 'Doughboys' and carry a fence rail [a rifle] all my life" (Samuel E. Chamberlain, *My Confession,* 1956).

The earlier *doughboys* may or may not have been so called because they wore uniforms with globular brass buttons. For example, it also has been suggested that the *doughboy* that is a soldier (as opposed to the flour or cornmeal *doughboys* mentioned by Mrs. Custer) comes from '*dobe* or *dobie,* common abbreviations of *adobe,* the different forms of the word once having been used interchangeably, as in "The Carpenters at Work getting the Doughboy tools ready" (1856 in *Montana Historical Society Contributions,* 1940). According to this theory, *adobe/doughboy* was applied to soldiers in the Southwest either because

(1) they spent a lot of time making adobe bricks for buildings on military posts; or (2) they lived in adobe barracks; or (3) they used the white adobe clay, or dough, to clean their belts and other leatherwork; or (4) their feet became encased in doughy masses as they marched through areas of adobe mud. Or then again, it has been posited that the name stuck because the soldiers were notably fond of eating Mrs. Custer's doughboys.

Out of this morass of speculation, one common strand emerges, and this is that *doughboy*—the most frequently used term for American soldiers in World War I—began life as an uncomplimentary word. Depending on which theory one prefers, the infantrymen were called *doughboys* because they were pasty-faced (as though frightened of something or because they were covered with white clay); or the name implies that they were sissies, always living in comfort in adobe barracks; or they were looked down upon (particularly by mounted dragoons, such as Samuel Chamberlain) simply because they were foot soldiers, who had to slog along through doughy mud (like *beetle crushers, blisterfoots, gravel pushers,* or *ground pounders,* which are other terms for infantrymen); or that the name began as a derisive reference to a staple of the soldiers' diet.

Of these possible motives, the last has the strongest ring of truth, principally because food terms loom so large in the lexicon of disparagement (witness *bean eater, chili chaser, fish eater, frog eater, limey, meatball, pork eater,* and *spaghetti bender,* among many other similar insults for different national and ethnic groups). Also, the culinary factor shows up clearly in another pre–Civil War example of the word's use. "It is noon; and Dough-Boy, the steward, thrusting his pale loaf-of-bread face from the cabin-scuttle, announces dinner to his lord and master" (Herman Melville, *Moby-Dick,* 1851). See also G.I.

dressed to the nines. This colloquialism for being very fashionably attired, equivalent to being *dressed to death, dressed to kill, dressed to the teeth,* or *dressed to an inch of one's life,* has caused much scratching of heads among etymologists. The Reverend Walter W. Skeat suggested that the pronunciation of the Anglo-Saxon *to then eyne,* to the eyes (with *eyne* being the plural of *eye*), gradually shifted, so that *dressed to then eyne* became *dressed to the nines.* The trouble with this is that it is a long reach from Anglo-Saxon times to 1820, when an early version of the phrase, "togged out to the nines," appeared in *London Magazine.* Other theories, even less convincing, are that the phrase derives from the nine muses of Greek mythology or from the smartly dressed Ninety-ninth Regiment of Foot.

A likelier explanation is that *dressed to the nines* comes from *up to the nines*, meaning "excellent" or "to perfection." This expression has been dated only to the late eighteenth century (it appears in poems that Robert Burns wrote and collected), but it fits with the connotations of perfection and completion that the number nine has enjoyed from ancient times. For example, something marvelous is a nine days' wonder; Hell has nine levels; a cat has nine lives; possession is nine points of the law; in Scandinavian mythology there were nine earths (as there are nine planets in our solar system); and three times three, a tripling of the Trinity, forms a mystical number with powerful associations. As the weird sisters sing in *Macbeth* (1606): "Thrice to thine, and thrice to mine, and thrice again to make up nine."

Against this background, the real mystery is why Bo Derek and other well-constructed ladies are *not* described as perfect nines even when they are *dressed* (or *undressed*, as the case may be) *to the nines*.

dumps. It seems logical to assume that the melancholy person who is *down in the dumps* is, figuratively speaking, in a depression filled with refuse—a sanitary landfill, as the old town dump is called today.

The melancholy *dumps* and those for refuse are separate words, however. People have been cast down in the former since the early sixteenth century: "What heapes of heauynesse, hathe of late fallen among us alreadye, with whiche some of our poore familye bee fallen into suche dumpes" (Sir Thomas More, *A Dialoge of Comforte Against Tribulation*, 1529). Captain Francis Grose reported that the word was "jocularly said to be derived from Dumpos, a king of Egypt, who died of melancholy" (*A Classical Dictionary of the Vulgar Tongue*, 1796). Though the term's origin is not entirely clear, it is much more likely to have a European than an Egyptian antecedent, coming instead from the Dutch *domp*, a haze or mist. The Dutch word is cognate to the English *damp*, which referred to a poisonous vapor or gas before it acquired the present senses of wetness and moisture. The true allusion in *down in the dumps*, then, is to a person whose mind is in a gloomy fog.

By contrast, the *dump* that refers to a place for depositing refuse is a comparatively recent innovation. The word first appeared with this meaning in the United States, with the oldest known example coming from the diary of Jacob Hiltzheimer: "Attended the sale of the street dirt at the dumps" (4/10/1784). This form of *dump* comes from the Middle English *dompen,* to drop, fall, or plunge, akin to the Norwegian *dumpa,* to fall with a thud or thump. Like *thump,* this *dump* may be basically onomatopoeic. In any event, the noun seems to come from the verb; refuse is *dumped* at a *dump.*

E

ear. An *ear* of corn sticks out from its stalk, and a person's *ear* stands out from his or her head, but the two are entirely different words even though spelled the same way. The first is from the Anglo-Saxon *ēar*, which has an Indo-European root, *ak-*, signifying that which is sharp or pointed. Related terms include the Latin *acus*, needle, and *ācer*, sharp, bitter, which produced such English words as *acuity*, *acumen*, and *acute*, on the one hand, and *acrid*, *acrimony*, and *vinegar*, on the other. The notion of sharpness also carries through in modern words that derived from this root through Greek, including *acanthus*, *acme*, *acne* (pimples are pointed), and *acrobat* (who walks on tiptoe).

The name of the organ of hearing, meanwhile, comes from another Indo-European root, *ous-*, which produced the Anglo-Saxon *ēare*, the Latin *auris*, and the Greek *ous*, all meaning "ear." Descendants of the Latin term include *aural*, *auricle*, and *scout* (from *auscultāre*, to listen, i.e., to incline the ear). Stemming from the Greek *ous* are a number of words that are of interest mainly to physicians and crossword puzzlers, including *otic* (having to do with the ear), *myosotis* (from the Greek word for "mouse-ear," this is the fancy, technical name of a plant genus, typified by the humble forget-me-not), and *parotid* (referring to a gland located near the ear).

earwig. The name of the insect is not related to the term for an artificial hairpiece, as logical as it might seem for a bug that likes to crawl into people's ears to take up temporary residence in their wigs. The insect's name derives instead from the Anglo-Saxon *ēarwicga*, where *wicga* means "insect." (*Wicga* also is the ancestor of *wiggle*, which is what these bugs seem to do as they perambulate.) *Earwig*, then, translates as "ear insect"—and it has the same name in French, *perce-oreille*, and German, *ohrwurm*, as well as in the official Latin nomenclature of Linnaeus, *Forficula auricularia*.

People have been worrying about getting these bugs in their ears for quite some time. Thus, Pliny the Elder (23–79) passed along an ingenious method for evicting such a loathsome tenant: "If an earwig be gotten into the eare . . . spit into the same, and it will come forth anon" (*Natural History*, Philemon Holland, tr., 1601). How to do this when camping in the woods by oneself, Mr. Pliny did not explain.

easel. Having an *easel* makes life easier for an artist, and the word's spelling apparently has been influenced by *ease*, but the name of the frame actually comes from the Dutch *ezel*, ass (the donkey kind), and ultimately the Latin *asinus*. The basic idea is that the *easel* is like a beast of burden, similar to the *horse* in *sawhorse*. See also DONKEY.

eat crow. The phrase was popularized during the presidential election of 1872 when Horace Greeley, a founder of the Republican Party, ran as a Democrat against Ulysses S. Grant. Many Republicans, and even some Democrats, found that they couldn't stomach Mr. Greeley, e.g., "The chief leader of the Democratic Party of Rhode Island, Hon. Thomas Steever . . . cannot and will not 'Eat Crow.' He prefers Grant to Greeley and made a speech at Providence recently to that effect" (San Diego *Daily Union*, 9/13/1872). Thus, *to eat crow* or *boiled crow* (as also was said) was to be humiliated. It meant that one had to recant one's principles—to "eat dirt," as the *Magazine of American History* explained in 1885—or, putting a better face on it, to EAT HUMBLE PIE.

Such a vivid expression naturally has inspired considerable specu-lation about its origin. The most popular explanation, as reported by Charles Earle Funk in *A Hog on Ice* (1948), dates the phrase to the War of 1812. According to Funk's account, which he based on a story that appeared in the Atlanta *Constitution* in 1888, a British officer came upon a Yankee just after he had shot a crow while hunting during an armistice on the British side of the Niagara River. Determined to punish the intruder, but unarmed himself, the officer complimented the Yank on the excellence of his marksmanship and asked to examine his fine weapon. As soon as the American handed it over, however, the officer took aim at the Yank and ordered him as punishment for trespassing to take a bite out of the crow. The American pleaded but finally com-plied, after which the officer warned him never to cross the river again and returned the weapon. Whereupon the Yank drew a bead on the Britisher and threatened to kill him if he didn't finish eating the crow. The officer did so, but next day he went to the American camp to demand that the soldier be punished for violating the armistice. Want-ing to get at the truth of the matter, the American commander had the soldier brought in and asked him if he had ever seen the British officer before. The soldier, not knowing quite what to say, hemmed and hawed, then blurted out, "W-w-why y-y-yes, Captin', I d-d-dined with him y-y-yesterday."

This makes a good story, but there is no reason to believe it. Equally possible is that the phrase arose as the punch line of a joke that made the rounds more than a quarter of a century prior to the *Constitution*'s report. As recounted in the *San Francisco Picayune* (12/3/1851), a man who boasted that he could eat anything had his bluff called. A bet was made and a crow was caught, roasted, and served. "Yes, I kin eat a crow," said the man, as he chewed away, "but I'll be darned if I hanker after it." This anecdote provides the earliest citation for *to eat crow* in *The Oxford English Dictionary*, but it is impossible to say for sure whether the phrase originated with the joke or the joke merely popularized the phrase.

eat humble pie. To dine on humble pie is to be very humble, the dish being a metaphor for profound apology, self-abasement, or some similar, equally abject form of submission. This unpalatable dish—the British culinary counterpart to the American *to eat crow*, discussed in the preceding entry—is an etymological pun.

Humble pie doesn't actually have anything to do with being humble, at least not linguistically. The name comes from *umble pie*, made from *umbles* or, the earliest English form of the word, *numbles*. The *numbles* were the edible innards of a deer or other animal. In medieval times, these parts—the heart, liver, kidneys, etc.—were considered something of a delicacy and often reserved for the huntsman. (He also got the head, shoulders, and shins, while milord and his lady had to content themselves with venison steaks.)

Starting in the fourteenth century, perhaps earlier, the *n* gradually migrated from *numbles* to the preceding article, so that *a numble pie* became *an umble pie*. The same thing happened to a number of other words, with *a nadder, a napron, a nauger, a noumpere,* and *a nuncle* becoming *an adder, an apron, an auger, an umpire,* and *an uncle*. (Sometimes the process worked in reverse; thus *an ewt* became *a newt* and *an innocent* turned into *a ninny*. See also NICKNAME and NINCOMPOOP.) Then, having dropped the *n*, the *umble* gradually acquired an *h*, there being no distinction between the Cockney pronunciation of *umble* and *humble*.

While all this was happening, the dish itself began to lose favor among those with educated palates. Samuel Pepys, who was not above serving umbles himself to guests, sometimes complained when presented with them: "He did give us the meanest dinner, (of beef, shoulder and umbles of venison)" (9/13/1665). Nineteenth-century Americans were even more persnickety, as indicated by James Russell Lowell's observation that "Disguise it as you will, flavor it as you will, call it what you will, umble-pie is umble-pie, and nothing else" (*McClellan or Lincoln?*, 1864).

The oldest example of *a humble pie* in the literal, consumable sense is dated to pre-1648 in the *Oxford English Dictionary*. The metaphorical dish is dated to 1830, appearing first in a list of words collected prior to 1825 in East Anglia. A similar expression used in Lincolnshire was *to eat rue*, punning upon repentance and the plant. Both phrases probably were fairly antique by the time lexicographers picked them up and wrote them down.

See also APPLE-PIE ORDER.

egg on. The expression does not come from the henhouse but from the Old Norse *eggja*, to edge. Both *egg on* and *edge on* were used through the nineteenth century in the sense of urging on, inciting, and provoking. Of the two, *edge on* was considered in some quarters to be the more proper, e.g., "To *Edge*, or as 'tis vulgarly call'd, to *Egg* one on" (*New Canting Dictionary*, 1725). Proper words do not always have the staying power of improper ones, however.

elope. Lovers do not lope away, despite the look of the word. A *lope* is a steady, easy gait. Lovers usually abscond much more quickly. They run. The word for their action is a cousin to *lope*, not a descendant of it. Both seem to be related to the Middle Dutch *outlōpen*, to run away, in turn from *lōpen*, to run, and, ultimately, some Scandinavian word, perhaps the Old Norse *hlaupa*, to leap, which is what lovers may also do if exiting via a window. *Elope* surfaced in English records in 1338 as *alopa*. It originally was a legal term, applying to an early form of women's liberation, i.e., to a wife who—horrors!—ran away from her husband with another man. The similar *interlope* began as a legal word, referring to one who intruded upon the trading rights or privileges of another by, in effect, running or leaping—not loping—into someone else's domain or sphere of interest. See also ANTELOPE and RUN THE GAUNTLET.

Ember days. The periods of fasting and prayer observed by some Christian churches have been associated with the wearing of ashes on Good Friday, but the name actually comes from the Middle English *Ymbre*

Days, in turn from the Anglo-Saxon *ymbryne,* a revolution or recurring period, as the rotation of the seasons. Introduced into Britain by St. Augustine, observance of *Ember days* was regularized by the Council of Placentia in 1095. The *Ember days* are the Wednesday, Friday, and Saturday of the four *Ember weeks,* following the first Sunday of Lent, Whitsunday or Pentecost (the seventh Sunday after Easter), Holy Cross Day (September 14), and St. Lucia's Day (December 13).

equerry. The *equerry* who is in charge of the horses of a noble household or who serves an attendant of the English royal family is so called because of mistaken association with the Latin *equus,* horse. Actually, the title derives from the Old French *escuier,* riding master, squire, in turn from the Late Latin *scūtārius,* guardsman, shield-carrier (Latin *scūtum* = shield). The gradual change in meaning and spelling of the word reflect the rising social position of this functionary. See also COMPTROLLER.

eyrie. The name for the nest of an eagle or other bird of prey, frequently encountered in crossword puzzles and occasionally in other works, as in "You ought not to be rude to an eagle, when you are only the size of a hobbit, and up in his eyrie at night!" (J. R. R. Tolkien, *The Hobbit,* 1937). *Eyrie* is a "corrected" spelling of *aerie,* introduced in the seventeenth century in the belief the word's true root was the Old English *ey,* egg, with *eyrie* translating as "eggery" or "repository of eggs." Actually, *aerie*—which has nothing to do with "airy," although the birds' nests typically are on windswept heights—has a more down-to-earth meaning, deriving from the Old French *aire,* in turn from the Latin *area,* open space, level ground.

F

faker. The deceptive or fraudulent *faker* is not related to the Muslim or Hindu *fakir*, a holy man who lives by begging. The two words have influenced each other, however. Thus, the pronunciation of *fakir* has been altered from *fah-keer* to *fay-ker* and it often is assumed that the fakir who lies down upon a bed of nails or walks across hot coals is faking the act in some way. Meantime, *faker* has been confused with *fakir*, as in the following proclamation issued in 1882: "To Thieves, Thugs, Fakirs and Bunkco-Steerers. . . . If found within the Limits of this City after Ten O'Clock P.M. this Night, you will be Invited to attend a Grand Neck-Tie Party" (in Sophie Poe, *Buckboard Days*, 1936).

The religious *fakir* actually comes from the Arabic *faqīr*, a poor man, in turn from *faqr*, poverty. It appeared in English as far back as 1609 (*OED*). *Faker*, meanwhile, is newer, having been dated only to 1851 in the sense of "thief," but is of less certain origin. Attempts have been made to link it to the Latin *facere*, to make, which would square, more or less, with such picturesque terms as *bit-faker*, a counterfeiter of coins; *mush-faker*, a mender of umbrellas; *twat-faker*, a pimp; and *poodle-faker*, a man who makes like a lap dog. (The first three have been dated to the nineteenth century and the fourth to 1902; see also GRASS WIDOW.)

Another, more likely possibility is that *fake* and *faker* derive from the German *fegen*, to clean, to sweep, via the obsolete but Standard English *feague* or *feak*, to thrash, but also to overcome by trickery (i.e., by polishing or cleaning up). Eighteenth-century horse dealers, whose reputation was similar to that of secondhand car dealers today, were noted especially for *feaguing*. Captain Francis Grose told how this was done in the first edition of his *Classical Dictionary of the Vulgar Tongue* (1785):

> FEAGUE. To feague a horse, to put ginger up a horse's fundament, and formerly, as it is said, a live eel, to make him lively and carry his tail well; it is said, a forfeit is incurred by any horse-dealer's servant, who shall shew a horse without first feaguing him.

fanny. Evidence for the use of this term to refer to the human posterior appears very late in the written record. "Parking her fanny in here," from *The Front Page* (1928) by Ben Hecht and Charles MacArthur, is the earliest recorded example of the word's anatomical sense in both *The Oxford English Dictionary* (1972 supplement) and the *Dictionary of American Slang* (1975). A number of possible etymologies for fanny have been proposed, including: (1) that the term derives from the fanning, or spanking, that is commonly administered to the buttocks of wayward youths; (2) that it comes from the overhanging stern, or fantail, of some ships, a parallel to *poop* and *stern*, both of which have been applied in the past to the rearward parts of people as well as of vessels (see CLINCHPOOP); (3) that it commemorates a particular Fanny, or Frances, with a notably large one; and (4) that it is a transferral from the British slang use of *fanny* since at least the middle of the nineteenth century to refer to the female pudendum (*keister* and *tail* are other words that have enjoyed the same double meaning). In the last case, the anatomical sense just might come from the name of the heroine of John Cleland's *Memoirs of a Woman of Pleasure* (1749), i.e., Fanny Hill. One regrets to have to report that none of these theories has been proven beyond doubt and that the origin of the human fanny thus remains a minor etymological mystery.

farthingale. The hooped frame for a skirt cost more than a *farthing* (one-fourth of a penny) even in Elizabethan times when the Queen and other women of fashion favored this garment. As noted in *The Spectator*, No. 478, on September 8, 1712: "We shall not for the future submit ourselves to the learning of etymology, which might persuade the age to come that the *farthingale* was worn for cheapness or the *furbelow* for warmth."

The "learning of etymology" led some others to derive the name of the garment from its effectiveness as a defense against onslaughts of the other sex. Jutting out at almost a right angle from the waist, the farthingale kept men at arm's length from the wearer. Accordingly, it was suggested that the term was a compound either of the French *vertu*, modesty + *gardien*, keeper, or of *virg*, virgin + *garder*, to keep or preserve.

Another, more intriguing theory is that *farthingale* comes from the aforementioned *vertu* + *galle*, growth, swelling. This ties in with the widespread belief that the device originated not so much for fashion's sake but as a means of concealing an embarrassing pregnancy. Thomas Fuller, the seventeenth-century English historian and divine, who was one of the most learned and witty men of his time, supported this derivation of *farthingale* on the grounds that "the first inventress thereof

76

[was] known for a light House-wife, who, under the pretence of modesty, sought to cover her shame and the fruits of her wantonness" (*History of the Worthies of England,* pre-1661).

Of the many candidates who have been proposed for the honor, so to speak, of inventress, the leader is Juana of Portugal, second wife of Enrique IV of Castile (1453–74). Circumstantial evidence favoring her includes the following: (1) the farthingale seems to have been worn first in Spain in 1468; (2) Henry was known to his subjects as "Henry the Impotent" on account of his having divorced his first wife on grounds of "mutual impotence"; (3) Her Majesty nevertheless managed to become pregnant and give birth to a daughter. The supposition, then, is that Juana tried to hide her pregnant condition with a hooped skirt and that the farthingale became the mode after her ladies in waiting copied her style of dress. (Fashion history note: The first farthingales were bell-shaped underskirts, with the hoops on the outside; later, the hoops were put inside and the upper part of the skirt was widened with a padded roll, which was tied around the waist. The effect of this additional underpinning, known to Elizabethans as a *bum bolster,* was to make the waist look smaller by enlarging the rest of the silhouette.) Whatever the truth about Juana and the farthingale, doubts about her daughter's legitimacy were so great that Henry was succeeded by his half-sister, Isabella, the same who married Ferdinand of Aragon in 1479, uniting the two kingdoms, and who backed Columbus in 1492; see ANGEL.

Fuller's "light House-wife" explanation fits so nicely with the facts surrounding Queen Juana and her impotent husband that one wants very much to accept his etymology. Sad to report, then, that the English word actually arose a different way. It is merely a corruption of the French name for the device, *vertugalle,* in turn from the original Spanish *verdugado,* literally, green stick or switch (*verde* = green), referring to the cane that was used to make the hoops before wood was superseded by whalebone and steel. Note, too, that while the farthingale might have helped conceal pregnancy, the tight bodice and corset worn with it could not have been very comfortable for Juana or any other mother-to-be. See also FURBELOW.

female. Appearance to the contrary, *female* has nothing to do with *male,* at least not etymologically. This knowledge should be of some comfort to the most ardent feminists, who abhor the thought that "their" word derives from the other one, as well as to misogynists, who have noticed with some concern that *male* is a lesser word than *female*, being contained in it.

Female actually comes from the French *femelle*, in turn from the Latin *femella*, the diminutive of *femina*, woman. The root is *fe*, to suckle, which also appears in such words as *fecund*, *fetus*, and *filial*. The present spelling of *female*, however, is the result of confusion in the fourteenth century with *male*, which has a similar sound but a completely different Latin ancestor, *masculus*, the diminutive of *mas*, male. See also WOMAN.

fink. This epithet for an odious person, especially an informer or strike-breaker, surfaced in the United States around the turn of this century. The oldest example of *fink* in writing comes from a 1903 story by George Ade ("Anyone who goes against the Faculty single-handed is a Fink," *People you Know*), but the term is reported to have been used during the 1892 strike against the Carnegie Steel Company's works in Homestead, Pa. Because the company tried to break this strike by importing some three hundred armed Pinkerton detectives, also known to unionists as *Pinks* and *Pinkies*, the standard explanation for many years (following a suggestion in the *American Mercury* in 1926) was that *fink* arose as a rhyme on *Pink*. In retrospect, however, this seems forced. More likely, the English word comes either from the German *fink*, a frivolous or dissolute person, or from the underworld use of the German-Yiddish *fink*, finch, to denote an informer. In the latter case, the point is that the finch is a songbird; like the *canary* (a member of the finch family) and the *nightingale*, which are other avian terms for an informer, it "sings" upon its companions. See also STOOL PIGEON.

P.S. The three hundred Pinks were beaten by the unionists in a battle on the shore of the Monongahela, but Carnegie upped the ante, eventually breaking the strike with the aid of some eight thousand state militiamen.

flack. Because of the barrages of releases put forth by public relations people, etymologists were content for many years with the assumption that *flack* derived from the German *flak*, a World War II acronym for *fliegerabwehrkanone*, antiaircraft fire. This theory fit comfortably with the oldest example of a publicity *flack* in *The Oxford English Dictionary*, dating from 1946, shortly after the war's conclusion.

But in language as in other fields, the best laid theories may be upset by new facts—in this case by the discovery that the show business weekly *Variety* was using *flack* as early as 1939 ("The Etymology of

Flack," Fred R. Shapiro, *American Speech*, Spring 1984). Long a hotbed of neologisms (the paper's staffers coined or popularized *brush-off, flopperoo, payola, pix,* and *tie-in,* among many other words), *Variety* based *flack* on the name of a motion picture publicity agent, Gene Flack.

The onset of World War II and the appearance of *flak* in the skies may have helped give momentum to *Variety's* coinage. Still, it seems clear from the chronology (as now known) that the word is basically an eponym.

flamenco. The fiery Spanish dance is not related to *flame* or the Latin *flamma,* nor does it come from the name of the peculiar, pinkish bird, the *flamingo,* called the *flamenco* in Spanish, despite the resemblance that some have seen between the strutting dancer and courtship rituals of the long-legged waterfowl. In Spanish, *Flamenco* originally meant *Fleming* (*Vlaming* in Dutch), and the dance name arose as an ethnic insult. The exact sequence of linguistic events has been lost in the mists of the sixteenth century, but it seems to have gone something like this: (1) the Spanish did not much like some of the Flemish nobles in the court of Holy Roman Emperor Charles V (1500–58), who also happened to be Charles I of Spain; (2) *Flamenco* became a disparaging term for any foreigner from the other side of the Pyrenees; (3) the word was applied to Gypsies who moved to Andalusia in the sixteenth century— and then to their vigorous style of dancing; hence, the *flamenco.*

As for the bird, its name in Spanish, *flamenco,* draws on the medieval stereotype of Flemings as sporting bright clothes and florid complexions. A *flamenco* turning red as it takes flight in the sun, then, resembles a Fleming—perhaps one with a feverish face from drinking. (The Flemings at the court of Charles V were reputed to be in their cups most of the time.)

Meanwhile, the English name for the bird, *flamingo,* seems to come from the Portuguese *flamengo,* in turn either from the Spanish *flamenco* or, an alternate suggestion, from the Old Provençal *flamenc,* fire bird, which probably does—closing the circle—descend from the Latin *flamma.*

flash in the pan. The suggestion has been made that this expression dates to the great California gold rush of 1849. After dipping his pan into water, any prospector who spotted a flash amid the sand, silt, and gravel had cause to become very excited. This explanation is doubly attractive because it ties in with the mournful complaint of the prospector who came up empty, i.e., "It didn't pan out."

As logical as all this seems, however, *flash in the pan* has another origin. The phrase comes from the age of the flintlock musket, when the priming powder in the pan on the outside of the weapon sometimes exploded without setting off the main charge inside the barrel. Thus, from Charles James's *A New and Enlarged Military Dictionary*, published in 1810, nearly forty years before the first prospectors showed up in California: "*Flash in the pan*, an explosion of gunpowder without any communication beyond the touch-hole."

flicker. The common name for any of several species of woodpecker may come from the bird's fitful, fluttering pattern of flight (several quick wingbeats, followed by a pause), as suggested by some etymologists. However, the real experts in the field—the bird-watchers—think the name comes from one of the creature's calls, *flick-a, flick-a, flick-a*, etc. Arguing in favor of the latter is the fact that the names of birds often come from the sounds they make. For example: the peewee goes *pewee* (or *pewit*, another name for the same bird); the Old World hoopoe goes *hoop-hoop* (a supposedly stupid bird, like the booby and dodo, *hoopoe* is the ancestor of the word *dupe*); and the hummingbird's wings beat so quickly, they produce a *hum*. On the other hand, the movements of birds may contribute to their names—witness the green heron, which has a tendency to defecate when flushed and taking to wing, and which is politely called the *shy-poke*, with *shy* serving as a euphemism. And see also LAPWING and QUAIL.

flounce. A woman may flounce along in a skirt with a flounce, but the word for her exaggerated method of locomotion is of obscure origin (perhaps akin to the Norwegian *flunsa*, to hurry, with an assist from *bounce*), while that for the gathered or pleated trim on her dress comes from the Old French *fronce*, wrinkle, as in the current *froncer les sourcils*, to frown, to wrinkle one's brows. See also FURBELOW.

foolscap. The outsize sheet of paper (usually about 13 × 16 inches) seems ideal for making hats for schoolroom dunces and other fools, but the term derives from the watermark—a fool's cap with bells—used from an early date for such sheets of paper. A German specimen of the fool's cap watermark has been dated to 1479, nearly four hundred years prior to the earliest recorded example in 1831 of a "paper fool's cap" for a dunce.

The story that the Rump Parliament, which created the court that tried and condemned Charles I to death, had the watermark in the paper used for the journals of the House changed from the royal arms to a fool's cap is a pretty one but, we are assured by *The Oxford English Dictionary*, without foundation in fact.

footpad. Not a mugger in sneakers, nor his forebear, a robber in padded shoes, but a hold-up man without a horse, from *foot* + *pad*, the latter meaning "path" or "road" in the slang of vagabonds and other sixteenth-century lowlifes. Other forms of *footpad* included *pad* and *padder*, as in (demonstrating the esteem with which learned counsel traditionally have been held): "Such as robbe on horse-backe were called high-lawyers, and those who robbed on foote, he called Padders" (Samuel Rowlands, *Martin Mark-all*, 1610).

forcemeat. It can take a strong arm to cram forcemeat into a turkey, but strength really has nothing to do with this finely chopped and seasoned stuffing, so tasty that it is sometimes served alone. Nor does forcemeat have anything to do with the forcing, or fattening, of turkeys or other animals on a farm.

The *force* in the stuffing on the table, as well as in the process of stuffing animals, began as *farce*, e.g., from an eighteenth-century recipe for breast of veal: "Farce it between the Skin and small Ribs." The present spelling of the culinary term is due to confusion of *farce* with the more powerful *force*. Thus, Shakespeare (or his printer) used the "o" spelling in "Wit larded with malice, and malice forced with wit" (*Troilus and Cressida*, 1601–2). The original *farce*, in turn, derives from the Latin *farcīre*, with the same meaning, "to stuff." This also is the ancestor of the dramatic *farce*, which began as an interpolation—a stuffing—in litanies and subsequently was extended to comic amplifications or interludes on stage, and then to a particular form of theatrical composition. A French farce, then, has a lot in common with forcemeat, which is no laughing matter. See also FORCEPS.

forceps. An obstetrician may use forceps with some force to extract a baby from the womb, but *forceps* and *force* are unrelated. *Force* derives from the Latin *fortis*, strong. *Forceps* itself is a Latin word for pincers or tongs. It comes from *formus*, hot + *capere*, to take. Obstetricians, then, got the instrument and its name from smiths, who used the first forceps for grabbing pieces of hot metal. The role of *force* also has been misinterpreted in FORCEMEAT, above.

foremost. The word looks like a combination of *fore* and *most*, but it actually derives from the Anglo-Saxon *formest*, a superlative of *forma*, first. Thus, its true meaning is *first-est*, not, as suggested by the spelling, *most-est*, and the common oratorical lead-in "First and foremost" is essentially a redundancy.

forlorn hope. Soldiers who volunteer to storm a fortified position may not have much hope of surviving, but this is not why the band of attackers is called the *forlorn hope*. Dating from the sixteenth century, and originally applied to those who led an attack of any kind, the phrase comes from the obsolete Dutch *verloren hoop*, which derives, in turn, from *verliezen*, to lose, and *hoop*, band, company. (*Hoop* is cognate to English "heap.") The literal meaning of *verloren hoop*, then, is "lost troop," so it is not difficult to see why English soldiers converted it into the equally mournful but more familiar-sounding *forlorn hope*.

fox trot. The name of the dance has been said to come from that of comedian Harry Fox, who appeared with fox-trotting dancers in the *Ziegfeld Follies of 1913*. The timing is about right, as the dance became the rage around the time of World War I. In March of 1915, it was described in a London weekly, *Truth*, as a new relation of ragtime, and fox trots were included for the first time in the *Victor Record Catalog* that was released in May of that year. However, *fox trot* was used much earlier (1872, *OED*) as the name of the shuffling gait of a horse, halfway between trotting and walking, and it seems more likely that the dance, with its alternating long and short steps, took its name from this. Since the equine term is based ultimately on the pace of the fox, which has to take short steps because it has short legs, this explanation for the origin of the human fox trot also has the advantage of fitting in naturally with the tendency to give animalistic names to the mating rituals we perform to music, e.g., *bunny hop, fish, monkey, snake dance*, and, of course, *turkey trot*.

frontispiece. The *piece* in *frontispiece* is a mirage—a foreign word with a different meaning, converted into a familiar one. The term entered English in the late sixteenth century as *frontispice*, referring originally to the front of a building rather than—in the usual sense today—to the illustration facing the title page of a book. It comes from the Medieval Latin word for the facade of a building, *frontispicium*, whose literal meaning is "looking at the forehead," from *frons*, forehead, and *specere*, to behold. Very early on, the English changed the spelling of the final syllable from *pice* to *piece*, perhaps influenced to some extent by *chimney-piece*, originally a picture or other decoration over a fireplace rather than—the primary sense today—the mantel shelf.

fuck. The strong desire of folk etymologists to trace the origins of words to acronyms has produced the suggestion that this one stands for *For Unlawful* (or perhaps *Unnatural*) *Carnal Knowledge*, supposedly used in medieval trials to refer to rape and sodomy. Unfortunately, no documentary evidence for the acronym exists. As theories go, this is on a par with the tongue-in-cheek suggestions that the Ford motorcar was so called because the name comes from *Fix Or Repair Daily* or perhaps *Found On Road Dead*. Nor is it at all likely, as most imaginatively suggested by James Barke in his notes on Robert Burns's *The Merry Muses of Caledonia* (with Sydney Goodsir Smith, eds., 1959), that the taboo term is "an onomatopoeic word equivalent to the sound made by the penis in the vagina."

The spurious explanations have flowered in the soil of ignorance, the term's true etymology being much less certain than that of Henry Ford's Ford. This is because the vulgar word, though most likely uttered frequently in anger and other contexts, was not recorded in written form until the early sixteenth century—comparatively late in its linguistic history. The term appears as "fukkit" in the oldest citation for it in *The Oxford English Dictionary*'s 1972 supplement. This is from a poem "Ane Brash of Wowing" ("A Bout of Wooing"), composed by William Dunbar prior to 1503. The first example of the word in its modern form comes from a poem by another Scot, Sir David Lyndesay: "Bischops . . . may fuck thair fill and be vnmaryit" ("Ane Satyre of the Thrie Estaits," 1535–36).

Why the earliest examples of the word come from Scotland is not known. It may be that the word did not carry as heavy a taboo in northern Britain as in the south (where people at this time were using—when committing their thoughts to paper, at least—such synonymous terms as *jape*, *sard*, and *swive*), or it may simply be that the Scots were bolder and reveled in lewdness.

The English word is most likely kin to, or borrowed from, the Middle

Dutch *fokken*, to strike, to thrust, to copulate with. It may also be related to the German *ficken*, to strike, to copulate with. Parallels in other languages include the French *foutre*, to thrust, to beat, to copulate with (from the Latin *futuere*), and its Italian cognate *fottere*, defined by John Florio in his Italian-English dictionary, *A Worlde of Words* (1598), as meaning "to jape, to sard, to fucke, to swive, to occupy." Then there is the obsolete English *firk*, whose diverse meanings included to cheat, to move sharply and suddenly, to urge oneself forward, to move about briskly, to beat, and to lash, and which also was used by Shakespeare and other Elizabethan writers as a euphemism for the copulative verb.

Whatever their linguistic relationships, the bond that all these words have in common is their joining of violent and sexual meanings within the same term. This is true, too, of many current slang terms for sexual intercourse, such as *bang, beat, boff, bop, bump, hit, jab, jump, knock, poke, slam, womp on,* and *zap,* all of which also are inherently physically aggressive. The close linkage of sex and violence seems to be one of the characteristic features of our culture, frequently exemplified in daily life as well as in language, alas.

furbelow. Warm underwear for women? Uh-uh. A furbelow is a showy piece of trimming—specifically, a ruffle or flounce on a dress or petticoat. It is possible that some furbelows in the past actually have been made of fur, but the word itself has an entirely different source. Dated to the early eighteenth century, it is a corruption of the French *falbala*, which also has appeared in English, e.g., "As many blue and green Ribbons . . . as would have made me a Falbala apron" (Colley Cibber, *The Careless Husband*, 1704).

Admittedly, *falbala* itself is of obscure origin, with different versions of the word also appearing in other languages, including German (*falbel*), Spanish (*farfala*), and Provençal (*farbello*). The word may be related to the Old French *frepe*, rag, or the Late Latin *faluppa*, fiber, valueless thing. But one thing is sure: There is no *fur* here, either above or *below*. See also AGITA, FARTHINGALE, and FLOUNCE.

G

gadfly. The fly is not so called because it *gads* about but because it bites, from *gad*, meaning a pointed stick or tool. The two forms of *gad* are unrelated. The first comes from the Middle English *gadden*, in turn probably from *gadeling*, companion, fellow, and later a wanderer or vagabond. The second comes from the Old Norse *gaddr*, a spike, a goad.

The confusion over the *gad* in *gadfly* shows up in the word's figurative uses. Today, a human gadfly usually is one who irritates others with continual criticisms, but in the past the term also has been applied to gadabouts, e.g., "Your Harriet may turn gad-fly, and never be easy but when she is forming parties" (Samuel Richardson, *Sir Charles Grandison*, 1754).

get down to brass tacks. It often is asserted quite confidently that this metaphor for getting down to basics comes from nineteenth-century retailing—that clerks in dry-goods shops measured lengths of material by stretching it between brass tacks, embedded a yard apart in the counters of their stores. Another theory is that the brass tacks are the ones used in upholstery, often not exposed until the outer layer of material is removed. Of the two, the latter suggestion seems the less likely, if only because purchasing yard goods is a more common task than reupholstery.

Eric Partridge has debunked both theories, however, reporting that *brass tacks* is Cockney rhyming slang for "hard facts" (*Adventuring Among Words*, 1961). Cockney speech features many such rhymes, e.g., *apples and pears*, stairs; *plates of meat*, feet; and *ham and eggs*, legs. Partridge's observation in the case of *brass tacks* is reinforced by the nonbrassy variants, *get down to nails* and *get down to tin tacks*, sometimes abbreviated to *get down to tin*. The *facts-tacks* rhyme also has received the imprimatur of a distinguished non-Cockney (and therefore presumably impartial) poet: "That's all the facts when you come to brass tacks: Birth, and copulation, and death" (T. S. Eliot, "Sweeney Agonistes," 1932).

ghetto. The term is of Christian origin, despite the resemblance to the Hebrew *get*, the official document dissolving a marriage in accordance with Jewish law, which has led some scholars to suppose that *ghetto*

85

must mean something like "place of our divorcement." Somewhat closer to the mark are theories that *ghetto* derives from the Italian *borghetto*, diminutive of *borgo*, borough, or from *Giudeica*, in turn from *Judaicam*, used in fourteenth-century Italy to refer to the Jewish quarter of a city.

In fact, the word *is* Italian, but it comes from *geto*, meaning "foundry" in the Venetian dialect, in turn from *ghettare*, to throw, or to cast, as metal is in a foundry, and ultimately from the Latin *jactum*, thing cast. The particular foundry in question, *il geto*, made cannon. Starting about 1500, Venetian Jews were required to live in the neighborhood of *il geto*. In 1516, walls were built around the area. Venetian practice was in line with the edict of the third Lateran Council (1179), which generally forbade Christians from having close contacts with infidels, and anticipated Pope Paul IV's bull of 1555, which formally instituted ghettos in Rome and other papal states.

Ghetto has been dated in English to 1611 as applied to a Jewish quarter. Toward the end of the nineteenth century it began to be used for any inner-city area inhabited mainly by members of a particular ethnic, minority, or social group, e.g., a *working-class ghetto*, *black ghetto*, or, referring to Manhattan's Upper East Side, home to many airline attendants and other young businesswomen, *girl ghetto*.

G.I. The term is the Second World War's counterpart of the First World War's DOUGHBOY. The abbreviation usually is regarded, even by the very highest authorities, as standing for *government issue* or *general issue* (with perhaps an assist from *garrison issue*). Thus, when an army surgeon happened to refer to the troops under General Douglas MacArthur's command as "G.I.s," Himself erupted: "Don't ever do that in my presence. . . . GI means 'general issue.' Call them soldiers" (William Manchester, *American Caesar*, 1978).

In the very beginning, however, *G.I.* stood for *galvanized iron*, referring to the cans for ashes, garbage, etc. that proliferate like mushrooms on army posts. The meaning of *G.I.* seems to have been extended gradually from cans to supplies to men. As an abbreviation for *galvanized iron*, it is dated to 1906 in *A Dictionary of Soldier Talk* (Colonel John Elting et al., 1984). By 1935, *G.I.* was being used to refer to other items, as indicated by a note in *American Speech* (2/36): "You can readily, after a few visits to the Quartermaster, understand that G.I. cans are made of galvanized iron and that G.I. soap is government issue soap; but it is pure slang to call a large artillery shell a G.I. can."

Just when the abbreviation began to be applied to soldiers, too, is not known, but it probably was about this time or shortly thereafter. By 1939, the soldierly *G.I.* was recorded as part of West Point slang. According to an unnamed regular army sergeant of many years' service, cited in *American Speech* (12/46), the galvanized abbreviation was applied to soldiers because "a man who was G.I. was crude or uncouth, and the term was [originally] considered insulting." Perhaps it was this subliminal association that so troubled General MacArthur.

gibberish. It seems perfectly reasonable to assume that *gibberish* should come from *gibber*, following the pattern of *English* from *England*, *Spanish* from *Spain*, and *Turkish* from *Turkey*.

Language, however, does not always follow logical rules. *Gibberish* appears in the written record almost fifty years prior to *gibber*. The oldest citation in the *OED* for the former is from *The Interlude of Youth* (ca. 1554): "What me thynke ye be clerkyshe For ye speake good gibbryshe." The first *gibber*, meanwhile, comes from *Hamlet* (1601–2): "The graues stood tenantlesse and the sheeted dead Did squeake and gibber in the Roman streets." This raises the possibility that the process worked the other way around, with Shakespeare cutting off the final syllable of *gibberish* to produce *gibber*. This is a standard method of creating new words—a back-formation, as linguists call it, when a prefix or suffix is lopped off a word under the mistaken impression that it is merely an affix to the real term.

Whichever came first, *gibberish* or *gibber*, the root word seems to be essentially onomatopoeic, similar to *jabber*, imitative of senseless chatter. Various lexicographers, including Dr. Samuel Johnson and Captain Francis Grose, have suggested that *gibberish* is actually an eponym, from *Geber*, a ninth-century alchemist (Jabir ibn Hazyan in full and in Arabic), but this seems much farther fetched, reflecting the popular opinion of the complicated jargon that these pre-scientists used for concealing their real thoughts from the uninitiated. See also BOMBAST.

give [someone] the cold shoulder. The phrase conjures up the image of demonstrating neglect or contempt by turning one's back upon another person. The original shoulder, however, was an inferior cut of meat, typically mutton. The point was that only servants or guests who overstayed their welcome would be served a cold shoulder rather than a warm and tasty roast. The phrase, probably a Scottish one, was popularized by Sir Walter Scott toward the beginning of the nineteenth century. Shakespeare had the essential thought in mind two hundred years earlier, however: in *Cymbeline* (1609–10) we meet a "base wretch, One bred of alms and fostered with cold dishes, With scraps o' the court."

glass slipper. The standard explanation for Cinderella's famous footwear is that it is the result of a mistranslation, someone having mistaken *pantoufle de vair*, fur slipper, for *pantoufle de verre*, glass slipper, when making an English version of Charles Perrault's *Histoires ou contes du temps passé avec des moralités* (1697). (The title of Perrault's collection—in English, *Stories or Tales of Olden Times with Morals*—also is known as *Tales of My Mother Goose*, after a line that appears on the frontispiece of the original, *Contes de ma mère l'oye*.)

The principal difficulty with the standard explanation is that *pantoufle de verre* appears in Perrault's original text, so this is definitely not a question of mistranslation. Nor does it seem to be a case of mishearing, with Perrault writing *verre* for *vair* when transcribing an oral account, since *vair*, a medieval word, was no longer used in his time. (*Vair*, variegated fur, from the Latin *varius*, varied, also is a root of *miniver*, originally *menu vair*, small vair, which referred initially to the fur—perhaps squirrel—used as trim on medieval robes and later was applied to the prized ermine, or winter weasel fur, on the ceremonial robes of peers.)

Finally, the glass slipper is peculiar to Perrault's telling of the story, which is one of the world's best-known and most widely distributed folktales. In most versions, Cinderella is helped by her dead mother, who reappears as a domestic animal, typically a cow or goat, rather than by her fairy godmother; often, she makes three visits to a ball, festival, or church; and her true identity is revealed by a ring that will not fit anyone's finger but hers. The story probably is of Oriental origin. In the oldest known version, from China in the ninth century, the heroine loses a slipper, as it happens, but it is of gold. The glass slipper, then, along with the use of the witching hour of midnight as the moment at which the heroine's finery will disappear, seems to be one of Perrault's own contributions—along with OGRE—to the Cinderella story.

See also CAT AND THE FIDDLE.

god. The term for a deity sometimes is said to derive from *good*, and, indeed, there is some overlap between the two words, e.g., *Good Friday*, which originally was written as *god Friday*, with *god* being used in the sense of "holy" or "sacred," and *good-by*, which is a contraction of "God be with ye."

The confusion results partly from the assumption that God must be good and partly from the similarity of the two terms, which were even spelled the same way (as *god*) in Middle English. The words have different Indo-European roots, however. *God* has been traced to *gheu-*, with the primordial meanings of to call, to invoke, to offer sacrifices or to pour libations to, while *good* derives from *ghedh-*, to unite, to join, to fit, to bring together. It should be of passing interest to women readers especially to know that *god* originally was of neuter gender, as in the Middle High German *abgott*, idol. The word became masculine following the conversion of the German tribes to Christianity.

For more about gender shifts, see HARLOT.

good scout. Boy Scouts are being good when they help little old ladies across the street, but the original *good scout* doesn't appear to have been a member of Scouting/USA, as the organization has called itself since 1977, when it dropped the increasingly objectionable "Boy" from its official title.

Founded by Sir Robert Baden-Powell in England in 1908, the Boy Scout movement did not become popular in the United States until after World War I, although the organization was incorporated in this country in 1910. The earliest example of *good scout* in *The Oxford English Dictionary*, meanwhile, strongly suggests the phrase's prior existence: "Dad's a good old scout and he's pretty sure to do it" (Meredith Nicholson, *A Hoosier Chronicle*, 1912). Most likely, *good scout* comes from the college slang use of *scout* for a servant, from the early eighteenth century at Oxford (and subsequently at Yale and Harvard), when students could concentrate on their studies, or whatever, without being distracted by the need to make their own beds or do other routine chores. World War II brought the glorious era of hired help to an end in the United States but not in the mother country, e.g., "Miss Bootes, who has been a scout at St. Hilda's College for 25 years, was presented with the teapot on Wednesday" (*Oxford Times*, 5/26/72).

gorp. The name of the high-energy mixture of raisins, nuts, dried fruits, etc., popularized by hikers, climbers, and other outdoors types, often is said to be an acronym for *Good Old Raisins and Peanuts*. This reeks of after-the-fact rationalization, however, the formation of acronyms being one of the most frequent ways of "explaining" the origins of words; see TIP. Admittedly, the situation in the case of *gorp* is complicated by the fact that the word's true origin is not known. Most likely, the name for the munchies (from ca. 1965–70) comes from the earlier use of the word as a verb. *Gorp*, to eat greedily, and *gorper*, a voracious eater, a glutton, are both included in the 1953 edition of *The American Thesaurus of Slang* by Lester V. Berrey and Melvin Van den Bark. And where did the verb come from? It may simply be that the *g* sound connotes quick consumption of food, as in *gobble, gorble* (? a combination of *gorp* and *gobble*), *gorge, gorm* (from the 1800s and perhaps from *gourmand*), *gulp*, and *guzzle*. G, it seems, is an intrinsically guttural ("pertaining to the throat") sound.

grain of salt, with a. The learned explanation is that this metaphor for moderate skepticism comes from the Latin *cum grano salis*. In truth, the case seems to be the reverse. The phrase, dated to 1647 in English (*OED*), has not been found in the writings of ancient authors. Thus, the Latin appears to be a modern rendering of the English expression. (A similar, pseudo-Latin construction is *illegitimi non carborundum* for "Don't let the bastards grind you down.") The underlying idea is that an exaggerated statement calls for a little skepticism before being accepted, just as slightly rank meat needs some salt to be made palatable. See also SALT CELLAR.

grass widow. The origin of the expression is obscure, but the *grass* part almost certainly does not come from *grace*, pronounced as though it were the French *grâce*, with the implication that the unwidowed woman in question is being treated by grace, or by courtesy, as though she were one. True, a *grass widow* is a woman without a man. Dated to 1528 in *The Oxford English Dictionary*, the phrase originally referred to an unmarried woman who had lived with one or more men. In time, the meaning was broadened, so to speak, to include an unmarried mother, a discarded mistress, and then a married woman with no spouse on the premises, either because she was divorced or permanently separated from him or simply because he was temporarily absent. The latter sense was popularized in Anglo-India, which was stocked with more soldiers than soldiers' wives, as in the somewhat regretful report that "Grass widows in the hills are always writing to their husbands when you drop in upon them" (John Lang, *Wanderings in India*, 1859). In our own century, it looked for a while as though the meaning of the expression might be extended further to include the wife of a pothead, but the best moment for this may have passed with the 1960s.

The theory that the *grass* in *grass widow* comes from *grâce* is contradicted by the existence of parallel forms in other languages, including the Low German *graswedewe;* the Swedish *gräsenka,* literally, "grass widow"; and the German *strohwittwe,* straw widow. Some etymologists have suggested that the *grass* here is rooted in the Scandinavian *gradig,* longing (in the sense of "greedy for"), in which case the underlying image is of a woman who yearns for her absent husband. This is the high-minded, sentimental, Victorian explanation. The low-minded explanation is that the *grass* should be taken at face value, with the original reference being either to the horse or other animal that is "turned out to grass" (and is free to roam) or to the grass (or straw) on which couples in haste have been known to make their beds prior to marriage.

By the bye: In British India, and subsequently elsewhere, the man who got all dressed up and went to call upon regimental grass widows was said to be *pea-cocking* (displaying himself) or *poodle-faking* (pretending to be a lap dog). See also FAKER.

Great Scott. The English sometimes like to think that this minced oath is short for *Great Scotland Yard,* but the earliest examples of its use (from 1885) come from the United States. It is much more likely, therefore, that the expression has an American referent. The case can't be proven, but the logical candidate is General Winfield Scott (1786–1866). Known as "Old Fuss and Feathers" on account of his attention to detail and his love of elaborate uniforms, Scott remained almost constantly in the public eye for half a century. A hero of the War of 1812, he fought in the Indian wars, conducted the spectacularly successful campaign against Mexico in 1847, ran unsuccessfully for president on the Whig ticket in 1852, and commanded the Union Army at the outset of the Civil War. He must have seemed to many to be an American Caesar, so it would be natural for his name to be used in the same way as *Great Caesar* or, for emphasis, *Great Caesar's Ghost.*

greyhound. The long-legged racing dog usually is pictured as being gray, although it comes in other colors, but its name derives from the Old Norse *greyhundr,* a compound of *grey,* bitch, coward, and *hundr,* hound. Based on the secondary meaning of the original *grey,* then, the dog's name reflects its speed (and ability to flee from danger) rather than its grayness.

gridiron. There isn't any *iron* here—at least not linguistically. The word comes from the Middle English *gridirne,* itself a variant of *gridel,* griddle. The false assumption that *gridiron* was a compound of *grid,* meaning an arrangement of crossed lines, and *iron,* referring to the material from which a grate or grill is usually fashioned, led to the splitting off of the first syllable, *grid,* as a separate word (1839, *OED*).

Gridirons were used in kitchens for many years before the term was applied to a football field (from the 1890s). The culinary context probably was the original one, though this is giving our ancestors the benefit of the doubt, as the reference in the word's very first appearance in English (ca. 1290) was to a frame for supporting a person being tortured by fire. The earliest English *griddle* (pre-1225) also was used for torture, not cooking. See also ANDIRON.

gringo. The contemptuous term for white, English-speaking Anglo-Americans, particularly those from the United States, has inspired one of the most picturesque, often-repeated folk etymologies, i.e., that it stems from a line in a song by Robert Burns, "Green grow the rashes, O," (i.e., "rushes, O"), as sung by Yankee soldiers during the Mexican-American War of 1846–48. In another version of this story, the song was "Green Grow the Lilacs," and the singers were homesick Yankee sailors during the same conflict. In either case, so the tale goes, the Mexicans heard the song so frequently that they began calling the Yanks "Greengrows," or, in Spanish, *gringos.*

In fact, *gringo* did enter English at the time of the war with Mexico, with the earliest known example of the word coming from the journal of John Woodhouse Audubon (son of the artist): "We were hooted and shouted at as we passed through, and called 'Gringoes' " (*Western Journal,* 6/13/1849). Moreover, transferences of this sort are not unprecedented. Thus, Joan of Arc commonly referred to English soldiers as *les Goddems,* and the French in World War I knew the Americans as *les sommombiches.*

Gringo existed in Spanish, however, before the Yanks invaded Mexico. It meant "gibberish" and, by extension, a foreigner who spoke Spanish so poorly that he sounded as though he were talking gibberish. Thus, the *Diccionario Castellano* of 1787 noted that in Malaga "foreigners who have a certain type of accent which keeps them from speaking

Spanish easily and naturally" were called *gringos*. The same word was used in Madrid, particularly for the Irish.

Gringo almost certainly comes from the Spanish *griego*, Greek, as in the proverb *hablar en griego*, to talk in Greek, which is the equivalent of our own "It's Greek to me," e.g., "those that understood him smiled at one another and shook their heads—but for my own part, it was Greek to me" (William Shakespeare, *Julius Caesar*, 1599). Both proverbs go back to the Medieval Latin *Graecum est; non potest legi*, If it is Greek; it cannot be read.

As a disparaging term for English-speaking Anglo-Americans, then, *gringo* springs from the same font of contempt as *barbarian*, which comes from the ancient Greek *bárbaros*, foreign, rude, non-Greek, i.e., one whose language can't be understood, in turn from the imitative *baba*, as in BABBLE. The *gringos*, of course, return the compliment when they refer to Spanish speakers as *spicks*, which may well derive from *no spik Ingles*.

grin like a Cheshire cat. The Cheshire cat, with its grin that stayed behind after the cat itself had vanished, is so closely associated with Lewis Carroll's *Alice's Adventures in Wonderland* (1865) that most people assume he invented the image. He did not. Carroll (a.k.a. Charles Lutwidge Dodgson) created the character out of an earlier saying. Thus, from the wit and wisdom of Peter Pindar (a.k.a. John Wolcot): "Lo, like a Cheshire Cat our Court will grin" (*A Pair of Lyric Epistles*, 1782). And the grin of the Cheshire cat was not a very pretty one, as noted in the *Lexicon Balatronicum* (Anonymous, 1811): "He grins like a Cheshire cat; said of anyone who shows his teeth and gums while laughing."

Many theories of the origins of the phrase have been advanced. For example: that Cheshire cheese was made in a round mold that formed the face of a grinning cat; that the crest of a county family featured a lion that sign painters, who had never seen such an exotic animal, depicted with catlike features; and that the expression comes from a forest warden in the time of Richard III, a Mr. Caterling, who grinned fiercely as he chased poachers with his sword. (Mr. Caterling also is said to figure in the rhyme about the CAT AND THE FIDDLE.) The truth of the matter is not known. "In fact, Mr. Newcome says to Mr. Pendennis, in his droll, humorous way, 'that woman grins like a Cheshire cat!' Who was the naturalist who first discovered that peculiarity of the cats in Cheshire?' " (William Makepeace Thackeray, *The Newcomes*, 1855).

Before Carroll made the phrase his own, fixing it permanently in its present form, Cheshire cats also were noted for other peculiarities, with the expression sometimes being extended into *to grin like a Cheshire cat chewing gravel* (or *eating cheese* or *evacuating bones*). The *evacuating*, however, though included in Farmer and Henley's *Slang and Its Analogues*, with a citation from 1859, looks very much like a Victorian euphemism.

See also DORMOUSE, MAD AS A HATTER, and TABBY CAT.

guinea pig. The tailless rodent so often used in scientific experiments is native not to the Guinea coast of West Africa but to South America, probably through confusion of *Guinea* with *Guyana*, formerly spelled *Guiana*. See also TURKEY.

Guinea pig has been dated to 1664 as *ginny pig*. The extended scientific sense of *guinea pig*, referring to a person or another (nonrodent) subject of an experiment, first appeared in 1913. This was foreshadowed, however, by the use of *guinea pig* to mean a midshipman in the East Indian service, as in "He sent his nephew at the age of fourteen, on a voyage as a Guinea-pig" (*Adventures of a Kidnapped Orphan*, 1747).

gung ho. This pidgin-English adjective for that which is zealous, eager, or enthusiastic, sometimes foolishly so, is derived in most dictionaries from the Mandarin *kung*, work, + *ho*, together. Even the 1972 supplement to *The Oxford English Dictionary* perpetuates this mistake, first made by the man who popularized the expression.

That man was Marine Lieutenant Colonel Evans Fordyce Carlson, an innovative military thinker and charismatic leader, who organized the Second Raider Battalion in 1942 to carry out guerrilla-type campaigns. Carlson's ideas were strongly influenced by his experience as an observer with the Chinese Communist Eighth Route Army during 1937–38. He was impressed particularly by the selflessness and dedication that enabled ordinary Chinese soldiers to accomplish feats that ordinary Americans might not—in one case marching fifty-eight miles in twenty-four hours, going up and down mountains without rest, and without a single man's falling by the wayside. The high morale of the Eighth Army soldiers was the result of what the Chinese called "political work" and what Carlson termed "ethical indoctrination." Each man knew why he was fighting and what his role was in the larger scheme of things. No one, whether officer, cook, or coolie, thought of himself or his job as being any more or less important than any other person or anyone else's job. Through mutual respect and confidence came the ability to work together wholeheartedly.

Carlson began introducing these concepts to the Raiders in his first speech to the battalion in February 1942. "The Chinese have two words for 'working together,' " he said. "*Gung*, meaning 'work'; *Ho*, meaning 'harmony.' *Gung Ho!* 'Work Together!' That is the end result of ethical indoctrination." (Michael Blankfort, *The Big Yankee: The Life of Carlson of the Raiders*, 1947)

Carlson's knowledge of Chinese was far from perfect, however. He had first heard the words *kung* and *ho*, which he rendered as *gung ho*, in a conversation with a coolie in 1937. He thought from the context in which the terms were used—how the Chinese could defeat the Japanese—that they meant "work together." (The actual Chinese expression for "work together" includes other words that Carlson did not understand at the time.) Carlson further assumed *kung ho* to be the motto of the Chinese Industrial Cooperatives, which began using the phrase following their establishment in 1939. The Chinese characters for these words fit neatly into a triangular sign that was displayed wherever the small manufacturing cooperatives were established. This was not a motto, however, but an abbreviation of the organization's full name, *Chung Kuo Kung Yeh Ho Tso Hsieh Hui*. Gerald Cohen broke down the full name this way in his *Comments on Etymology* (12/89):

chung kuo—china (*chung*, middle + *kuo*, country)
kung yeh—industry (*kung*, work + *yeh*, industry)
ho tso—cooperative (*ho*, harmony + *tso*, do)
hsieh hui—association to negotiate for a common cause, in
    this case industrial cooperation (*hsieh*, negotiate +
    hui, association)

Following the principles of *gung ho*, as interpreted by Carlson, the Raiders functioned more democratically than the usual military unit. Carlson deemphasized saluting and didn't pay much attention to pitching tents in neat rows. He and his officers tried to encourage initiative by giving as few orders as possible. The idea was to get men in the habit of thinking for themselves so that they could take charge if the occasion arose in combat. The Raiders also attended Friday night *Gung Ho* forums. These had some elements of revival meetings, with songs and music, but the most important part of the evening always was a talk by Carlson about the *gung ho* philosophy or by his executive officer,

Major Jimmy Roosevelt, one of the President's sons, about the meaning of democracy, the reasons for the war, and what the world might be like after it.

"My motto caught on and they began to call themselves the *Gung Ho* Battalion," Carlson told *Life* magazine (9/20/43). "When I designed a field jacket to replace the bulky and orthodox pack, they called it the *Gung Ho* jacket. And they named every new thing *Gung Ho*. It became the watchword."

Gung Ho was used as the name of the battalion's camp in the New Hebrides, as an expression of reassurance, as an attack cry in battle, and eventually—in other units—also as a term of disparagement for the seemingly overzealous.

Carlson's belief that the men with *gung ho* spirit would be braver and more resourceful in battle than other troops appeared to be justified by combat results. In a raid on Makin Island (8/17/42) and later that year during a monthlong patrol through the jungles of Guadalcanal (11/4–12/4), the Raiders inflicted much damage upon the enemy while keeping their own losses low. On Guadalcanal, the battalion harried a large column of retreating Japanese, marching 150 miles, living off the land, fighting a dozen skirmishes, and killing 488 of the enemy, before returning to American lines, counting just 17 dead and 18 wounded.

The exploits of the Raiders attracted much media attention. Carlson and *gung ho* were featured in newspaper editorials; a national radio broadcast by Raymond Swing (11/11/42); articles in the *New York Times Magazine*, *Liberty*, and the *Saturday Evening Post*, plus the one in *Life*; and, finally, a flag-waving movie, *Gung Ho!*, starring Randolph Scott, which still shows up on TV, sometimes in a colorized version.

By the time the film came out at the end of 1943, however, Carlson was no longer with the Raiders. Marine headquarters was uneasy on a number of counts: about all the publicity, about having an elite unit within what was supposed to be an elite corps, about Carlson's admiration for the Chinese Communists, and even about the use of guerrilla tactics. Carlson was kicked upstairs to a staff position, and a new colonel, unsympathetic to the *gung ho* spirit, took command of the Raider battalion on April 1, 1943.

Never again given direct command of troops, Carlson still managed to insert himself into the action at Tarawa and at Saipan. During the latter invasion he was shot through the arm and thigh as he helped carry a wounded enlisted man to safety. (In the words of Colonel—

later Commandant—David Shoup, "He may have been Red but he was never yellow.") Carlson retired as a general in 1946 and died of a heart attack in 1947. *Gung ho* lives on.

gun moll. Despite appearances to the contrary, and occasional confusion by crime writers who don't know better, this kind of moll does not ordinarily pack a weapon. Rather, she is a pickpocket, typically a member of a *gun mob*. The *gun* part comes from the Yiddish *gonif*, thief, recorded with various spellings (e.g., *ganef, ganov, gonoph*) from the 1830s in England and the 1840s in the United States. *Moll*, meanwhile, a diminutive of *Mary* (similar to *Molly*) has been used as a generic term for any woman, especially a prostitute or thief's companion, since at least the early 1600s. The combined *gun moll* has been dated to 1908 (*OED*). See also GUNSEL.

gunsel. Usually thought of today as referring to a hoodlum or other criminal with a gun, *gunsel* had nothing to do with armament when it appeared in English around the time of the First World War. Originally, *gunsel* was tramp slang for a young male homosexual. Variants (deviants?) include *gonsil, gonzel, guncel, gunshel, guntzel, gunzel,* and *gunzl*, e.g., "*Gonsil*, a young tramp, not yet taken in hand and bent to his will by an older man. A boy. A passive male homosexual, usually a youth or younger man" (G. Irwin, *American Tramp & Underworld Slang*, 1931). Whatever the English spelling, the word comes from the Yiddish *genzel*, little goose, gosling, in turn from the German *gänslein*, with the same meaning. The underlying image is similar to that of *silly goose*, the point being that the inexperienced youth is easily lured into a homosexual relationship.

The shift in the word's meaning is due to Dashiell Hammett. Angry at a prudish editor who had been blue-penciling his hard-boiled prose, Hammett slipped this word into *The Maltese Falcon* (1930): " 'Another thing,' Spade repeated, glaring at the boy: 'Keep that gunsel away from me while you're making up your mind or I'll kill him.' " Since Sam Spade is referring here to Kasper Gutman's young hit-man companion, Wilmer Cook, it was easy for the editor to assume that *gunsel* meant "gunman." Most other readers made the same mistake. The word also was admitted into the 1941 film starring Humphrey Bogart that was made of the book—and this was at a time when the Motion Picture Production Code specifically forbade the use of such "vulgar expressions" as "chippie, fairy, goose, nuts, pansy, S.O.B., [and] son-of-a." Which goes to show that the Hollywood censors didn't know the true meaning of *gunsel*, either. Hammett probably got a good laugh out of his private joke. But bluenoses never give up: When *The Thin Man* (1934) went into paperback, another editor replaced "get an erection" with the decidedly limp "get excited." See also GUN MOLL and SON OF A GUN.

H

half-seas over. Attempts have been made to derive this expression for tipsiness from the Dutch *op zee zober*, oversea beer, i.e., beer for export, as well as from the late-sixteenth-century English phrase *upsy friese*, to drink up, or drink heavily, in the Frisian fashion (with many variants, such as *upsee freeze, upsie Dutch*, and even *upsy English*).

Op zee zober is not a standard Dutch phrase, however, and the other expressions parallel the disparaging use of *Dutch*, dating from the same period, when the English competed with the Dutch for supremacy of the seas. Similar slurs of the Hollanders include *Dutch courage*, false courage, inspired by alcohol; *Dutch draught*, a big swig; and *Dutch feast*, a party at which the host manages to get drunk before the guests do.

Half-seas over, meaning inebriated, has been dated to 1690. This sense probably comes from the earlier use of the same phrase (1551, *OED*) to mean halfway across the sea and, by extension, halfway to one's destination. Technically speaking, then, the person who is *half-seas over* is only fifty percent drunk.

But there probably is a pun lurking here, too, comparing the reeling sailor to the vessel that is on its beam-ends, half sloshed and ready to keel over. Certainly, *half-seas over* fits in well with a raft of other nautical expressions for inebriation, a number of which remain current although the age of sail is long gone. Among them: *a full cargo aboard, on the lee lurch, overboard, three* (or *four*) *sheets in* (or *to*) *the wind, waterlogged*, and *with the main brace well spliced*.

halt. The *halt* in "bring in hither the poor, and the maimed, and the halt, and the blind" (*Luke*, 14:21) has nothing to do with crippled people coming to the *halt* that is a temporary stop. The crippled *halt* derives from the Anglo-Saxon *healt*, to be lame; the other comes from the German *halten*, to hold, to stop, as in the military command *halt machen*, to make halt. The command was adopted prior to 1600 in other languages, e.g., the Spanish *allo hacer*, the Italian *far alto*, and—the immediate source of the English *halt*—the French *faire halte*.

ham. The term for the thespian who overacts, or *hams it up*, has been dated only to 1882, which means that it is most unlikely to come from the *ham* in *Hamlet* (1601–2), despite what some actors have done in and to the role of the melancholy Dane. The suggestion that the term is a clipping of the Cockney *hamateur* also seems far-fetched, considering that the theatrical *ham* appeared first in American English.

The origin of the theatrical *ham* is obscure, but it probably is a shortening of *hamfatter*, "a term of contempt for an actor of low grade" (*The Century Dictionary*, 1899). *Hamfatter*, in turn, came from a minstrel song, "The Ham-Fat Man." The reference may be to the use of ham rind instead of a more expensive but nicer-smelling oil as a base for makeup by low-grade, poorly paid actors.

Meanwhile, amateur radio operators are *hams*, as were amateur telegraphists before them, because many of the early ones were as bad as amateur actors. They were all thumbs—ham-handed, so to speak.

hangnail. The small dead flap of skin at the base of a toenail or fingernail originally was called an *agnail*, from the Anglo-Saxon *angnægl*, a corn on the foot. In the very beginning, ca. 1000, the *nægl* was not a toenail or fingernail but an iron nail, and the *ang* implied pain or angst. In other words, the hard corn hurt like a nail in the foot. *Agnail* eventually was applied to any painful swelling or sore around a toenail or fingernail and then, by the seventeenth century, specifically to a partially detached piece of skin. Thus, the sense of iron in the *nail* was lost, and the *ang*, whose original meaning had been forgotten by most people, was converted by folk etymology into the familiar *hang*, producing *hangnail*. This is the word that everyone uses today, except for lexicographers, who continue to list *agnail* in many dictionaries. One suspects that even the most fastidious scholars stoop to using the folk expression when visiting the doctor, however, since most physicians wouldn't know where to begin operating on an agnail.

harlequin. The origin of the name of the British pantomime character (*Arlecchino* in the older Italian *commedia dell'arte*) has inspired many guesses—among them, that it comes from the French town of Arles; from the Flemish *hellekint*, child of hell; or from the Italian *arlotto*, glutton, and *lecchino*, meaning the same.

The name was recorded first in 1130 in the form of *Herlechin*, referring to a giant-size, *Hercules*-like demon who terrorized the medieval countryside. Mounted and armed with a huge club (also like Hercules), he was accompanied by a band of riders, including women who rode on sidesaddles studded with white-hot nails.

Harlequin also has been associated with other historical and mythological personages, including the biblical Herod; a shadowy Count Hernequin of Boulogne; Hennequin, another medieval demon; the Erlking (*Herla rex* in Latin, but probably a corruption of *elverkonge*, king of the elves); Herne the Hunter, also a leader of a spectral band, who supposedly haunted Windsor Forest (he is mentioned in *The Merry Wives of Windsor*, 1597); and King Charles V (i.e., *Charles Quint*) of France, even though he did not appear on the scene until the fourteenth century (1337–80), long after the earliest references to *Herlechin*.

Given this tangle of possibilities, it is difficult to say for sure which etymological thread should be followed. Certainly, the myth of the demon hunter is a common one, and this may well be the source of the word and the pantomime character. Ultimately, as Ernest Weekley suggests in *Words and Names* (1932), *harlequin* probably is based on a personal name, perhaps the Flemish *Henekin*, Johnny, a diminutive of *Hans*, John. This would be in accord with standard naming practice for spirits, e.g., *hobgoblin*, where *hob* is a diminutive of *Robert*; *Robin Goodfellow*, where *Robin* is another diminutive of *Robert* and *Goodfellow* is a propitiatory euphemism; and *will o' the wisp*, a.k.a. *jack o' lantern*, not to mention the *dickens*, *Old Harry*, and *Old Nick*, which are bywords for Satan himself. See also DICKENS and OLD NICK.

harlot. Etymologists once pinned this word on Arlette, daughter of Fulbert, a tanner in the Norman town of Falaise, and mother of William the Bastard, normally characterized in schoolbooks today as William the Conqueror. As delicately described in a pamphlet on sale at the site of William's castle in Falaise: "it is in a small rush-strewn cell of the keep that Robert the Magnificent embraced Arlette and made her the mother of William, the founder of an immense empire" (Léonce Macary, *Falaise*, 1958).

Actually, *harlot* derives from the Old French *herlot* or *(h)arlot*, vagabond, beggar. Dating from the thirteenth century, this originally was a masculine term, not a feminine one. The usual reference was to a boy or servant, a buffoon, a rascal, fornicator, itinerant jester or juggler, but sometimes to a regular fellow, a good guy, which is how Chaucer used it in describing the Sumonour in the *Prologue to the Canterbury Tales* (1387–1400):

> He was a gentil harlot and a kynde,
> A bettre felawe sholde men noght fynde.

Not until the early fifteenth century was *harlot* applied to women, and then it encompassed actresses, dancers, and jugglers, as well as prostitutes. The feminization of *harlot* and the narrowing of its meaning probably were speeded by sixteenth-century translators of the Bible. Where the Wyclif versions of the 1380s used "hoore" and "strumpet," for example, the widely used Geneva Bible of 1560 (the first English Bible to break chapters into verses, and the edition read by Shakespeare, among many others) employed the softer term, as in "How is the faithful city become an harlot!" (*Isaiah*, 1:21). Within another twenty years, the suggestion—frequently repeated—that the word was based on *Arlette* was proposed by William Lambarde (1570–76, *OED*), thus demonstrating that the earlier, nonwhorish meanings of *harlot* already had been largely forgotten.

Harlot's semantic sex change is typical of what often happens to words with negative meanings: other feminine terms that once were masculine or neutral include *hoyden*, once an ignorant chap, boor, or bumpkin, from the Dutch *heiden*, heathen; *shrew*, originally a wicked man; *termagant*, from the name of an imaginary Muslim deity in medieval mystery plays; *wench*, from the ninth-century *wenchel*, a child of either sex; and even *girl*, applied to male children, who were *knave girls*, as well as to female children, or *gay girls*, up to the middle of the fifteenth century. Meanwhile, men have arrogated neutral words with "good" meanings for themselves; for example, see GOD and the etymology of the *man* in WOMAN.

hat trick. Spectators at ice hockey games have been known to throw their hats upon the rink to show their appreciation for a player who has scored three goals in a single game, but the phrase comes from another sport, cricket, where it had a different meaning.

Hat trick has been dated to 1877 (*OED*); the idea in the beginning was that the cricketeer who took three wickets with successive balls was considered to have performed a feat that entitled him to presentation with a hat or its equivalent by his club. As originally adopted in ice hockey, the expression had a similar meaning, *hat trick* at first referring to the feat of making three goals in a row, without anyone else's scoring in between. This is now called a *pure hat trick*.

By the early twentieth century, *hat trick* was extended to triple feats in horse racing and other activities. It is a purely homonymous coincidence that the cricket player who performs the *hat trick* by delivering the ball at the wicket is known as the BOWLER.

have [one's] ass in a sling. The inability of donkeys to stand on three feet when being shod is said to have inspired this picturesque metaphor for defeat, incapacitation, or other serious trouble. The supposition is that the old-time smith had to erect a sling to support the critters while putting new shoes on them. This makes such a nice story that one would like very much to believe it. Unfortunately:

1. Slang specialists have traced the phrase only to the 1930s, after the great age of smiths and smithies had passed.
2. Archaeologists have yet to discover the remnants of a sling in the ruins of any smithy.
3. Anatomists have determined that donkeys actually are capable of lifting one foot off the ground at a time without toppling over.

In the absence of supporting (so to speak) evidence, it seems more likely that the metaphor is just a fanciful variation upon the familiar sling that supports a broken arm. Certainly, the phrase is comparable to such others as *[someone's] ass is on the line, no skin off my ass, pain in the ass,* and *smart-ass,* wherein mention of the part refers to the whole man (or woman). Technically, this is what is known as synecdoche, a figure of speech in which a less-inclusive term stands for a more inclusive one, or vice versa. "Three sail" for "three ships" and "the law" for "a policeman" are other examples. The allusion in *ass in a sling,* then, is fundamentally anatomical rather than animalistic. See also DONKEY.

helpmate. This is an example of folk etymology at its best: a corruption of a corruption. To begin at the very beginning, in *Genesis* (2:18): "And the Lord God said, *It is* not good that man should be alone; I will make him an help meet for him." By this, which is from the King James Bible of 1611, the Lord meant that he would furnish Adam with a help, or helper, that would be meet, or suitable, for him. The intent of the passage is clearer in earlier translations of the Bible, e.g., "an help lijk to hym silf" and "an help, to beare him company," which is how the passage appears in the Wyclif and Coverdale bibles of 1388 and 1535, respectively.

Hearing *help meet* pronounced, however, churchgoers began running the two words together. Before the end of the seventeenth century, the terms were being joined by a hyphen, as in "If ever woman was a help-meet for man, my Spouse is so" (John Dryden, *Marriage à la Mode*, 1673). And within another fifty years, people began to drop the hyphen (while occasionally extending the sense of the expression to include helpers of another sort). For example: "Socrates had the like Number of Helpmeets; and Anthanæus concludes it was no Scandal in those Times" (*Entertainer*, No. 15, 1718).

Meanwhile, people also began to confuse the *meet* in the new *helpmeet* with the *mate* that is a spouse. This second mistake produced *helpmate*, used in its first recorded appearance in print (1715, *OED*) to refer to a helper, and shortly thereafter in the currently dominant sense, i.e., "A woman is to be a helpmate, and a man is to be the same" (Daniel Defoe, *Religious Courtship*, 1722).

The *mate* in *helpmate* also is of interest. It comes from the Anglo-Saxon *gemetta*, guest, and is cognate to *meat*, from Anglo-Saxon *mete*, referring to food generally rather than to the flesh specifically. (As late as the seventeenth century, animals were being fed *green meat*, meaning grass or other fodder.) Originally, then, a *mate* was, in modern parlance, a *messmate* or *companion* (a parallel formation, based on Latin *panis*, bread), not a *helpmate* or *help-meet*, let alone *help meet*.

hocus-pocus. This pseudo-Latin phrase for deceptive nonsense often is described as a perversion of the words uttered during the Mass at the moment of transubstantiation, when water and wine are transformed into the presence of Christ: *hoc est corpus*, this is the body. This theory, suggested prior to 1694 in a sermon by John Tillotson, an Archbishop of Canterbury, is attractive, if only because it creates such a nice parallel with the magician's *patter*, from the opening words of the Lord's Prayer in Latin, *Pater Noster*. See PATTER.

Firm evidence for Tillotson's theory is lacking, however, and it seems certain that the immediate source of the phrase is the stage name of a conjurer, as evidenced by the use of capital letters in its earliest appearances in print, i.e., *Hocas Pocas* (1624), *Hokos Pokos* (1625), and then *Hocus-pocus* (1634). This magician is said to have practiced in the time of James I (1567–1625), which squares with the title of the first illustrated book in English on magic, *Hocus Pocus Junior, The Anatomy of Legerdemain* (1634).

The original Hocus Pocus may have gotten his name from a longer nonsense incantation that he uttered when performing tricks, *Hocus pocus, tontus talontus, vade celeriter jubeo* or even—a longer stretch—*hax pax max Deus adimax.* By comparison, twentieth-century American children have been heard to say *hocus pocus dominocus,* and according to Ernest Weekley, Norwegians and Swedes recite *hookuspokus-filiokus* (*An Etymological Dictionary of Modern English,* 1921). The modern expressions hint at blasphemy, so perhaps the older ones do, too. Still, it would seem to have been a brave conjurer to risk an indictment for blasphemy in the early seventeenth century, when the penalties included fines, imprisonment, and bodily punishment.

Another possibility, then, is that *hocus-pocus* is simply a reduplication, similar to *claptrap, fiddle-faddle, flimflam, hotch-potch, twiddle-twaddle,* etc., based in this instance on the small bag, or poke, into which magicians place coins and other objects, and from which those objects vanish. As described by an early observer: "His very fingers cryed 'give me the gold!' which . . . he put in his hocas pocas, a little dormer under his right skirt" (James Shirley, *Captain Underwit,* 1640). See also HOOK OR BY CROOK, BY.

Whatever its source (yet another suggestion is Ochus Bochus, a supposed demon-wizard in Scandinavian mythology), *hocus pocus* has been fecund. It probably inspired *hoax* (from 1796); it influenced *hanky-panky* (1841), which may also allude to the hanky, or handkerchief, a standard magician's prop; it undoubtedly is responsible for *hokey-pokey* (1847–78), originally a deception and later a cheap ice cream and then a dance; and it apparently blended with *bunkum* to form *hokum* (1917), which makes it ancestral to *hoke* (1935) and *hokey* (1945).

See also TEDIUM.

hogwash. Not the water in which hogs have been bathed, but the swill—a mixture of leftover liquids, table scraps, and other garbage—that is fed to them. The term has been dated to ca. 1440 as pig feed (*hoggyswasch*); to 1712 as weak liquor, rotgut, and other worthless stuff; and to 1893 as inferior or insincere writing.

homosexual. The *homo-* does not come from the Latin *homo,* man, but from the Greek *homós,* same. (The *-sexual* part is Latin, however, from *sexualis.*) The belief that the word meant "lover of men," in effect, reflects the reluctance of proper Victorians to admit that women ever engaged in what our ancestors referred to as *unnatural, unspeakable,* or *nameless acts.* For example, the pertinent section of British criminal law, enacted in 1885, did not contemplate the prosecution of women. It specified only that "Any male person, who in public or private, commits, or is party to the commission of, any act of gross indecency with another male person, shall be guilty of a misdemeanour." (This is the law that sent Oscar Wilde to Reading Gaol for two years of hard labour in 1895–97.)

Scholarly students of sexual behavior knew the real meaning of the word and used it correctly from the start. Thus, C. G. Chaddock's 1892 translation of Baron Richard von Krafft-Ebbing's *Psychopathia Sexualis*, the first English work in which the term is known to have appeared, includes a reference to "homo-sexual women." H. Havelock Ellis also used the term in its proper "same-sex" sense at an early date, noting in *Studies in the Psychology of Sex* (1897), "Among animals in a domesticated or confined state it is easy to find evidence of homosexual attraction."

Ellis did not really approve of the term, also declaring in *Studies* that " 'Homosexual' is a barbarously hybrid word and I claim no responsibility for it." He employed it in preference, however, to *inversion, perversion, abominable offense, gross indecency*, and other synonyms of the time, all of which were freighted with negative connotations. Since then, *homosexual* also has acquired pejorative connotations, of course, with the result that it has largely been superseded by *gay*.

Time marches on, and words continually evolve new meanings.

honeymoon. Once upon a time, so it is said, the custom was for newlyweds to drink nothing but mead, made of fermented honey and water, during the first month, or moon, of their marriage. The liquor is supposed to have an especially strong aphrodisiac effect, though it is not clear just why an aphrodisiac is needed at this stage of marriage.

A simpler, more likely explanation for the term (from 1546, *OED*) is that the first month of marriage is the sweetest. Dr. Johnson had a more jaundiced view of the proceedings, however, suggesting in his *Dictionary of the English Language* (1755) that the *moon* alluded to the changeability of that heavenly body. According to this interpretation, then, the term is essentially ironic: No sooner is the moon full but it begins to wane, as does the mutual affection of the newly married pair.

One regrets to have to report that Johnson's view is seconded by *The Oxford English Dictionary* (Section Hod–Horizontal, Volume V, 3/1899).

honky (honkey, honkie). The most likely explanation of the origin of this derogatory term for a white person is that it is a variant of *hunky*, in turn from the *Hun* of *Hungary*, but applied generally, usually disparagingly, to Middle European immigrants to the United States and their descendants. Thus, Milton (Mezz) Mezzrow, a white jazz musician from Chicago, translated *honky* as "factory hand" when re-creating a conversation with a black hipster buying marijuana from him in Harlem in the 1930s. In Mezzrow's jive talk, "I'm down with it [marijuana], sticking like a honky," meant "my pockets are as full as a factory hand's on payday" (Mezzrow and Bernard Wolfe, *Really the Blues*, 1946). This is the earliest example of *honky* in *The Oxford English Dictionary*.

Blacks themselves have tended to relate *honky* to the sound of an automobile horn, however. Several connections have been adduced: (1) that whites have tinny voices; (2) that the term was first applied to whites who honked the horns of their cars when they stopped outside the houses where their black girlfriends worked as maids; and (3) that whites honk their own horns a lot, especially so-called liberals who claim to favor integration but aren't willing to fight for it.

Finally, it also has been suggested that *honky* comes from *honky-tonk*, presumably referring to white customers of black jazz joints, but firm evidence is lacking for this as well as for the other theories, leaving the true origin of the term in doubt.

hoodlum. The word originated in San Francisco around 1870 and within a short time inspired one of the most fanciful of all folk etymologies. As retailed by John Russell Bartlett in his *Dictionary of Americanisms* (1877): "A newspaper man in San Francisco, in attempting to coin a word to designate a gang of street Arabs under the beck of one named Muldoon, hit upon the idea of dubbing them *noodlums*—that is, simply reversing the leader's name. In writing the word, the strokes of the *n* did not correspond in height and the compositor, taking the *n* for an *h*, printed it *hoodlum*."

This story, best characterized as noodleheaded, has been given more credence than it deserves because of the parallel with nearly synonymous *hooligan*, which really is based on a family name. The latter word first appeared in London newspaper accounts of the activities of street toughs in the summer of 1898. Modern etymologists lean toward the theory that it comes from *Houley*, as in *Houley's gang*, or *Houlihan*, sometimes spelled *Houlighan*. But Ernest Weekley, who heard about this "lively" Irish family ca. 1896 "from a surgeon at Guy's who spent some of his time patching up the results," believed that it came straight from the surname Hooligan (*An Etymological Dictionary of Modern English*, 1921). In any case, the transition of the word from proper to common noun probably was aided by the popularity of a music-hall song of the time about a rowdy family named Hooligan.

Meanwhile, theories of *hoodlum*'s creation go on practically forever. For example, it has been proposed that the term comes from *Hood*, referring to the leader of a San Francisco gang; or from the hoodlike caps of the city's militia; or from *hooligan* as pronounced by someone with a speech defect (absurd on the face of it, considering that *hoodlum* is the older word); or from an unspecified Spanish word; or from *hood lahnt*, a pidgin-English expression meaning "very lazy mandarin"; or from the Bavarian *hudelum*, disorderly, in turn from *Huddellump*, a slovenly or careless person, a ragamuffin. Of these, the last is the most commonly accepted today, in part because Germans seem to have constituted the largest group of non-English speakers in San Francisco when *hoodlum* first appeared on the scene.

hooker. General Joseph ("Fighting Joe") Hooker, who commanded the Army of the Potomac for five months in 1863, frequently is credited with lending his name to denote the professional women who attached themselves to his camp. And we do have it on the authority of Charles Francis Adams, Jr., grandson of one president and great-grandson of another, that Hooker's headquarters was "a place where no self-respecting man liked to go, and no decent woman could go. It was a combination of barroom and brothel." It also was apparently in tribute to the General's character that the women who worked in Washington's brothels in this period became known collectively as "Hooker's Division" or "Hooker's Brigade."

The circumstantial evidence in favor of General Joe (or disfavor, if you prefer) certainly seems strong. But, alas, the case is punctured by the existence of pre–Civil War examples of the word's use in this sense, e.g., from 1845: "If he comes by way of Norfolk, he will find any number of pretty Hookers in the Brick row not far from French's hotel" (N. E. Eliason, *Tarheel Talk*, 1956). And John Russell Bartlett defined *hooker* as a "strumpet" or "sailor's trull" in the prewar, 1859 edition of his *Dictionary of Americanisms*.

All this leaves the term's true origin in doubt. Bartlett speculated that it derived from *Corlear's Hook*, a section of New York City that was notorious for its "houses of ill-fame" (a fearsome gang of river pirates, the Hookers, also lived there). Other possibilities are that *hooker* is a spin-off from the British slang use of the same word to mean a petty thief (also called an *angler*), who employed a stick with a hook on the end to remove goods from shop windows, or that it derives from *hooker*, originally (from the seventeenth century) a fishing boat and later applied depreciatingly or fondly to any ship, usually in the form of *old hooker*. In the first case, the connection would be the practice of many whores to supplement their earnings with thievery; in the second, it would be the common comparison of ships to women, particularly to the lady who is a *tramp* (a vessel that does not follow a fixed route but makes frequent stops at different ports, picking up whatever business she can).

More likely yet is that *hooker* arose because of the way in which a working woman, like an angler, hooks approaching customer-fish, e.g., quoting a British prostitute in 1857: "I've hooked many a man by showing him an ankle on a wet day" (Henry Mayhew, *London Labour and the London Poor*). It may be coincidental—a case of semantic convergence—but a point in favor of the last theory is that the technical term for the man employed to steer customers to whorehouses in Paris is *accrocheur*, i.e., hooker.

hook or by crook, by. This phrase has attracted so many "explanations" over the years that it qualifies as a lexicographic lightning rod. The most popular one, repeated in many books, is that it stems from a medieval custom of allowing peasants to gather as much deadwood from the trees in manorial forests as they could reach with a shepherd's crook and cut down with a billhook. A variant of this story cites a particular charcoal burner by the name of Purkiss who was given the right to remove all the wood he could get from New Forest by hook or by crook as a reward for finding the body of King William II (William Rufus), assassinated by an unknown archer while hunting in the forest on August 2, 1100, and then carting the corpse to Winchester.

Another theory is that the phrase arose among shepherds: a shepherd who happened to leave his crook at home would use a branch as a hook to keep sheep from straying.

Yet another suggestion is that this originated as an underworld expression, referring to thieves who used sticks with hooks to steal goods from open windows or from behind shop grills. This method of pilfering was popular from the sixteenth to the nineteenth century; its practitioners were termed *anglers* or *hookers*.

It has even been said, apparently with a straight face, that the phrase honors the exploits of two rival nineteenth-century barristers, Hook and Crook. Both had such good records in court, so the story goes, that people who had to go to law swore that they would win their cases either by Hook or by Crook.

If all this sounds like nonsense, that is probably what it is. The phrase has been dated to ca. 1380, appearing first in the works of John Wyclif, with the same meaning as today—by fair means or foul, by one way or another. None of the examples of the phrase in *The Oxford English Dictionary* have anything to do with deadwood, William Rufus, lost sheep, shoplifters, or barristers.

Most likely, repetition is as important as reason in the origin of the expression, with the sound of *hook* and *crook* reinforcing each other in the same way as do the elements of *dilly-dally*, *fiddle-faddle*, *flimflam*, *highways and byways*, *hoity-toity*, *namby-pamby*, *rack and ruin*, *wishy-washy*, and so forth. Both *hook* and *crook* are old words for bent instruments for catching things. In view of the meaning of the phrase, it seems significant that *crook* also once denoted a trick, deceit, or wile, with the sense of a crooked piece of conduct having been dated to ca. 1200, about two centuries prior to the first appearance in literature of a bishop's crook (ca. 1386) or a shepherd's crook (ca. 1430). See also HOCUS-POCUS.

hopscotch. The word conjures up an image of Scottish children, kilts flying as they hop back and forth in the playground game. But this is all wrong. *Scotch* here has nothing to do with the inhabitants of the northern portion of the island of Great Britain. Rather, it is a moderately old (fifteenth-century) word for a cut, incision, scratch, or score on the ground, which is how the boxes were made before kids got their hands on chalk. Schoolchildren have been playing *scotch-hoppers* since at least 1677 (*OED*).

The same non-Scottish sense of *scotch* appears in *butterscotch* (the butter candy is scored, or cut, into squares) and the phrase *to scotch a rumor* (that is, to cut it off). The etymology of this form of *scotch* is a matter of some guesswork. It probably comes from the Anglo-French *escocher*, to notch or nick, and perhaps ultimately from the Latin *coccum*, berry of scarlet oak (notched or notchlike in appearance),

See also SCOT-FREE.

horse latitudes. Spanish ships transporting horses to the New World sometimes were becalmed for so long in this part of the Atlantic, approximately thirty to thirty-five degrees north of the equator, that it is said that many animals died and had to be tossed overboard. Coming upon the carcasses floating in the ocean, sailors in other vessels naturally called this region the *horse latitudes.*

The part about becoming becalmed is true enough. Sailing vessels certainly may be caught for long periods in this area between the prevailing westerlies to the north and easterlies to the south (or in the corresponding zone at the same distance south of the equator). It is most unlikely that the sea was ever littered with horse corpses, however. The becalmed sailors, fed up, so to speak, with hardtack, would have eaten the animals first.

Unfortunately, the best of the alternative explanations—that the name derives from the Spanish *El Golfo de las Yeguas,* the Gulf of the Mares—is not entirely satisfactory either. The idea here is that the Spanish name alludes to the fickleness of the region's winds in contrast to those of *El Golfo de las Damas,* whose smooth and stately breezes, suitable for *damas,* ladies, propelled ships quickly from the Canaries to the West Indies. The first difficulty with this theory is that the term *Golfo de las Yeguas* wasn't recorded until 1883, more than a century after *horse latitudes* (1777), which makes *Yeguas* look like an afterthought. Second, as Laurence Urdang points out in *The Whole Ball of Wax* (1988), extensive research in old maps and modern gazetteers has not turned up any other references to *El Golfo de las Yeguas.* For the time being, then, the origin of *horse latitudes* remains one of the mysteries of the sea. Could it be—just a guess, you understand—that the *horse latitudes* were so named because sailors welcomed the change in rations when they became becalmed there?

hurricane. The spelling has led to the supposition that the storm is so called because it *hurries* away the *cane* from sugar plantations in the West Indies. The present form of the word, however, represents only one of several attempts by the English at rendering Spanish and Portuguese terms into their own language. English variants include *furacan* (the oldest English version, from 1555) and *hurricano,* used by Shakespeare in *The Tempest* (1611) with reference to a waterspout rather than a storm with violent winds. The modern spelling was not fixed until about 1688 (*OED*). The ultimate source is the Arawakan *hurakán,* an evil spirit of the sea.

husky. The dogs that pull Eskimo sleds are stout and sturdy, but their name has nothing to do with their physique; rather, it is a variant of

Eskimo, as in "Carl Peterson no speak Husky" (C. F. Hall, *Life Among the Esquimaux*, 1864). The term has been dated in its canine sense to 1852 as *huski*, which preceded *huskie* (1878) and *husky* (1886).

Eskimo, meanwhile, is an Algonquian word, variously translated as "eaters of raw fish" (*American Heritage Dictionary*), "eaters of raw meat" (*Barnhart Dictionary of Etymology*), and "snowshoe-netter" (*Random House Dictionary*). The Eskimo themselves prefer to be known as *Innuit*, the men, which is at once chauvinistic and ethnocentric, but not especially unusual. As noted by Mario Pei: "The Chantku of Siberia, the Lolos or Ne-su of China, the Tule Indians of Panama, even the Germans, whose *Deutsch* comes from an earlier *tiutisk* ('pertaining to the people'), bear national names which in their own respective languages mean 'men,' 'we men,' 'persons,' [and] 'people' " (*The Story of Language*, 1965).

I

idyll. King Arthur did not have a lot of time on his hands, despite the Tennyson title *The Idylls of the King.* Nor was Tennyson alluding to the way Lancelot and Guinevere *idled* (from the Anglo-Saxon *idel*, empty, trifling, useless) time away.

The literary *idyll* usually is a narrative work, either prose or poetry, about a pastoral scene or some charmingly picturesque episode. The *idyll* typically is brief, but it may be extended to epic length, which is what Tennyson did. The word comes from the Latin *idyllium*, in turn from the Greek *eidýllion*, short pastoral poem. The Greek root is *eidos*, form, shape, which also is the ancestor of *ideal* and *idol*.

ignoramus. An *ignoramus* by definition is *ignorant*, but the first word does not descend from the second, nor vice versa. Rather, they are cousins, both coming from the Latin *ignōrāre*, to have no knowledge, to disregard.

Ignorant, which comes from the present participle of *ignōrāre*, was the first of the two to appear in English. Chaucer used it in the fourteenth century. *Ignoramus*, which translates as "we do not know," is the first-person plural of *ignōrāre*. It entered English in the sixteenth century as a legal term. When members of a grand jury refused to approve an indictment because they didn't think there was enough evidence to warrant going to trial, they reported *ignoramus*, we do not know, when returning the prosecutor's charge to him.

The presently dominant sense of *ignoramus*, meaning an ignorant person, is due to a play by George Ruggle that was produced in 1615. Entitled *Ignoramus*, after the name of its lead character, a lawyer, it satirized attorneys of that era as ignorant and arrogant fellows. Unlikely as it may seem to the members of the bar today, distinguished and learned counsel all, Ruggle's unflattering portrayal of their predecessors struck a sympathetic chord with his public. Francis Beaumont quickly glommed on to the word, using it as a term of personal disparagement, albeit still with a capital *I*, in *Vertue of Sack* (pre-1616), referring to a "silly *Ignoramus*." And within a quarter of a century (1641, *OED*), full-fledged "ignoramuses" began appearing on the scene generally, not just in courts of law.

installment. By purchasing goods on an *installment* plan, one can *stall* off debts, but the two words are only distantly related. *Installment* is from the Old French *estaler*, to fix, or set (as payments); it has been dated in the pecuniary sense to 1732. *Stall* meaning a delaying tactic is early-nineteenth-century slang (1812, *OED*). It comes from the word's use among pickpockets since at least the sixteenth century (1591) to refer to the person who distracts the victim, or mark, maneuvering him or her into a position where the chief pickpocket, or tool, can do his job. *Stall* remains current in this sense among the so-called light-fingered gentry. The underworld term derives from—and here is where *installment* and *stall* finally come together—the Anglo-French *estale*, decoy, so called because it was fixed, or installed, permanently in a particular place.

internecine. The most common modern sense of the term, involving a bitter or disastrous struggle within a group, stems from a mistake by Dr. Samuel Johnson. He assumed that the *inter-* came from the Latin *inter*, between, among, as in *interchange* or *intermediate*. Accordingly, Johnson defined *internecine* as "endeavouring mutual destruction" in his *Dictionary of the English Language* (1755). In this case, however, the *inter-* serves as an intensive. *Internecine* comes from *internecīnus*, murderous, destructive, in turn from the verb *internecāre*, to slaughter, to massacre, where the function of *inter-* is to accentuate *necāre*, to kill.

Samuel Butler introduced *internecine* into English in his mock-heroic poem *Hudibras* (1663), basing it on the Latin phrase *internecīnum bellum*, murderous war, war of extermination, war for the sake of slaughter. Later writers also used the word in Butler's original sense, e.g., "Rome has written on her banners . . . the alternatives only of internecine war or absolute surrender" (William Ewart Gladstone, *Gleanings of Past Years*, 1843). Johnson's influence on the language was so great, however, that his error eventually was accepted as correct. For more about the original Dr. J. and etymology, see BONFIRE, CURMUDGEON, and SEDAN.

isinglass. The gelatin, or isinglass, obtained from the air bladders of sturgeon and other fish is transparent or translucent like glass. Mica also is called *isinglass* when cut or flaked in thin sheets, and named for its resemblance to the fishy substance. In neither case, however, does the word reflect the item's glasslike qualities. Nor does *isinglass* derive from the English *icing* and the French *glacé*, glazed, even though the gelatin is used in confectionery as well as in making jellies.

Isinglass actually is an import from Holland, linguistically as well as literally, deriving from the Middle Dutch *huysenblas*, sturgeon bladder. It appears first in English as *isom glass* in a customs regulation of 1545. The *m* in *isom* apparently was a typo, since other early references are to *ison glass*, but the English consistently interpreted the *-blas* as *-glass* on account of the item's transparency.

island. An *isle* is a small *island*, but the two words have a closer connection geographically than linguistically. *Isle* comes from the Old French *isle* and the Latin *īnsula*, island. *Island*, by contrast, is an Anglo-Saxon word, from *īgland*, where *īg* means "island" and *land* means "land." Thus, the Anglo-Saxon *īgland* actually translates as "island land."

Medieval clerks, influenced by their knowledge of French, mistakenly assumed that *isle* and *igland* were related, and began dropping the *g* from the English word to make *iland* and *yland*. Thus, John Milton wrote in *Paradise Lost* (1667): "Down the great River to the op'ning Gulf, And there take root an Iland salt and bare." Then, with the *g* gone, the French form edged further into English, producing *isle-land*, *ysle-land*, and the present *island* spelling, which became standard toward the end of the 1600s. (Curiously, while the English word gained an *s*, the Old French word lost the same letter, with the result that the word for island in French today is *île*, not *isle*.)

The Anglo-Saxon *ig* was not completely eradicated, however. It survives in the *ey* of such British place names as Chertsey, Hackney, and Romsey, as well as in the *y* of Runnymede, the meadow in Surrey beside the Thames associated with the signing of the Magna Carta by King John in 1215. Historians have argued over whether the signing ceremony actually took place in the meadow, which is mentioned in the document, or on Charter Island, the *ig* facing it, which was a traditional meeting place.

For a similar clerkish error, see DEBT.

J

jerked beef. Daniel Boone and other pioneers preserved meat by cutting it into long slices and drying it in the sun; no sharp tugs, pulls, or jerks were involved. The culinary term comes from *charqui*, the American Spanish word for meat that has been cured in this fashion. The Spanish, in turn, learned the method from the Inca and adopted their word for it—*ch'arki*, in Quechua.

The term has been dated in English to 1612, first appearing as *jerkin beefe* in Captain John Smith's *A Map of Viginia, with a Description of the Countrey.* Captain Smith's rendering of the Spanish word may have been influenced by the *jerkin* that is a short, sleeveless jacket, usually made of leather, which seems to say something about the chewability of jerked beef.

jerry-built. The origin of this adjective denoting flimsy construction has been a subject of debate almost from the time of its first recorded appearance in print (1869, *OED*). Most of the theories of the term's origin, though sometimes confidently asserted, depend upon unsupported suppositions and speculations. They are, in a word, jerry-built. Some of the more imaginative guesses, in more or less ascending order of likelihood:

1. The *jerry* refers to the tumbling down of the walls of the biblical Jericho.

2. It alludes to the prophet Jeremiah, known for his forecasts of doom, gloom, and disaster.

3. *Jerry* comes from a Gypsy word for excrement.

4. It is basically an ethnic insult referring to shoddy construction techniques of the *jerries,* as German soldiers were known from the time of World War I. The soldiers apparently were so called because the English thought their helmets looked like chamber pots, also called *jeroboams*— or *jerries,* for short. In turn, the porcelain utensil and the extra-large wine bottle known as a *jeroboam* were named after Jeroboam I, the first King of Israel, a mighty man—but a sinful one, according to the Bible.

5. *Jerry* is a corruption of the French *jour,* day, via *joury,* implying that the building is not likely to stand for more than twenty-four hours.

6. The term is an eponym, for a developer named Jerry or Jerrey, who put up cheap and insubstantial houses in Liverpool in the first half of the nineteenth century. (This theory appeared in a British newspaper as early as 1884, but has not been confirmed.)

7. *Jerry* is a nautical term, a corruption of *jury* in the seagoing sense of "temporary" or "makeshift," as in jury-mast, jury-rig, jury-rudder, and the jocular jury-leg, i.e., a wooden leg. (The nautical term is itself of obscure origin. It may come from the Old French *ajurie* and the Latin *adjūtāre*, to aid, to give help, whence also *adjutant*, the staff officer who assists a commander.) Arguing in favor of the marine origin are the facts that *jury* in its makeshift sense predates the *jerry* of *jerry-built* by more than two centuries (*jury mast* is dated to 1616 in the *OED*); that *jerry-built* (and *jerry-builder*) are recorded as appearing first in Liverpool, an important port; and that the makeshift *jury* has been converted to *jerry* in other instances, e.g., from a novel set in Vietnam, "At one point the trail became so steep the point squad had to cut vines and jerryrig ropes for the boonierats to pull themselves up" (John M. Del Vecchio, *The 13th Valley*, 1982).

8. Finally, there is the theory that *jerry*—perhaps, again, from the proper name Jeremiah or Jeremy—became attached to *built* in keeping with its general use as a pejorative prefix in such combinations as *jerry-go-nimble*, diarrhea; *jerry-mumble*, to shake or tumble about; *jerry-shop*, a cheap beer joint; and *jerry-sneak*, originally a henpecked husband and later any mean, sneaking fellow. Certainly, jerry-built houses, and those who put them up, have never been in good repute—and with good reason, e.g., from the London *Daily Telegraph* of March 23, 1883: "Houses of the jerry-built sort especially, when the builders have a difficulty in raising money to finish 'em, are singularly liable to catch fire."

There is nothing much new under the sun, as insurance underwriters, among others, will tell you.

Jerusalem artichoke. The plant, a species of sunflower with an edible root that tastes something like an artichoke, is a native of the Americas, not the Holy Land. The plant was introduced to Europe in 1617 and cultivated in Italy, where the sunflower is called the *girasole*, sun turner, from *girare*, to turn, plus *sole*, sun. The name is descriptive, of course, since sunflowers are sun followers, constantly turning during the day in order to keep their faces toward the light. The English, with their well-known facility for foreign languages, almost immediately managed to mangle the Italian *girasole* into a more familiar-sounding word, e.g., "Artichocks of *Jerusalem*, is a roote vsually eaten with butter, vinegar, and pepper" (1620, *OED*). See also ARTICHOKE.

Jew's harp. This small, metal mouth instrument looks a bit like a lyre or harp; it is played by striking a prong with one's finger while holding the lyre part between the teeth. From the very beginning, the instrument has been associated with Jews, but it is not at all clear why. The earliest known mention of the instrument in English is in a customs regulation of 1545, where a rate is set for the importation of "Iues trounks."

The "trounk" in this case was a mistranslation for *trompe*, trumpet, which is what the French used to call the same instrument; the modern French word for it is *guimbarde*. It has been speculated that the full French name might have been *jeu trompe*, play trumpet. *The Oxford English Dictionary*, however, pooh-poohs the idea that the *Jew* here is a corruption of either *jeu* or *jaw*, describing these conjectures as "baseless and inept."

Well, perhaps. The instrument has been called a *jaw harp*, as well as a *juice harp*. Admittedly, both seem to be later developments—euphemisms devised to avoid articulating "Jew." At the same time, the rendering of *jeu* as *Jew* would not be at all surprising, considering what the English did to the Italian *girasole*; see the preceding JERUSALEM ARTICHOKE, as well as, for similar mistranslations, BOOTS AND SADDLES, BRIAR PIPE, CRAYFISH/CRAWFISH, and FURBELOW.

Other origins for the instrument's name have been suggested, i.e., that Jewish merchants were the first to import these items into England; that the reference is to the harp of David; and that the *Jew* was intended as a term of derision, alluding to the inferiority of cheapness of the mouth harps. Of these, the last seems to have the most "merit" in view of the ancient and widespread use of ethnic terms as pejorative modifiers. This is true not just of *Jew* (*Jew bail*, insufficient bail; *Jew flag*, a dollar bill; and *Jew canoe*, a Cadillac), but of all nationalities and ethnic groups, from *American cards*, as *French postcards* have been called in France, to *Zulu* as a derogatory term for an American of African descent. Everyone does this, even Jews, who do not mean it as a compliment when observing that someone is acting *goyish*, like a gentile, or has *goy* brains.

In the end, it seems quite possible that *Jew's harp* is the product of more than one factor. Perhaps it was the human tropism toward insult that motivated the conversion of *jeu* to *Jew*.

jingo. Etymologies suggested with tongue in cheek may lead the unwary astray. For example, Richard H. Barham thought he was making a joke when he asserted in *The Ingoldsby Legends* (pre-1845) that *jingo* came from St. Gengulphus, "sometimes styled 'the living jingo' from the great tenaciousness of vitality exhibited by his severed members." But at least one etymologist swallowed this fanciful explanation whole and passed it along to other readers as fact, according to Ernest Weekley's *Words and Names* (1932). A kind man as well as a great scholar, Weekley did not mention his gullible rival's name. (This is the same Weekley whose wife Frieda, née von Richthofen, abandoned the professor and their three children in 1912, running away with one of his former students, a certain D. H. Lawrence. Kindness, it seems, is not always the quality most appreciated by women.)

Jingo has been dated to 1670 (*OED*). Efforts have been made to link it to the Basque *Jinko*, God, the theory being that sailors learned the word from Basques, who often were employed as harpooners on English whaling vessels. Maybe the Basques exclaimed "By *Jinko!*" as they thrust their harpoons home, but if so, no one appears to have bothered to mention it in a ship's log, journal, letter, or whatever. As far as the written record goes, the word seems to have been used originally by conjurers, who said, "Hey [or "high"] jingo," when causing objects to appear. This was the opposite of "Hey presto," for making things vanish. In this and later uses (e.g., the 1694 Motteux translation of Rabelais's works, where *Par Dieux* is rendered as "By jingo"), the word seems to be essentially euphemistic, a form of "By Jesus" analogous to *gosh, golly,* and *egad,* all of which are minced oaths for "God." See also DICKENS and OLD NICK.

The modern political sense of *jingo,* meaning a bellicose superpatriot, derives from a music-hall song, written by G. W. Hunt in 1878, when it looked for a while as though Great Britain might go to war to defend Turkey against Russia. (Disraeli sent the fleet to the Mediterranean, and the Russians backed down.) The song's refrain:

We don't want to fight yet by Jingo! if we do,
We've got the ships, we've got the men, and got the money too.

We've fought the Bear before, and while we're Britons true,
The Russians shall not have Constantinople.

john. The name of the john that flushes sometimes is attributed to the Reverend Edward Johns, who exhibited his "Dolphin" toilet at the Centennial Exposition of 1876 in Philadelphia. As an inventor, the Reverend Johns was aptly named, but the common term for the sanitary convenience, as well as the room in which it is located, derives from the masculine personal name, not the surname, and it was in common use well before 1876. For example, a Harvard regulation of 1735 directed: "No freshman shall mingo against the College wall or go into the fellows' cuzjohn." (*Mingo* comes from the Latin *mingere*, to urinate; it is the first-person singular, as in *mingo, mingas, mingat*.) Meanwhile, the *john* in the *cuzjohn* or, in full, *cousin john* probably derives from *jakes* or *jacques* (that is, *jack* or *john*), meaning a privy or a chamber pot, as in the punning title *The Metamorphosis of Ajax*, in which Sir John (sic) Harington set forth plans for a flushing, valve-controlled toilet. This was in 1696. Sir John, by the way, was godson to Queen Elizabeth, who is said to have installed one of Harington's devices in her palace at Richmond. See also CRAP.

jolly boat. "There is *nothing*—absolutely nothing—half so much worth doing as simply messing about in boats," declares Mr. Rat in Kenneth Grahame's *The Wind in the Willows* (1908). To Mr. R., boats are jolly. Even so, there is nothing particularly fun about a *jolly boat*, which is a small boat kept at the stern of a larger vessel. The term is a fairly recent addition to English, having been dated only to the first half of the eighteenth century. It apparently is a corruption of the *jolywat*, dated to the late fifteenth century, with the *joly-* part equivalent to the Danish *jolle*, the Dutch *jol*, and the modern *yawl*. The other, jovial *jolly*, meanwhile, derives from the Old French *joli, jolif*, with a range of merry meanings: gay, festive, lively, festive, amorous, brave, finely dressed, handsome. The connections are obscure, but the Old French term probably comes from the Old Norse *jōl*, the name of a midwinter festival now known to us a *Yule*. See also LAUNCH.

journeyman. Not necessarily an itinerant worker, who journeys from job to job, but one who is hired by the day, from the Old French *journée*, a day's work. The *journeyman* was originally (from the early fifteenth century) a craftsman or mechanic who had finished his apprenticeship but had not yet qualified as a master of his trade or business. The term has been used pejoratively, referring, since the mid-sixteenth century, to uninspired, hack work by people who have not mastered their professions. Of course, the *journeyman* occasionally may take a trip, or a *journey*, also from the Old French *journée*, in the sense of day's travel.

jug, in the. A prison—or correctional facility, as such institutions generally are called nowadays—contains many people and lets out only a few at a time, so the analogy to a kitchen jug, a large-bodied vessel with a small opening, seems apt enough. The image is wrong semantically, however, the result of confusing two similar-sounding words.

The jug that is a prison comes from *jougs*, a kind of pillory once used in Scotland. It consisted of an iron collar that was put around the culprit's neck, then attached with a short chain to a tree, post, or wall (often the wall of a church, as the punishment was used for ecclesiastical as well as civil offenses). The collar was constructed in two pieces, which is why the now-obsolete term usually is found in court and other records in the plural form. The Scottish word came from the French *joug*, a yoke, and by extension, slavery or bondage. The Latin root is *jugum*, a yoke.

The transition from *joug* and *jougs* to *jug* seems to have begun during the eighteenth century. Captain Francis Grose defined "stone jug" as "Newgate, or any other prison" in *A Classical Dictionary of the Vulgar Tongue* (3rd edition, 1796). Within a generation, *jug* also appeared in the United States in the penal sense: "A full grown villain, who with an accomplice, were shortly after safely lodged in the jug" (*Niles Weekly Register*, 1815–16 supplement).

The jug for holding liquids, meanwhile, apparently comes from the *Jug* that is the pet form of the feminine names *Joan* and *Judith*. The argument is by analogy, since other vessels for liquids have borne other personal names, e.g., DEMIJOHN, *jack* (usually made of waxed leather), *jeroboam* (a large wine bottle—and also a chamber pot—from *Jeroboam I*, a King of Israel), and *jill* (a variant of *Gill*, short for *Gillian*, and with a pun on *gill*, the liquid measure). *Jug* is recorded as having been used from the sixteenth century onward for both a vessel for liquids and a woman—often, in the latter instance, in a disparaging way as a general term for a female servant, a homely woman, or a mistress. (*Juggins*, a simpleton, and *jug-head* also share this origin.) Meanwhile, the modern slang use of *jugs* for breasts (a.k.a. *ninny-jugs* or, in British English, *cream-jugs*) nicely combines the presumptively original feminine sense with that of large-bodied containers for liquids.

K

keep your pecker up. The British phrase always sounds odd to American ears. It is *not* an exhortation to remain in priapic splendor, but merely an expression of encouragement, tantamount to "be of good cheer" or "keep your chin up." In British English, *pecker* translates as "courage" or "resolution." The underlying image seems to be of *pecker*, in the sense of a hearty eater, i.e., one who keeps pecking away, thereby demonstrating a good appetite. The earliest known example of the phrase occurs in the colorful *Adventures of Mr. Verdant Green:* "Keep you pecker up old man . . . and don't be down in the mouth" (E. Bradley, a.k.a. Cuthbert Bede, 1853). The American *pecker*, meanwhile, alludes to the well-known virility of the barnyard pecker, or rooster, formerly known as the cock. And for more more about the many ways of avoiding mention of the pecker's original name, see APRICOT.

kick the bucket. The "obvious" explanation—that the reference is to standing on a pail and kicking it away in order to hang oneself from a rafter—may not be correct. *Bucket* also is an antique word, perhaps from the Old French *buquet*, balance, for a beam or yoke from which anything may be carried or hung. Thus, the reference might also be to the beam from which slaughtered pigs are suspended by their heels, so that the blood will drain out after their throats have been cut. Shakespeare refers in *Henry IV, Part II* (1596) to "he that gibbets on the brewer's bucket," but it is not clear from the context what kind of bucket he had in mind.

The earliest known example of *kick the bucket* in print is from Captain Francis Grose's *A Classical Dictionary of the Vulgar Tongue* (1785), where the phrase is defined simply as "to die." The use of the expression at this date to refer to death in general rather than suicide in particular argues in favor of the bucket-as-beam theory, as does the existence of such similar phrases as *kick up [one's] heels* and *kick [one's] clogs,* also meaning simply "to die."

kitty-corner. Any self-respecting cat will walk a beeline, so to speak, cutting diagonally across a yard or field rather than go around its edges, but the expression does not have a feline origin. The *kitty* here comes from *cater,* which is how fifteenth-century English gamblers pronounced the French *quatre*, four. Thus, when playing cards or dice, a four was *cater* or *cater-point*. (We still use much French terminology at the card table, where the two and the three are the *deuce* and the *trey*, and in the casino, where a *quarter bet* in "little wheel"—*roulette* in French—is not a twenty-five-cent bet but one that is made by placing a chip at the intersection of four, i.e., *quatre*, spaces on the multicolor roulette layout.)

The easiest way of connecting the four pips in the corners of a die or playing card is with two straight lines, drawn on the diagonals, which probably is what led to the use of *cater* as a verb (1577, *OED*) for moving or arranging in slanting, corner-to-corner fashion. The verb blossomed in such combinations as *catercross, caterways, caterwise,* and *cater-corner,* the last of which eventually evolved into *catty-corner* and, finally, *kitty-corner.*

The trail continues: *Cater* also is responsible for *catawampus* (the *wampus* may be akin to the Scottish *wampish*, to wriggle, twist, or swerve about), used widely in the southern and western parts of the United States to characterize diagonal or oblique relationships, as well as that which is askew, awry, or wrong, e.g., "It looked like all the white brains were catawampus that day, all except Mrs. Effingham's" (1947, *Dictionary of American Regional English*). And *catawampus*, in turn, has had a huge number of offspring, including *caddywampus, caliwampus, cankywampus, catawampit,* and, inevitably, *kittywampus.*

See also CAT'S-CRADLE.

knuckle under. On the face of it, this expression for submitting and acknowledging defeat doesn't seem to make much sense. The standard explanation of the phrase is that *knuckle* once had a broader meaning than it does today. Back in the fourteenth century, the term applied to any joint in the body. A knuckle could be an elbow, knee, or even vertebral joint. The term did not begin to be limited to the finger joints until the fifteenth century. Hence, according to this theory, *to knuckle under* or, a variant, *to knuckle down,* at first meant to kneel in humble submission.

The trouble with this explanation is that it doesn't square well with the dates for the changes in *knuckle*'s meaning. The latest example in the *OED* of *knuckle* in the broader sense—an "Elbows-Knockle," as it happens—comes from a medical text of 1658. Meanwhile, *knuckle down* and *knuckle under* don't show up in the written record until 1740 and 1882, respectively.

The *OED*'s citations are no more than rough benchmarks for when words change in meaning, but the generational gap suggests that the expression may have another source, perhaps *truckle under* or *knock under*, either singly or in combination. Both were used earlier (from the 1660s) in the same sense as *knuckle under*. The first derived from the low, truckle bed that rolls beneath a higher one, while the second was a shortening of *knock under board* (or *the table*), originally referring to the submissive posture assumed by the losers of drinking bouts.

L

landlubber. Landlubbers feel queasy when they go to sea, but not because, as the term seems to suggest, *lubbers* are *lovers* of land. Among sailors, a *lubber* originally (from 1579, *OED*) was a clumsy seaman. Earlier, the term was used as an epithet for an idle lout or big, clumsy fellow. It is recorded first in *Piers Plowman* (ca. 1362–87), where it refers to lazy monks—*abbey-lubbers* in the vernacular of the day. *Lubber* probably comes from the Old French *lobeor*, a deceiver, parasite, as influenced by *lob*, a bumpkin or clumsy person. The *lubber*, then, was one who behaved like a *lob*, the latter being an onomatopoeic word for anything heavy, lumpish, or pendulous, including the arched *lob* still seen on tennis courts.

lanthorn. Back in the sixteenth and seventeenth centuries, those who ventured abroad at night generally lit their way with *lanthorns*. This is because they had confused the ending of *lantern* with the translucent *horn* that had been used for making lanterns since Roman times. Thus, from Robert Burton's *The Anatomy of Melancholy* (1621): "To thy judgement [she] looks like a mard in a lanthorn, whom thou couldst not fancy for a world, but hatest, loathest and wouldst have spit in her face." (Burton was a good man with invective, the *mard* in the *lanthorn* being a piece of excrement, equivalent to the French *merde*.) As late as the middle of the eighteenth century, Samuel Johnson noted that "*Lantern*... is by mistake often written lanthorn." The correct *-ern* spelling reflects the word's Latin root, *laterna*, in turn from the Greek *lamptēr*, torch, and *lampein*, to shine (hence also the modern *lamp* for reading).

lanyard. The word comes from the French *lanière*, a strap or thong, but was corrupted into its present form by sailors who thought in terms of *yards*, meaning the spars at right angles to a vessel's mast from which its sails are suspended. The word was adopted into English, first as *layner* and then as *lanyer*. Chaucer used the original spelling in *The Knight's Tale* (ca. 1387–1400) when referring to fastening straps of shields "with layneres lacinge," meaning "laced with thongs." The middle *y* and *n* were reversed early on, however (1483, *OED*), and by 1626 Captain John Smith used the word in essentially its present form, describing short pieces of rope as "lanyeards" (*An Accidence or the Pathway to Experience Necessary to All Young Sea-Men*, 1626). See also BOONDOGGLE.

lapwing. The name of this Old World member of the plover family comes from its wavering pattern of flight, not from the way its wings lap over one another. *Lapwing* arose as a result of people's changing a strange word into a more familiar one. The bird's name comes from the eleventh-century Anglo-Saxon *hlēapwince*, leaper-winker, where the *wince* is akin to the Old High German *winkan*, to totter, to waver. The Anglo-Saxon term was converted to *lapwyng* by 1430 (*OED*) and to the present *lapwing* by 1592. The folk etymology was well enough established by 1617 for John Minsheu to explain in his *Guide into the Tongues* that the "lappe-wing" was so called because "he lappes or clappes the wings so often." See also FLICKER.

lark. A person who goes on a *lark,* or *larks about,* is full of high spirits, resembling the lark that sings as it soars into the sky, but the words for the spree and the bird are not really related. Nor is there any truth to the pleasant story that the term for a frolic comes from medieval times when young people supposedly went into the fields to catch larks, then considered to be dainty morsels, but often caught each other instead.

The name of the bird has been dated to ca. 725, appearing in various forms. (Chaucer used both *laverokke* and *lark* for the same creature.) The other kind of *lark* appears to be an early-nineteenth-century development. It is recorded first as a slang term in the *Lexicon Balatronicum* (1811), by "a member of the Whip Club," where it is defined as "A piece of merriment. People playing together jocosely." This kind of *lark* probably represents an English attempt to pronounce the Scottish *lake*, meaning play, sport, fun, and, in the plural, games and tricks generally. Given the bluntness, if not lewdness, of the inhabitants of north Britain, as noted in the entry on the F-word, the Scottish term may also be the ancestor of *larking*, defined in the first edition (1785) of Captain Francis Grose's *A Classical Dictionary of the Vulgar Tongue* as "a lascivious practice that will not bear explanation." In the second and third editions of his dictionary, Grose not only declined to define *larking* but omitted the entry altogether. Later lexicographers have brushed up against the term, but delicately, explaining the "lascivious practice" variously as "irrumation" and "cunnilingism."

Meanwhile, *skylark* in the sense of indulging in frolic or boisterous sport was popularized by sailors, who may well have had the bird in mind, since *skylarking* (from 1809, *OED*) often featured displays of agility in the rigging high above a ship's deck. The bird also seems to have been the model for the *skylarker*, who was a bricklayer working for a gang of burglars. His modus operandi was to rise early in the morning (like the lark) after a stormy night, and gain admission to houses by offering to repair chimneys and tiled roofs for a small fee. The skylarker's ruse was described as early as 1789 by George Parker in a chapter on "Low Life in the Neighbourhood of St. Giles's" in *Life's Painter:*

> Now, it is most probable, this man belongs to a desperate gang of house-breakers, if so, he surveys the house, how, or in what manner it can be robbed, and reports it to the gang accordingly, and they insert it in a list, with many more of the like purpose, and nothing so likely as the house being robbed the same night: at any rate, the sky-larker is a thief, and will rob the house, somehow or other, by slipping into the chambers, &c.

Which is a lark for the skylarker, perhaps, but not for the householder, who was poorer for the experience.

launch. Ships are launched, but the name of the motorboat or other *launch* has nothing to do with how the vessel first was introduced into the water. It comes, rather, from the Portuguese word for a small sailing vessel, *lancha*, in turn from the Malay *lancharan*, with the same meaning. The Malay root is *lanchār*, quick.

The *launch* at which one may break a bottle of champagne over a ship's bow is related to *lance*, deriving from the Middle English *launchen*, to hurl or pierce, in turn from the Old North French *lancher*, and the Old French *lancier*. See also JOLLY BOAT.

lay an egg. The provenance of the metaphoric egg that is laid when something flops is not entirely certain, but one thing is sure: It does not come from a chicken. Most often used today when theatrical productions fail, the expression is dated in *The Oxford English Dictionary* only to the famous *Variety* headline about a flop of another sort: "Wall Street Lays an Egg" (10/30/29). Best guess is that the expression comes from *goose egg* as employed on the sports pages to mean "zero," e.g., from an 1886 report of a baseball game in the *New York Times:* "The

New York players presented the Boston men with nine unpalatable goose eggs in their contest at the Polo Grounds yesterday." (Cricket players used *duck's egg* in the same nihilistic sense, but they usually abbreviated the phrase to *duck,* not *egg.*)

Another possibility is that the expression comes from the punch line of a nineteenth-century minstrel-show joke that was retold so often that it imprinted itself indelibly on the collective psyche of the theatergoing public. As recalled by Mark Twain in his unfinished autobiography, Mr. Bones, one of the end men (Banjo was the other), related how he had been caught in a storm at sea, which lasted so long that the ship ran out of provisions. Asked by the middleman, who was the spokesman for the show, how in this case the people had managed to survive, Bones replied that they had lived on eggs. This led to the following deathless exchange:

MIDDLEMAN: You lived on eggs! Where did you get the eggs?
MR. BONES: Every day, when the storm was so bad, the Captain laid *to.*

This joke convulsed audiences for the first five years of its life, according to Twain, but was afterward received "in a deep and reproachful and indignant silence, along with others of its caliber which had achieved disfavor by long service."

See also BAD EGG, LOVE, and PATSY.

lemon sole. The fish typically is served with a slice of lemon, but it is a kind of flounder, not a true sole, and its name has nothing to do with the fruit. It comes from the French *limande,* flatfish, which London fishmongers misheard as *lemon.* The French name probably derives from *lime,* file, rasp, referring to the fish's skin, which is so rough that it could be used as sandpaper. Another possibility is that the French term comes from the Latin *limus,* mud, flatfish being bottom dwellers. Whatever the truth here, the theory that the name comes from the fruit is, as they saying goes, a lemon.

limerick. The name of the five-line light verse form is the same as that of the chief town of the county of Limerick in Ireland, but the art form was not invented there. Though poems in limerick meter appeared earlier in English and French, credit for popularizing the verse form goes to Edward Lear, whose *Book of Nonsense* (1846) included such tame specimens as:

> A flea and a fly in a flue
> Were imprisoned, so what could they do?
> Said the flea, "Let us fly!"
> Said the fly, "Let us flee!"
> So they flew through a flaw in the flue.

Not surprisingly, verses of this sort generally were known as "nonsense rhymes" or "nursery rhymes." So closely was Lear associated with them that a Father Matthew Russell, S.J., described them as "learics" in 1898. This coinage never caught on, however, perhaps because this breed of verse had already developed during the 1870s into its modern, bawdy form—leerish, not learish.

The earliest known example of *limerick* as applied to the verse comes from a letter written by Aubrey Beardsley on May 1, 1896: "I have tried to amuse myself by writing limericks on my troubles." The name may have been inspired by "Will you come up to Limerick?" the refrain of a ballad that was often sung on convivial occasions when Victorian gentlemen got together for cigars, drinking, and the extemporary production of poetry that could not be recited when ladies were present.

Readers who wish to know more about limericks are referred to G. Legman's massive collection, *The Limerick* (1949), containing some seventeen hundred examples. We have it on Legman's authority that Arnold Bennett (1867–1931), distinguished English novelist, playwright, and journalist, believed the following to be "the best limerick of all":

> There was a young plumber of Leigh
> Who was plumbing a girl by the sea.
> She said, "Stop your plumbing,
> There's somebody coming!"
> Said the plumber, still plumbing, "It's me."

Despite the best efforts of untold numbers of mostly anonymous versifiers, it does not seem that the art of the limerick has progressed substantially beyond this in the last sixty-odd years.

limey. The nickname for a Britisher often is connected falsely with the Limehouse district in London's East End, ancient home of the Cockney and later the city's Chinatown. Thus, a reviewer of this author's *Wicked Words* complained in the *Los Angeles Times*, "One wonders how he could write of *limey* without reference to the Limehouse district of London" (2/18/90).

Well, it really wasn't so hard. The epithet is of fairly recent vintage, most likely an Americanism, though recorded first in Australia as *lime juicer* (1859). It almost certainly was applied originally to British sailors, who were dosed with lime juice from 1795 onward as protection against scurvy. (Earlier, they had been given lemon juice mixed with seawater, but Admiralty penny-pinchers apparently found limes to be less expensive.)

Now it is true that London's docks once were in the Limehouse area, and that the Navy stored many items there, perhaps even a few bushels of limes. The name of the district is much older, however. It already had a reputation as a tough part of town in 1613, when Shakespeare wrote in *Henry VIII:* "These are the youths that thunder at the play-house and fight for bitten apples; that no audience but the tribulation [troublemakers] of Tower Hill, or the limbs of Limehouse, their dear brothers, are able to endure."

The place name, then, refers not to the fruit, which probably hadn't been imported to England in Shakespeare's time, but to the part of London where kilns, or oasts, were once located for burning limestone to make lime for cement. John Ciardi suggested the following progression: *Lime oast* to *Lime oas'* to *lime 'ouse* to *Limehouse* (*A Browser's Dictionary*, 1980).

links. A golf course is not called a *links* because, as is sometimes said, the holes are linked together by fairways or because, back in Scotland, courses were laid out on sandy seaside terrain, as at St. Andrews, thus serving as a link between land and sea. The flexible, connecting *link* comes from the Anglo-Saxon *hlence,* a coat of chain mail, akin to the German *lenk,* joint. The golf *links* is a topographical term, from the similar-sounding Anglo-Saxon *hlincas,* plural of *hlinc,* rising ground, ridge. The two words are remotely related, however, both deriving from the Indo-European root *kleng-,* to bend, to turn, which has spawned a number of words that imply sloping and bending, including *flinch,* to turn aside; *lean,* thin (and flexible); and *flank,* the hip or side (where the body curves).

loo. The standard British euphemism for the toilet (also a euphemism, being a conversion of the French *toilette,* dressing room) is of comparatively recent vintage but unknown provenance. This has not prevented—on the contrary, it has encouraged—a wealth of speculation about its origin. Among the more frequently encountered theories, arranged in more or less descending order of probability:

1. *Loo* is a mangled translation of the French *lieu,* place, as in *lieux d'aisance,* places of comfort, i.e., comfort stations. This theory accords with the tendency of English speakers to lapse into French when touching on delicate topics. Thus, we resort to *brassiere, chemise, latrine, liaison, lingerie, paramour,* and the aforementioned *toilet.* On the other hand, the evidence for *lieux* as the source of *loo* is only circumstantial, and it is odd that the conversion into English was not made much earlier than seems to have been the case.

2. *Loo* is a clipping of *Waterloo,* a word that is never far removed from the patriotic Briton's consciousness, possibly with an allusion to yet another euphemism—*W.C.* or *water closet.* The association certainly was in the mind of James Joyce, whose *Ulysses* (1922) provides the earliest reference to *loo* in *The Oxford English Dictionary:* "O yes *mon loup.* How much cost. Waterloo. Watercloset." But Joyce was always making connections of this sort, and the fact he made this one is not a proof of the *Waterloo* origin.

3. *Loo* derives from the French *l'eau,* water, perhaps as used in *gardyloo,* an old Scottish warning (from 1662) to people on ground level that a chamber pot or slop pail was about to be emptied out of an upper window. The warning itself probably came from some such phrase as *gardez l'eau,* watch out for the water. The trouble here is that *gardyloo* seems to have faded from use in the early nineteenth century, a casualty of improved municipal sanitation, leaving a considerable gap between its use and the appearance of the term for the toilet.

4. *Loo* is an abbreviation of *leeward,* commonly pronounced *loo-ard,* referring to the side of a ship (away from the wind), to which one resorts when—yet another euphemism—nature calls. Sailing vessels traditionally had two places to go, so to speak, one on either side of the bowsprit. The sailor wanting to relieve himself always went to the *loo-ard* side, since no one who pees into a stiff wind is likely to make the same mistake again. The principal difficulty here is that mariners usually speak of visiting a ship's *head,* not its *loo.*

5. *Loo* is—and here we're starting to make much longer etymological reaches—an abbreviation of *ablutions,* the euphemistic washing up performed in a lavatory (still another euphemism, deriving from the Latin *lavare,* to wash).

6. *Loo* stems from the supposed practice of Continental hotels of assigning the number *00* to rooms containing the, er, facilities. British tourists, so it is said, prefaced the number with the article *l',* thus making *l'00* and then *loo.*

7. And, finally, *loo* is a shortening of the eighteenth-century French *bourdalou,* a portable, concealable (small enough to fit in a lady's muff) chamber pot. *Bourdalou* itself is said to be an eponym, honoring Father Louis Bourdaloue (1632–1704), a French Jesuit whose sermons were exceedingly popular but also very long, requiring that people with small bladders come to church with such hidden utensils—or conveniences, as they also were called.

The various "explanations" for *loo* often are passed along with confident but sadly misplaced assurance. Permanent linguistic fame awaits the person who can discover the word's true origin. This is an etymological holy grail, albeit wrought not of gold or silver but of more humble porcelain. See also CRAP.

love. The use of *love* in tennis and other games to mean no score has been a minor puzzlement for at least a couple hundred years, e.g., from *Gentleman's Magazine* in 1780: "We are not told how, or by what means Six love comes to mean Six to nothing." Searching for an answer, people have looked to other languages. One suggestion is that *love* in this sense derives from the Icelandic *lyf,* something small or worthless. Another, more common "explanation" is that the term comes from the French *l'oeuf,* egg, the reference supposedly being to the *l'oeuf* of an *oie,* goose, since *goose egg* in American English is slang for zero or nothing. (See LAY AN EGG.) Unfortunately, evidence for the first theory is lacking, while the second runs against the factual grain, since the French themselves have never used *l'oeuf* in this way.

More likely, the *love* that amounts to nothing is a spin-off of a seventeenth-century expression, *to play for love,* to play without stakes; that is, for nothing. This phrase, in turn, probably evolved from *for love or money,* by any means, at any price, which dates to before A.D. 1000. A related expression is *labor of love,* meaning work that is performed

133

for the love of the work itself, or for the love of those who benefit from it, but in neither case for payment. Popularized by its use in the King James Version of the Bible (e.g., "Remembering without ceasing your work of faith, and labour of love," *I Thessalonians*, 1:3), *labor of love* is the direct counterpart of *play for love*, and in both instances the *love* amounts to nothing, or zero, just as it does in tennis scoring today.

M

mad as a hatter. The phrase is linked popularly with Lewis Carroll's Hatter, cohost with the March Hare of the mad tea party in *Alice's Adventures in Wonderland* (1865). The technical, medical explanation is that hatters used mercury in making felt. The mercury fumes affected their nervous systems. After a while, they developed uncontrollable twitches and trembles. To casual observers, many hatters must have seemed to be demented.

Mad as a hatter predates *Alice's Adventures,* however. Thackeray used the phrase in *Pendennis* (1849); still earlier, and on the other side of the Atlantic, Thomas Chandler Haliburton, a judge in Nova Scotia, employed it in *The Clockmaker; Or, The Sayings and Doings of Samuel Slick, of Slickville* (1837): "Sister Sal . . . walked out of the room, as mad as a hatter." The expression probably was influenced by such similar, apparently older phrases as *mad as March hare, mad as a buck, mad as a weaver, mad as Maybutter,* and *mad as a wet hen.* It also has been suggested that *hatter* here comes from *atter,* an obsolete term for poison or venom, as from—a closely related word—an *adder.*

Carroll may have modeled his Hatter to some extent on a real person, Theophilus Carter, according to Martin Gardner's *The Annotated Alice.* As it happens, Mr. Carter was a furniture dealer, not a hatter. Gardner reports that he was known around Oxford as the Mad Hatter, however, "partly because he always wore a top hat, and partly because of his eccentric ideas." The latter included an "alarm clock bed," which was exhibited at the Crystal Palace in 1851. It woke sleepers by tipping them onto the floor.

See also GRIN LIKE A CHESHIRE CAT and DORMOUSE.

main chance. The *main* that is the best or most advantageous opportunity is only tangentially related to the *main* that refers to that which is largest, most important, principal, or leading.

Main chance was popularized by sixteenth-century gamblers when playing hazard, the dice game from which craps evolved. Play began by selecting a *main,* which was any number from five through nine. Then the dice were rolled. If the shooter failed either to win by "nicking" his main or to lose by crapping out, the number thrown became the *chance*, or point, on which wagers were made. If the player rolled the *chance* again before the *main*, he won; if not, he lost.

Main chance is dated in *The Oxford English Dictionary* to 1579, but it obviously is older, as the first example, from John Lyly's *Euphues, the Anatomy of Wit*, is of the phrase's use in an extended sense: "Good Father, either content your selfe with my choice [of a husband], or lette me stande to the maine chance." (By the way: The modern *hazard*, meaning a risk or danger, comes from the gambling game, whose name has been traced back through the Old French *hasard* and the Spanish *azar*, an unlucky card or throw of the dice, to the Arabic *al-zahr*, the die that is rolled.) See also CRAPS.

malinger. The person who shirks work by pretending to be ill or injured may *linger* around the barracks (typically, this is a military maneuver), but the resemblance between the two words is only coincidental. *Linger* derives from the Anglo-Saxon *lengan*, prolong, lengthen. *Malinger* is a much newer word, coming from the French *malingre*, sickly, possibly via the Old French *malingrex*, a beggar with artificial sores. (Reflecting the onetime preeminence of the French Army, our military lexicon includes many words of French origin—*materiel, personnel, sortie, triage,* and *maneuver*, to name just a few.) *Malinger* has been dated to 1820. As *malingeror*, it was recorded even earlier by Captain Francis Grose, who defined the noun in *A Classical Dictionary of the Vulgar Tongue* (1785) as "A military term for one who, under pretence of sickness, evades his duty."

Mandarin. The Chinese national language is called *Mandarin*, based on the dialect spoken in and around Beijing, originally and principally by the mandarins, the educated, official class of Imperial China, but the word itself is not Chinese. Dated to 1589 in English in the form of *mandelines*, the term is the end product of a series of borrowings from the Spanish *mandarin*, the Portuguese *mandarim*, the Dutch *mandorijn*, the Malay and Hindi *mantrī*, and, ultimately, the Sanskrit *mantrin*, adviser, and *mánas*, mind—all of which makes Mandarin Chinese, mandarin duck, and mandarin oranges cousins to the sacred Sanskrit formula or prayer known as a *mantra*.

manner born, to the. Probably because of confusion with the *manor* that is a lord's estate, the phrase has taken on highfalutin' airs, with the implication that the person *to the manner born* is accustomed from birth to occupying a leading position in society. Literally, and originally, the phrase did not have this connotation. The essential meaning of *manner* is more lowly, referring simply to the way something is done or handled. It comes from the Latin *manus*, hand. The phrase was popularized by Shakespeare in *Hamlet* (1600–1). For him, *manner* connoted established practices. Thus, when Horatio asks if it is a custom of the country to mark the King's toasts during his nights of carousing by sounding trumpets and discharging cannon as he drains his cup, Hamlet replies:

> Aye, marry, is't.
> But to my mind, though I am native here
> And to the manner born, it is a custom
> More honored in the breach than the
>   observance.

marmalade. One of the most famous of spurious etymologies has it that when Mary, Queen of Scots, was feeling sick, she would refuse to eat anything but this tasty concoction made by boiling the pulp and rind of oranges, quince, and other fruits. The Queen's maid, so it is said, would call for the delicacy, explaining in courtly French that Her Majesty was *malade*, ill. As a result, *Marie malade* became the name of the preserve itself, with the two words eventually being combined to form *marmalade*.

If you believe this story (recently retailed to the unwary in Peter Shaffer's play *Lettice and Lovage*), you will believe almost anything. In truth, *marmalade* comes from the French *marmelade* and the Portuguese *marmelada*, quince jam, and ultimately from the Greek *melimēlon*, honey apple, i.e., the fruit of an apple tree grafted upon a quince. The English taste for marmalade by that name has been dated to 1524 (*OED*)— eighteen years before the birth of Mary, Queen of Scots.

Mars Bar. It is easy to assume, as a reviewer of John Noble Wilford's *Mars Beckons* did in a notice in *The New York Times Book Review* (7/15/89), that the candy was named after the planet. Alas, as pointed out by Gary Haynes, of Philadelphia, Pa., in a letter to the *Times* the following August 12, the family that makes the candy named it after themselves. See also BABY RUTH.

Mass. The origin of the name of the religious service has been much debated, but most likely can be attributed to misunderstanding by parishioners who didn't know Latin. The service concludes (at least it did in olden times, when the Roman Catholic Church still used Latin) with the incantation *Ite, missa est,* Go, it is the dismissal. The Latin root is *mittere*, to send away. The vulgar soon began to assume that the *missa* in the priest's parting words was the name of the service itself, and the phrase came to be translated, "Go, the mass is done."

The earliest written examples of *missa* in the eucharistic sense come from the Epistles of St. Ambrose, Bishop of Milan from 374 to 397. *Missa*, in turn, produced the English *mass*, the French and German *messe*, the Spanish *misa*, and similar words in other languages. It also is responsible for the related *missal*, the book containing the prayers for celebrating Mass, and the last syllable of the names of such festivals as *Candlemas, Michaelmas*, and, of course, *Christmas*. See also MESS, PATTER, REQUIEM SHARK, and XMAS.

massacre. A *mass* of people are slain in a *massacre*, but the two words are not related. The killing term comes directly from the Middle French *massacre*, with the same meaning. It appeared first in English in 1581 as a verb and was apparently popularized (so to speak) by references to the wholesale slaughter of Huguenots in France in 1572, beginning August 24—the St. Bartholomew's Day Massacre—and continuing through October of that year. The word is related to the Old French *macecre*, a shambles, a slaughterhouse, but its prior antecedents are not clear; it might go back to the Latin *macellum*, a butcher shop. Meanwhile, the *mass* that is a large agglomeration of something, or a group of people, as the so-called *masses*, is an unrelated word. It derives from the Latin *massa*, mass, and the Greek *mâza*, barley cake, cognate to *mássein*, to knead.

mayonnaise. Because many dishes are named after people, such as peach Melba for the opera singer Dame Nellie Melba, and because the French originally called the salad dressing *sauce mahonnaise*, it seems logical to assume that the condiment name honors Marie Edmé Patrice de MacMahon, Marshal of France and President (1873–79) of the Third Republic. *Sauce mahonnaise* has been dated to 1807, however, the year before Marie Edmé Patrice's birth. More likely, the name of the dressing commemorates the capture of Mahon, principal port of Minorca in the Balearics by an earlier Marshal of France, the Duc de Richelieu. Mahon fell in 1756, and the sauce may well have been invented by the victor's chef. The oldest example of the word in English in the *OED* is from an essay of 1841 by Thackeray, in which he refers to a "mayonnaise of crayfish."

The suggestion that *mayonnaise* really should be called *bayonnaise* because it was first made in Bayonne can be dismissed out of hand, since, as Ernest Weekley has pointed out, "Initial *b-* does not readily become initial *m-*, though one could imagine a nation with an endemic head cold bringing about the opposite transformation" (*Words and Names*, 1932).

mess. The preferred military term for a meal, or a group of people who eat together, does not come from the Latin *mensa*, table, as some have speculated, or from the messy appearance of food when it is served to troops in the field, or even from the biblical "mess of potage," referring to the lentil soup for which the hungry Esau traded his birthright to his brother Jacob. (Esau also got a piece of bread, but there is no denying that Jacob drove a very hard bargain. The story is told in *Genesis*, 25:29–34. The phrase "mess of potage" is not in the King James Version of 1611, but appears in earlier translations of the Bible and in other works dating back to the fifteenth century.)

Mess, in the sense of a serving of food, comes from the Old French *mes*, the past participle of *mettre*, in turn from the Latin *mittere*, to send away, in its extended sense of "to put." Thus, the underlying image is the putting or placement of a portion of food on the table. (*Mittere* also gives us the religious Mass, so it and *mess* are cognates.)

As for the messy, untidy sense of *mess*, this is a fairly recent, nineteenth-century addition to the word's array of meanings. The line of development seems to have been from a mixture of foods, to a jumble, to a state of confusion, to a cluttered, dirty, or untidy condition. Food words often evolve in this way. Other terms for mixtures of foods that have acquired pejorative meanings include, just to name a few, *balderdash* (originally a mixture of liquids, as milk and beer), *farrago* (mixed fodder for cattle), *gallimaufry* (a stew of leftovers), *hodgepodge* (once a stew of vegetables and meat), and, of course, that compound of meats known as *baloney*.

mind your P's and Q's. People have been admonishing other people, usually younger ones, to pay attention to their *P's and Q's* since at least the eighteenth century, with the earliest example of the expression in the *OED* coming from 1779: "You must mind your P's and Q's with him, I can tell you" (Hannah Cowley, *Who's the Dupe*). No one knows exactly how the letters *P* and *Q* came to stand for correct behavior in general and for saying the proper thing in particular. Inevitably, the mystery has served as a lightning rod for etymological theorizing. The most popular explanations come from the barroom, the ballroom, and the classroom.

Probably the most common theory is that the letters stand for "Pints" and "Quarts." Pub keepers, according to this explanation, once kept a running tab of how much customers owed by chalking up their consumption in pints and quarts on a blackboard behind the bar. Naturally, the tipplers looked sharply (or as sharply as one can look through bleary eyes) to be sure that the publican did not charge them for a quart when delivering a pint. Thus, this theory goes, the phrase came to stand for an honest measure—and it is true that it was used in that sense from an early date. Meanwhile, another barroom explanation is that the letters originally stood for "Prime Quality."

All things are possible, but the main thing these suppositions have going for them is that both are consistent with an early version of the phrase in a seventeenth-century pamphlet: "Boy y'are a villaine, didst thou fill this Sacke? Tis flat you Rascall, thou hast plaid the Jacke, Bring in a quart of Maligo, right true: And looke, you Rogue, that it be Pee and Kew" (Samuel Rowlands, *The Knave of Harts,* 1612).

From the world of fashion, we get—and from an even earlier date— the idea that the *P* stands for *pee,* meaning a coat of coarse cloth, as in the modern *pea jacket.* This seems to be what Thomas Dekker meant by "Now thou art in thy pee and cue" (*Satiro-mastix, or The Untrussing of the Humorous Poet,* 1602). But the *cue* here poses a problem. Does it mean the tail of a wig (usually called a *queue*)? Did some Elizabethan housewife start the linguistic ball rolling by telling her husband *to mind his P's and Q's,* meaning that he should take care not to get powder all over the collar of his newly cleaned coat of pea? Or did Dekker mean *cue* in the sense of the right or proper course to follow, an established sense of the term that flows from its use in the theater to denote the word or other signal for an actor to make an entrance or begin speaking? The answer is not readily apparent. See also PEA JACKET.

Yet another "fashionable" explanation is that the phrase alludes to the deep curtseys and huge wigs in vogue at the time of Louis XIV. Supposedly, French dancing masters advised newcomers to court: "Mind your *pieds* [feet] and your *queues* [wigs]." Which would make a very pretty explanation, except that Rowlands and Dekker seem to have been making plays upon *P and Q* before the Sun King (1638–1715) saw the light of day.

Finally, from the classroom, it has been suggested that the expression might allude to the reminder to students of classical languages to beware of the shifts that sometimes occur between the Latin *qu*, as in *quintus*, fifth, and the Greek *p*, as in *penta* (e.g., *pentagram*, a five-sided star-shaped figure, and *the Pentagon*, a five-sided office building in Arlington, Va.).

Another schoolroom theory is that the phrase originally referred to the shapes of the letters, which are mirror images when written in lower case, differing only in that the descenders are on opposite sides of the *p* and the *q*. Certainly, it does not take much imagination to visualize generations of teachers telling generations of students "to mind their p's and q's" when learning to read and write.

Supporting evidence for the last of these views does not go back very far. The phrase has been dated in an educational context only to 1820 in William Combe's *Second Tour of Dr. Syntax in Search of Consolation:* "And I full five-and-twenty year Have always been school-master here; And almost all you know and see, Have learn'd their *Ps* and *Qs* from me." The *pq* theory would be the most appealing except for the common confusion of *bd*, and no one ever says, "Mind your B's and D's."

mosaic. Moses came down from the mountain bearing the Ten Commandments on two tablets, but he has nothing to do with the designs or pictures, known as *mosaics*, that are made by setting small pieces of stone, glass, tile, etc. in mortar. *Mosaic* comes via the Old French *mosaïque* and the Old Italian *mosaico* from the Medieval Latin *musaicum*, as in *musaicum opus*, work of the Muses, so called on account of the use of this form of decoration in grottoes dedicated to them.

moxie. This nifty American slang term for courage, energy, and shrewdness comes from the soft drink Moxie, marketed since 1884, mainly in New England, but not, as sometimes claimed, because it takes a lot of nerve to drink the bittersweet beverage. True, Moxie is an acquired taste. Even Frank Anicetti, Jr., organizer of the annual Moxie festival in Lisbon Falls, Maine, admits this: "On the first taste, you may want to spit it out. Don't! On the second taste, you may want to do the same. Don't! Wait for the third taste, to allow the true flavor of Moxie to tickle the taste buds" (*Maine Sunday Telegram*, 7/21/91).

The slang use of the term derives from the way the cola was marketed rather than its taste. The drink was created as a patent medicine by Dr. Augustine Thompson, who founded the Moxie Nerve Food Company in 1876. His ads claimed many virtues for Moxie, among them that it "feeds the nerves," "makes you eat better, sleep better, feel better," and "will build up your nerve." Ultimately, the word may be of Native American origin, "based on a New England Indian term found in several Maine place names" (Robert Chapman, *New Dictionary of American Slang*, 1986). In any event, the advertising campaign—"What this country needs is plenty of Moxie"—was so successful that the brand name became a generic term.

mugwump. A *mugwump* often is said to be a man—or sometimes a bird—that sits on a fence with his mug on one side and his wump on the other. The term was popularized in the presidential campaign of 1884, when independent Republicans who declined to support the GOP's nominee, James G. Blaine, or—worse yet—actually crossed party lines to support the Democratic candidate, Grover Cleveland, were characterized by right-thinking Republicans as *mugwumps.* The label was not intended as a compliment, but the mavericks accepted it anyway. (A not uncommon development: *muckraker, Tory, Whig,* and YAN- KEE are other once-derisory terms whose sting was lost when they were adopted by the people who were supposed to have been insulted.)

Mugwump has nothing intrinsically to do with mugs, wumps, or the art of fence-sitting, however. It is a Native American term for a great chief or other leader. It appeared in print as far back as 1663, when John Eliot rendered "duke" as "mugquomp" in his translation of the Bible into Algonquian.

N

name is mud, [one's]. The expression often is described as an eponym, deriving from the name of Dr. Samuel A. Mudd, whose name became mud because of his involvement in the assassination of Abraham Lincoln on April 14, 1865. When John Wilkes Booth showed up at Mudd's farm in Maryland at four-thirty on the morning after he shot Lincoln in Ford's Theater in Washington, the doctor set the ankle that the actor-assassin had broken when leaping down to the stage from the presidential box. The extent of Mudd's prior knowledge of Booth's plans has been debated, but he was convicted as a conspirator in the plot to kill the President.

The doctor did not help himself by denying that he recognized Booth, with whom he was proven to have been acquainted. He also was well known as a Confederate sympathizer. Four of the conspirators were hanged (but not Booth, who either was killed or killed himself while being arrested), and four, including Mudd, were sentenced to hard labor for life. Mudd was pardoned in 1869, however, for having helped stop an outbreak of yellow fever at Fort Jefferson in Florida, where he was imprisoned. More than a century later, Dr. Mudd's descendants were still petitioning to have his conviction erased, thereby removing the mud from the family name.

Dr. Mudd's notoriety may have helped popularize *name is mud* as a way of characterizing a person who is distinctly out of favor, in trouble, or not to be trusted, but the phrase was in use more than forty years before Lincoln's assassination. Thus, the 1823 slang dictionary by "Jon Bee" (the euphemistic pen name of John Badcock) contains the following entry: "*Mud*—a stupid twaddling fellow. 'And his name is mud!' ejaculated upon the conclusion of a silly oration, or of a *leader* [the main article] in the Courier."

As an epithet for a person—a fool or blockhead—*mud* has been dated to 1708 (*OED*), and it is probably a good bit older, the term having been used since at least the sixteenth century to characterize the lowest or worst of anything, the dregs, so to speak, as in "An ordinary person (borne of the mud of the people)" (Sir Philip Sidney, *Arcadia*, ca. 1580).

nap. Napoleon is said to have been very good at taking a *nap* whenever there was a lull in the day's activities, but the word is not, as was once suggested, an abbreviation of his name. Rather, it is a good old Anglo-Saxon word, dating from the ninth century in the form of *hneappian*. Amateur etymologists do not always give up very easily, however. When the Anglo-Saxon root was brought to the attention of a gentleman who was convinced of the term's Napoleonic origin, the true believer huffed and puffed, maintaining that the Emperor's *nap* and the Anglo-Saxon *nap* were actually two quite different words. The first, he insisted, according to Ernest Weekley's *Words and Names*, derived from Napoleon's ability to go to sleep at will, while the other referred to involuntary sleep. "We have therefore," he concluded, "an instance, rare if not unique in etymology, of two words spelt and pronounced in the same way, derived from two completely different sources, but with meanings so similar that they may be confused even by an expert." A deadly riposte, indeed.

neat's foot oil. There is nothing intrinsically neat about *neat's foot oil*, which is made by grinding up the feet and shinbones of cattle. As evidenced by the apostrophe, the oil comes from *neat*, an archaic, Anglo-Saxon term (as *nēat*) for oxen and other bovines. A popular etymology for the Anglo-Saxon word, in turn, is that it derives from *nitan*, i.e., *ne witan*, no wit, meaning that the animals know nothing or have no understanding in the human sense. The word actually alludes to the value of these animals, however, not their ignorance. It is related to the Anglo-Saxon *nēotan*, to enjoy, to possess, to employ, meaning that *neat* are useful property to own.

news. One of the more persistent word myths is that the *news* that comes to us from near and far is an acronym for the names of the four cardinal points of the compass: North, East, West, South. In truth, it is merely the plural of *new*. The oldest example of the term in the *OED* is from John Wyclif's translation of the Bible (ca. 1380), where the Latin *novorum*, the genitive of *novus*, new, is rendered into English as "of newes." The English construction may have been modeled upon French, in which the word for news, *nouvelles* (or *noveles* in Old French), is simply the plural of that language's word for "new."

nickname. Although many nicknames are short forms of personal names, such as Hank for Henry or Tom for Thomas, the pet name is not truly clipped, or *nicked*, from the full name. And while everyone knows what familiarity breeds, nicknames are not basically contemptuous, as might be the case if the term derived from *nick* in the sense of to cheat, to defraud. This applies, too, to the derivations that have been proposed from the French *nique*, as in *faire la nique a quelqu'un*, to make fun of someone, and *nom de nique*, said by Captain Francis Grose to derive from the *nique* that is "a movement of the head to mark a contempt for any person or thing" (*A Classical Dictionary of the Vulgar Tongue*, 1796).

Actually, a nickname is just an additional name, originally (from the fourteenth century) *an eke-name*, or "also-name." People began splitting the *an* incorrectly, producing *a neke name* (ca. 1440) before arriving at the present form of the word (1580, *OED*). For other incorrect divisions of this sort, see EAT HUMBLE PIE and NINCOMPOOP.

nightmare. This term for a very bad dream inevitably conjures up the image of a wild mare, trampling or running away in the night with the dreamer. The trampling part, at least, is not far off the mark. *Mare* here is a very old (pre-700) word for a demon, corresponding to the *mar*, evil spirit, in *cauchemar*, the French word for nightmare—and *caucher* does mean "to trample." Specifically, this kind of *mare* is, or was, an incubus—that is, a goblin that descended upon women while they slept (so they said) and had sexual intercourse with them. The original sexual sense of *nightmare* (from ca. 1290, *OED*) gradually was watered down, progressing from a sense of suffocation while asleep (presumably as a result of the goblin's weight), to a dream that produced a feeling of suffocation, to the modern sense (from ca. 1830) of any frightening (i.e., oppressive) dream or, for that matter, similarly distressing experience while awake.

Male sleepers also claimed to be taken unawares by evil spirits in nights of yore. A female goblin that descends upon men as they sleep is known technically as a *succubus*, a word whose etymology is not quite what might first come to mind. The term derives from the Late Latin *succubāre*, to lie under. This is the obverse, of course, of *incubus*, from the Late Latin *incubāre*, to lie down upon, as in the related *incubate*. Thus, etymology serves to demonstrate the antiquity of the missionary position as well as its widespread popularity, even among goblins.

nincompoop. The origin of this colorful term for a fool or blockhead is a vexing question, thanks largely to a bad guess by Dr. Samuel Johnson.

The Grand Cham of Literature (as Smollett called him) had only a few chinks in his armor, and etymology was one of them. Dr. Johnson (the LL.D. was honorary, not earned academically) maintained in his great *Dictionary of the English Language* (1755) that *nincompoop* came from the Latin *non compos [mentis]*, of unsound mind. This assertion does not accord well, however, with earlier forms of the word, such as *nicompoop* (pre-1676, *OED*) and *nickumpoop* (from 1685).

More likely, the term is based on a personal name, either *Innocent*, via the incorrectly divided *Ninny* (i.e., an *inno [cent]*; see NICKNAME) or *Nicodemus* (in French, *nicodème* = fool). In either case, the *poop* part, meaning "to cheat," is essentially an intensifier, deriving from the Dutch *poep*, a fool.

Whatever the precise origin, it is hard to improve upon Captain France Grose's definition of the term: "NICKUMPOOP, or NINCUMPOOP. A foolish fellow; also one who never saw his wife's ****" (asterisks in the original, *A Classical Dictionary of the Vulgar Tongue*, 1796). See also PICKANINNY.

nitwit. This Americanism for a stupid person sometimes is said to be a scornful approximation of *niet wit* in the Dutch *Ik niet wit*, I don't know, presumably uttered whenever the non–English-speaking colonists of New Amsterdam were asked a question by their British conquerors. The theory seems implausible, however, considering that the British captured New Amsterdam and renamed it New York back in 1664, while *nitwit* has been dated in writing only to 1922 (*OED*). A better guess is that the term is based on the English *wit*, understanding, intelligence, plus either the Yiddish or German slang *nit*, in turn from *nichts*, nothing. Alternatively, the *nit* might also refer to the egg of a louse or other insect. Depending on which choice is made, the literal meaning is that the *nitwit* either has no brain at all or just an exceedingly tiny one.

Nosey Parker. Most often cited as the inspiration for this epithet for a snoop or busybody is Matthew Parker (1504–75), successively chaplain to Anne Boleyn and Henry VIII, then Archbishop of Canterbury under Elizabeth I. He is said to have stuck his long archiepiscopal nose into everybody's affairs as he sought to defend the high Anglican middle ground against Roman Catholics to the right and Puritan dissenters to the left.

Others say that the original Nosey Parker was a sailor, a cashiered midshipman named Richard Parker who stuck out his neck as well as his proboscis by leading a mutiny in 1797 of the British fleet stationed at the Nore (a sandbank at the mouth of the Thames). The Nore mutineers were following the lead of the Channel fleet at Spithead, which had refused earlier that year to put to sea, even though the nation was at war with France. Leaders of the Spithead mutiny adopted a respectful tone in their communications with the Admiralty and prudently kept their identities secret, however, while Richard Parker made truculent demands and signed his name to them. Largely because of their differences in style, the episodes had very different endings. The Admiralty negotiated an amicable settlement to the Spithead mutiny, which led to many reforms in the service, while Richard Parker was hanged from the yardarm of H.M.S. *Sandwich.*

Unfortunately, neither of the suggested eponymns, as picturesque as the stories are, is likely to be the source of the phrase, for *Nosey Parker* has been dated only to 1907—more than three hundred years since the first Parker preached and over a hundred since the second Parker swung. The silence over the centuries, like the dog that didn't bark in the night, argues in favor of another origin.

Best guess is that *Parker* is an abbreviation for *park keeper* or anyone else who frequents a park. In this case, the original reference probably was to London's Hyde Park (hence the capital *P*), where the *Nosey Parker* loitered in order to spy upon courting couples. In this connection, it seems significant that the inquisitive sense of *nosey* dates from roughly the same period (1882).

It is possible, too, that *Parker* is a corruption of the dialectical *pauker*, in turn from *pauk*, to be inquisitive—in which case *Nosey Parker* would class as a redundancy or, as linguists call it, a reduplication.

O

oakum. Appearance to the contrary, oakum, long used by mariners for caulking the seams of wooden vessels, does not come from oak trees. Rather, it is made of hemp, obtained by unraveling and picking apart old ropes, and often mixed with tar or another binding agent. The word derives from the Anglo-Saxon *ācumba*, off-combings, meaning flax fibers separated by a *camb* or, as the implement is called today, a *comb*.

obscene. A scene may be deemed obscene, but not, as some have argued, because it can't be shown in a theater. The term is not a compound of the Latin *ob*, against + *scena*, stage (or *ob* + *scaena* in Greek). It comes from the Roman augur's trade, not the dramatist's, deriving from *obscēnus*, repulsive, inauspicious, or offensive, especially to modesty. The augur's word, in turn, probably is based on *caenum*, filth, or a variant of it.

Obscene is not recorded in English until the late sixteenth century. (The absence of the word from people's vocabulary suggests that society was less concerned with this subject than we are today; in fact, Great Britain and the United States were both so benighted as to lack laws against obscenity until the nineteenth century.) In its initial appearance, and for some time thereafter, the term referred to that which was generally foul, disgusting, filthy, and repulsive. This is what Shakespeare meant in *Richard II* (1595–96) when he has the Bishop of Carlisle characterize Bolingbroke's seizure of the throne from the anointed king as "heinous, black, obscene."

The more particular, now dominant senses of indecency and lewdness are virtually as old as the general meaning, however, with the first example of the word's employment in this manner in the *OED* coming from John Marston's *The Metamorphosis of Pygmalion's Image* (1598): "Be not obscene though wanton in thy rimes." The question of how to draw Marston's fine distinction continues, of course, to vex legislators and Supreme Court Justices, who have long sought to ban obscenity but have not been able to devise a satisfactory definition of what it is.

ogre. The name for this hideous monster with an appetite for human flesh has been interpreted as an ethnic slur upon the Ugrians, a nomadic people of Asia. The point is that the Ugrians scared ninth-century Europeans out of their wits when one of their divisions, the Magyars, moved west and settled in what is now Hungary (i.e., the land of the Ugrians, the modern name descending from Ugri, via Ungari, Hungri, and Hungari). This theory makes a pleasing parallel with Philistine, Tartar, Vandal, and other ethnic names that have acquired pejorative meanings, but there is no paper trail to indicate its validity.

The earliest use of *ogre* in literature comes in the first collection of Mother Goose stories, *Tales of Olden Times* (1697), by Charles Perrault, who seems to have invented the word. He may have been inspired by an Old French term for a demon, deriving from the Latin *Orcus*, the Roman equivalent of Hades, god of the underworld. See also GLASS SLIPPER.

O.K. Without a doubt the greatest Americanism of them all, this expression of approval, correctness, and acceptability is understood by speakers of other languages around the world. *O.K.*'s source was shrouded in mystery for more than a hundred years, however. It was Professor Allen Walker Read, of Columbia University, who finally unveiled its origins in a series of magisterial articles in *American Speech* in 1963 and 1964. Even so, many people continue to believe—and one frequently sees in print—explanations of the term that preceded Read's great work of detection. All in all, the multiple strands in the story of *O.K.* make up a veritable tapestry of American history. Herewith, a sampling of the more colorful theories of the expression's origin:

1. *O.K.* dates to the election of 1840 and stands for "Old Kinderhook," sobriquet of President Martin Van Buren, who hailed from Kinderhook, N.Y. This theory was advanced initially by Professor Read himself in 1941, but had to be abandoned after the discovery of pre-1840 examples of the abbreviation's use in nonpolitical contexts.

2. The abbreviation was first used by Andrew Jackson when he was a young man in Tennessee. Supposedly, the future president wrote it on legal documents, meaning "Ole Kurrek," "Oll Korrect," or—depending on who is telling the story—"Orl Kerrect." This explanation was much favored by Jackson's political opponents, who liked to remind the public of Old Hickory's educational disabilities.

(Jackson was perfectly capable of spelling the same word four ways on the same page.)

3. *O.K.* comes from a Choctaw term, either *hoke* or *okeh*, pronounced with the accent on the second syllable, and meaning "It is so." Jackson figures in this theory, too, the supposition being that he learned the Choctaw term on his travels up and down the Mississippi prior to the War of 1812. Woodrow Wilson, a scholar as well as a president, favored this explanation, signifying his approval of memos and other papers with an "Okeh." Asked why he didn't use *O.K.*, he answered, "Because it is wrong."

4. It comes from Old Keokuk, the name of a Fox chief, who is said to have initialed treaties in the opening decades of the nineteenth century with his "O.K." The actual documents are missing, however.

5. The abbreviation is for *Oberst Kommandant*, German for "Colonel in Command," used by either—take your pick—a General Schliessen or Baron von Steuben when initialing letters and orders during the American Revolution.

6. *O.K.* is an English rendering of *aux quais*, at the quays, referring to the place in port typically selected by French sailors during the American Revolution when arranging assignations with colonial dames.

7. The term derives from Aux Cayes (or Les Cayes), a port on the southern coast of Haiti, where American sailors in the nineteenth century obtained such good rum that the place name evolved into a general term of approval.

8. It comes from the name of a railroad freight agent, Obadiah Kelly, whose initials were widely disseminated on bills of lading.

9. The abbreviation is for Open Key, popularized by telegraphers in the 1860s.

10. It stands for Orrin Kendall, supplier of exceptionally tasty crackers—in boxes with the firm's initials upon them—to Federal troops during the Civil War.

11. It is a contraction of a Scottish expression, *och aye*, i.e., *okay*.

12. The expression derives from the word for "good" in Ewe, a West African language spoken by slaves in the American South.

13. It comes from the names of Lords Onslow and Kilbracken, who initialed bills after they were read and approved in England's House of Lords ... or from a misreading of "Order Recorded" on official documents ... or from the Finnish *oikea*, correct ... or from the Greek *olla*, all, plus *kalla*, good ... or from some other word or phrase in Cockney, Danish, Greek, Norwegian, or Wolof (another West African language).

And though this list may seem exhausting, it is by no means exhaustive. More could be added.

What Professor Read discovered was that the abbreviation arose in a humorous manner at a time when Americans were indulging in a great deal of wordplay, including abbreviations, acronyms, puns, and intentional mispronunciations and misspellings. The earliest example of *O.K.* that he unearthed (and it is so far still the oldest known specimen) is from the Boston *Morning Post* of March 23, 1839. It appears in connection with a note by the paper's editor, Charles Gordon Greene, about a visit to New York of some members of the local Anti-Bell-Ringing Society. (The A.B.R.S., as it was usually known, was itself something of a joke, having been formed the previous year to oppose—its name to the contrary—an ordinance of the Boston Common Council against ringing dinner bells.) In an aside, Mr. Greene suggested that if the Bostonians were to return home via Providence, they might be greeted by one of his rivals, the editor of that city's *Journal*, who "would have the 'contribution box,' et ceteras, *o.k.*—all correct—and cause the corks to fly, like *sparks*, upward." The next month (April 12), the expression appeared in the Salem *Gazette* without explanation but clearly in the modern sense: "The house was O.K. at the last concert, and did credit to the musical taste of the ladies and gents."

Thus, it appears that *O.K.* was invented, possibly by Greene, as an abbreviation of the jocular "Oll" or perhaps "Orl korrect," meaning "All right." This explanation would seem farfetched, except for Read's finding that it dovetails with such coinages of the period as *O.W.* for "All Right," as though spelled "Oll Wright" (this appeared in the Boston *Morning Post* in 1838, the year before *O.K.*'s debut); *K.G.* for "No Good"; and *K.Y.* for "No Yuse." Conveying the flavor of the time and place is the following note from the *Morning Post* of June 12, 1838:

> *Melancholy.*—We understand that J. Eliot Brown, Esq., Secretary of the Boston Young Men's Society for Meliorating the Condition of the Indians, F.A.H. (fell at Hoboken, N.J.) on Saturday last at 4 o'clock, p.m. in a duel W.O.O.O.F.C. (with one of our first citizens). What measures will be taken by the Society R.T.B.S. (remains to be seen).

Other abbreviations commonly encountered in newspapers of the era include *G.T.D.H.D.* (Give The Devil His Due), *I.S.B.D.* (It Shall Be Done), *K.K.K.* (Commit No Nuisance), *N.S.M.J.* ('Nough Said 'Mong

Gentlemen, or Jintlemen), *O.F.M.* (Our First Men), and *O.K.K.B.W.P.* (One Kind Kiss Before We Part). A great many others could be cited, as the rage for them spread from Boston to New York and thence to the nation at large.

Besides *O.K.*, living remnants of this fad include *N.G.* (No Good) and *P.D.Q.* (Pretty Damn Quick). Read has dated the latter to *The Mighty Dollar*, a play by Benjamin Woolf. This warhorse is said to have been performed some 2,500 times prior to 1891, when its long tour was terminated by the death of its star, William Jermyn Florence. Its humor depended largely on such lines as:

"That's right, you'd better step, P.D.Q., pretty damn quick."
"That's what I call the D.S., the dirty shake. No, sir, it's a D.D.S, a damn dirty shake."
"I will prepare him an H.O.T., a high old time, by a large majority."
"He is a P.A., a perfect ass, and I will tell him so."
"Murder! G.I.C. Our goose is cooked!"
"I will be your E.F., your everlasting friend. . . . We shall be A.H., all hunky."
"You are K.K., quite correct, by a large majority."

As for *O.K.*, though not standing originally for "Old Kinderhook," the abbreviation certainly was popularized—as Read explained in his initial, 1941, foray into this field—by the coincidence of the initials with those of Van Buren's nickname. During the election campaign of 1840, Van Buren's supporters in New York organized a Democratic O.K. Club. The expression became their rallying cry. Thus, the New York *Herald* reported on March 28, 1840: "About 500 stout, strapping men marched three by three, noiselessly and orderly. The word O.K. was passed from mouth to mouth, a cheer was given, and they rushed into the hall upstairs like a torrent."

Whig supporters of William Henry Harrison and John Tyler ("Tippecanoe and Tyler Too") retaliated with the assertion that *O.K.* actually meant "Out of Kash, Out of Credit, Out of Karacter, and Out of Klothes." The Harrison-Tyler ticket won, with Democrats regarding the election outcome as an "Orful Kalamity" or "Orrible Katastrophe," while the victorious Whigs said it just showed that *O.K.* really stood for an Arabic phrase which, when read backward, meant "Kicked Out."

Thus, *O.K.* entered the American lexicon, proving in time to be a fecund term as well as an enduring one, its progeny including *oke, okie-dokie, okie-dory* (with an assist from *hunky-dory*), *okle-dokle*, and, the newest strand in the tapestry, the astronautical *A-O.K.*

Old Nick. One of many nicknames for Satan, whose real name is often avoided ("Speak of the Devil, and He may appear"), *Old Nick* has been identified with such diverse characters as Niccolò Machiavelli, Santa Claus, and a heretic mentioned in the Bible. In the first case, however, Samuel Butler probably was writing with tongue in cheek in *Hudibras:* "Nick Machiavel had ne'er a trick/(Though he gives name to our Old Nick)." As for Santa, the original St. Nicholas did have a dark side, as patron saint not only of scholars in general, and poor ones in particular, but of highwaymen, once known as *St. Nicholas's clerks*. Meanwhile, students of the Bible have leaned toward the heretical Nicholas on the strength of the denunciation in Revelation, 2:6: "thou hatest the deeds of the Nicolaitanes, which I also hate."

All these are just guesses, however, with no real evidence to back them up. The devilish *Nick* probably is short for *Nicholas,* but not for any particular one. This would be in keeping with such similar evasions as *The Old Boy, The Old Gentleman, Old Harry, Auld Hornie* (in Scotland), and *Meister Peter* (in Germany). The selection of the name might also have been influenced by the German *nichol,* goblin, as Ernest Weekley suggests in *An Etymological Dictionary of Modern English.* See also DICK-ENS, JINGO, and PUMPERNICKEL.

orange. The color of the fruit may have affected the spelling of the word, which comes from the Sanskrit *nāranga* via the Persian *nārang* and the Arabic *nāranj.* The *n* has been retained in the modern Spanish *naranja,* but in Old French, from which the English term derives, the initial *n* was dropped, probably through assimilation with the preceding article, *une.* Then the following *a* was converted to *o,* as in *orenge,* thanks to the influence of Old French *or,* gold. The original Sanskrit term may be related to the Tamil *naru,* fragrant. The fruit itself was known to Europeans for some centuries before the word became associated with the reddish-yellow color we now know as *orange* (from the late sixteenth century in English).

oust. The similarity of *oust* and *out* in spelling and meaning is close enough that it is easy to assume that the two are related. (Of course, readers who have penetrated this far into this book will not make this mistake.) For the record, *oust* began as a legal term, appearing in English in the thirteenth century in the sense of to dispossess or to eject. It derives from the Old French *oster*, in turn from the Latin *obstāre*, to block, to hinder (*ob-*, against + *stāre*, to stand). *Out*, meanwhile, dates to before 1200, deriving from the Anglo-Saxon *ūt* (from before 725).

P

passionflower. Some species of the tropical flower bear edible berries, but the fruit is not, as some would-be seducers have fondly hoped, an aphrodisiac. Rather, the name refers to the Passion of Christ. This is because medieval monks and others with a strong religious bent saw a resemblance between the characteristics of the showy flower and the nails, whips, crown of thorns, spear, and other instruments and circumstances surrounding the crucifixion. The flower's English name is a straight translation (from ca. 1613) of its New Latin name, *flor passionis*, flower of the Passion.

patsy. As a dupe, an easy mark, a fall guy, the American *patsy* (from 1903, *OED*) looks as though it could come from the Italian *pazzo*, fool, but there is no proof of this. Another suggestion is that the term derives from a given name, either the Irish *Patrick* or the Italian *Pasqualino*, the diminutive of *Pasqual*. The latter theory is credible, considering the pejorative uses to which personal names often are put. *Biddy* from *Bridget, billy* as in *hillbilly,* the anonymous *john* who patronizes a prostitute, *rube* from *Reuben*, and *tom* as in *tomcat* are only a few of the many that could be cited.

Elaborating on the idea that *patsy* is of Italian extraction, Robert L. Chapman noted in *The New Dictionary of American Slang* (1986) that the diminutive "is used to designate a vulnerable, weak, and small boy or man, and is probably based in this sense at least partly on the relation between *Pasqua* 'Easter,' and the derivative names *Pasquale* and *Pasqualino*, and the notion of the Paschal sacrifice or Paschal lamb as an innocent victim." Which is a poetic notion.

A more likely, more down-to-earth explanation of the word's origin has since been uncovered, however, in the form of a nineteenth-century minstrel-show character, Patsy Bolivar, who looks very much like the progenitor of *patsy*. In a communication to *American Speech* (Summer 1990), Louis Phillips included the following entry on the minstrel character, from Henry Frederic Randall's *Fact, Fancy, and Fable* (1889):

> *Patsy Bolivar.* A party of minstrels in Boston, about twenty years ago, had a performance in which they presented the scene of a

country school. There was a little fellow named Patsy Bolivar, who sat in the corner, who was inoffensive, quiet, and generally well-behaved. The older boys took occasion to annoy the master in many ways; and when the pedagogue asked, in a rage, "Who did that?" the boys would answer "Patsy Bolivar!" Then Patsy was chastised. As soon as that was over, some of the older boys would throw a wad of paper at the master's head, when, raging with anger he would repeat the query, "Who was that?" Again the answer came, "Patsy Bolivar." The phrase, as many phrases have done, spread beyond the limits of the minstrel performance; and when a scapegoat was alluded to, it was in the name of "Patsy Bolivar," an inoffensive person who is always in trouble, brought about by mischievous associates,—the one who is always blamed for everything.

Poor Bolivar, then, seems to have been very much a *patsy* in the present sense of the word. For another possible contribution of minstrel shows to language, see LAY AN EGG.

patter. The magician's hand may be quicker than the eye, and his patter quicker than the ear, but *patter* does not come from the pitter-patter of fast-falling raindrops or from the quick patter of little feet. Rather, it is a shortening, from ca. 1400, of *Pater Noster*, Our Father, the opening words in Latin of the Lord's Prayer. The allusion is to the rapid, mechanical way in which prayers sometimes are recited. See also CANT, HOCUS-POCUS, and MASS.

pea jacket. The name of the thick, woolen sailor's coat has nothing to do with turning pea green from seasickness, nor does it derive, as suggested by the distinguished mariner-turned-author Captain Francis Marryat (creator of *Mr. Midshipman Easy*), from *P.-jacket*, as an abbreviation of *pilot-jacket*. The clothing term is of American origin, dating from 1721 as *pee-jacket*. It probably comes from the Dutch *pijjekker*, where *pij* is the kind of cloth and *jekker* is the jacket. Alternatively, the *pea* part might represent a survival of the English use of *pee* or *py*, referring to coarse woolen fabric, as in the *pee-gown* and *py-doublet*, worn by men, especially in the sixteenth century. See also MIND YOUR P'S AND Q'S.

pencil. The name of the writing instrument is not related to *pen*. The latter comes from the Latin *penna*, feather, referring originally to a quill pen. *Pencil* also has an anatomical origin, but a human one. It comes from the Latin *pēnicillus*, a small tail, a brush, from *pēnis*, the Roman word for "tail" as well as for that other thing.

pennyroyal. The plants (the name is given to different species of similar appearance in the Old and New Worlds) do not look like pennies, royal or otherwise. The name reflects the difficulty that the English often have with foreign languages, the term coming (ca. 1520–30) from the Old French *pouliol* via *puliol real*. Ultimately, the name describes the plant's use by our forefathers and foremothers. It derives from the Latin *pūlegium*, flea-bane, based on *pūlex*, flea.

penthouse. The rooftop residence has a rather lowly origin and nothing to do, etymologically speaking, with a house for *Penthouse* pets—or for anyone else, for that matter. The term comes from the Latin *appendere*, to hang, to append (also the root of *appendix*, the anatomical one as well as that found at the back of a book). The Latin word was taken into Middle English as *pentice*, via the Old French *apentis*, attached building, referring to a lean-to, shed, porch, or covered way, placed against the wall of a larger building and having a sloping roof.

The word has been dated to 1232 as a surname, *de la Pentic*, and to the fourteenth century as *pendize*, *pentiz*, and *pentys*. Thus, the anonymous author of a sermon from ca. 1325 about Christ's birth described the shelter found by Joseph and Mary as "a pendize that was wawles" (a shed without walls). Apparently because of the structure's sloping roof, the first syllable of the word for it was confused with the French *pente*, slope. The second syllable then was converted by folk etymology into the more familiar "house." The word has been dated in its present form to 1579–80. The *penthouse* that is a separate apartment on top of the roof of a tall building is a much more recent development (1921, *OED*).

pester. The current meaning of the word—to annoy, to bother, to harass—is due to false association with *pest*. The two actually are quite different words. *Pester* (1536, *OED*) originally meant to clog, obstruct, hamper, or encumber, as by overloading or overcrowding. Thus, referring to a problem that still exists, an Elizabethan law (1572) noted that "the common gaoles . . . are like to bee greatly pestered with a more number of prisoners than hithertofore hath beene." *Pester* apparently arose as a shortening of the Middle French *empstrer*, to hobble (as an animal), and ultimately from the Latin *pastoria*, the rope used to keep an animal from straying.

Pest, meanwhile, comes from the Latin *pestis* and the Middle French *peste*, a disease, plague, or pestilence. In the sixteenth century, to be visited by the *pest* was no minor matter, as the reference usually was to the bubonic plague, and the imprecation "Pest upon you" amounted to "May you catch the plague." The diminished but now dominant sense of *pest* as a noxious, destructive, or troublesome person or thing does not show up among the *OED's* citations until 1609, but it is apparent that the word was used this way at least a generation earlier, since the same dictionary shows that *pester* had already begun to acquire its modern array of irksome meanings by 1586.

Pester is related to *pastor* (shepherd, in Latin), *pasture*, and, a technical term of some fame in the dictionary business, *pastern*. The last is the part of a horse's foot between the hoof and the fetlock. It is so called because this is where a tether, or—another, older meaning of the word—a *pastern*, was attached to keep the animal from roaming in the pasture. Thus, Dr. Samuel Johnson goofed when he defined *pastern* as "The knee of an horse" in his *Dictionary of the English Language* (1755). The mistake is remembered, however, mainly for Johnson's reply when a lady who knew more about horses than he did asked about the definition during his visit to Plymouth in 1762. Supposing Johnson to be almost infallible, she had, as Boswell relates, "expected to hear an explanation (of what, to be sure, seemed strange to the common reader,) drawn from some deep-learned source with which she was unacquainted." Instead, Dr. Johnson—unusually for a man with so great a reputation—freely confessed that the error was due simply to "ignorance, pure ignorance."

He didn't bother to correct the mistake, however, until his dictionary went into its fourth edition in 1773.

peter out. The least likely of the various explanations that have been offered for this phrase is that it comes from St. Peter, the idea being that the apostle *petered out* on the night of Christ's betrayal, first drawing his sword to defend Jesus but then denying three times that he knew Him.

The phrase is an Americanism, dated to 1846 and apparently popularized by miners who spoke of veins of ore as *petering out* when they became exhausted and dwindled away. In this context, it is much more probable that the *peter* comes either from *saltpeter*, used in explosives in mining operations, or from the French *péter*, to explode weakly, to fart, as in *péter dans la main*, to come to nothing. (The French verb also is the ancestor of *petard*, an explosive device for blowing holes in fortifications that frequently misfired, hence the phrase "to be hoist with one's own petard," which is to be defeated by a plan of one's own making.)

The possibility of the French origin is especially attractive because it would make *peter out* an exact counterpart to *fizzle out*, i.e., to tail off, to end weakly, deriving from *fizzle*'s original meaning of, as the *OED* delicately puts it, "To break wind without noise."

philander. This term for the pursuit of women, typically by a cad with no intention of marrying his quarry, has undergone a dramatic change in sexual orientation. The word derives from the Greek *philandros*, lover of man or, as applied conjugally to a woman, lover of one's husband. It entered English, however, as a male name, Philander, often paired with Phyllis in seventeenth-century love ballads. It was the association with the fictional character that apparently led people to think the name meant "man who loves," with "woman," not "man," as the object of affection.

phony. Many attempts have been made to connect this term for that which is fake, sham, or counterfeit with the telephone. The underlying assumption usually is that words spoken into early telephones came out sounding like gibberish or that telephone conversations are not worth very much. For example, the New York *Evening Telegram* declared in 1904 that *phony* "implies that... a thing so qualified has no more substance than a telephone talk to a supposititious friend." And in 1922 the Boston *Traveler* opined, "A statement is phoney if it is like the practical jokes and false impersonations that are so frequently perpetrated over the telephone."

Other suggestions are that *phony* comes from *funny*, as in "funny business," or from *Forney*, the name of a nineteenth-century manufacturer of cheap jewelry—brass rings, specifically.

Phony has been dated only to 1902, but word sleuths, led by Peter Tamony and Eric Partridge, have uncovered its roots in the eighteenth century—and the origins may go back considerably further. The surname is a clue, since *forney* is an old slang term for ring and also a variant of *fawney*. Thus, in nineteenth-century American tramp slang, a *fawney man* was a peddler of imitation jewelry, while in Britain, a *forney* or *fawney* was a ring, as in "He sports a diamond forney on his little finger" (Pierce Egan, *The Finish of Tom, Jerry, and Logic*, 1828).

Specifically, a *fawney* was a counterfeit ring, of copper or brass made up to look like gold, and it was featured in a con game known as the *fawney rig* or *fawney dropping*. Captain Francis Grose described the ploy this way in the third edition of his *Classical Dictionary of the Vulgar Tongue* (1796):

> FAWNEY RIG. A common fraud, thus practised. A fellow drops a brass ring, double gilt, which he picks up before the party to be cheated, and to whom he disposes of it for less than its supposed, and ten times more than its real, value.

The deception was by no means new in the eighteenth century, the machinations of the *ring-faller* (also called a *ring-dropper*) having been described in detail in 1561 in *The Fraternity of Vagabonds* (John Awdeley?). The game also has been played, probably since ancient times, with pocketbooks, meerschaum pipes, and other objects of value. In each case, the swindler pretends to find the supposedly valuable item at the same time as his victim, eventually selling his share—as a great favor, of course—to the mark, whose greed has been piqued to the point that he thinks he is cheating the cheater.

The phony *fawney*, finally, probably derives from the Irish word for a finger ring, *fainne*—which implies that many of the con men in eighteenth-century England were fast-talking Irishmen. The word, pronounced like *fawney*, apparently was brought to the United States during the mass emigration of Irish that followed the great potato famine of 1845. By 1851, *fawney dropping* was being practiced in New York in the same way as in London. But after all this, it has to be added that the present spelling and pronunciation of *phony* may be partly due to the influence of *telephone*, invented in 1876. See also CALL GIRL.

pickaninny. The pejorative impact of the term for a black child is enhanced by association with *ninny*, a fool or dummy, but the two words are not connected. The first is a West Indian creole word, based on the Portuguese *pequenino*, little child, or its Spanish counterpart, and employed affectionately by its creators. The second probably is the result of running together *an innocent* (in the same way an *an ewt* became *a newt*), with reinforcement from *Ninny* as the nickname for *Innocent* (parallel to *Ned* for *Edward*). See also NINCOMPOOP.

pickax. The heavy tool for loosening earth and breaking up rock has a sharp point (two points if it is double-ended, or one point and a broad blade if it is not really a pick but a mattock). The implement's design never featured an ax, however. That part of its name stems from a misunderstanding, dating from the fifteenth century, when people began to confuse the second syllable of the tool's Middle English name, *pikoys* (from the Old French *picois*) with the more familiar-sounding name of the tool for chopping.

piggyback. The carry-all term, suitable for practically anything that rides along with another thing, from children on parents, to truck trailers on railroad flatcars, to ideas on other ideas, has nothing to do with pigs. Rather, *piggyback* is an alteration of *pick-a-back*, which itself evolved from the sixteenth-century forms, *pick back* and *pick pack*. It is impossible to tell from the literary record whether the original reference was to the *pack* that was *picked* (that is, pitched or thrown) on the back or to the *back* on which the pack was *picked*. The *OED* dates *pickbacke* to pre-1565, *pig back* to 1783, and *piggyback* to 1838. In the last example, from a May 31 article in the New York *Voice*, the term is enclosed in quotation marks, indicating that the writer believed it to be a new one.

pin money. The origin of the expression has been attributed to the practice of merchants and other tradesmen of concluding a bargain by giving the other party something toward the purchase of pins.

Maybe this was sometimes done, but the phrase arose in a different way, referring originally to the allowance bestowed upon a woman, especially a married one, for all her household expenses. *Pin-money* has been dated to 1697 in this sense, while *pins* or *pynnes* alone had the same general significance, going back to the mid-sixteenth century.

In olden times, pins were made by hand, of course, and priced accordingly, so *pin money* could represent a substantial sum. Thus, the playwright William Wycherly referred in *The Gentleman Dancing Master* (1672?) to an allowance of "five hundred pounds for pins," and a later diarist, Thomas Hearne, noted in an entry for August 29, 1718, "Mr. Calvert tells me, that the late princess of Orange (wife of him that they call King William III.) had fifty thousand pounds per annum for pin money (as they commonly call ordinary pocket-money)."

In the nineteenth and early twentieth centuries, the expression acquired a rather different meaning in British slang, referring to the money that women picked up on the side, so to speak, through adultery or occasional prostitution. Presumably smaller sums were involved here, the price of pins having dropped considerably after the 1830s, when machines for producing them in large quantities began to go on-line.

pistol. The origin of the name of the sidearm (from ca. 1570, *OED*) frequently is ascribed to Pistoia, a town in Tuscany once famous for metalwork in general and gunsmithing in particular. This theory fits hand in hand with the presumed origin of *pistolet*, a sixteenth-century weapon, either a dagger or a pistol, which may well stem from the place name, via the French *pistolet* and the Italian *pistolese*, referring to Pistoia. (The use of the same word for a cutting weapon and a handgun may reflect the lack of trust that soldiers put in early firearms. In the sixteenth century, the pistol often was combined with a mace, sword, crossbow, or other weapon, so that the user was not left defenseless if the handgun failed to fire.) But *pistol's* true line of descent is from the Middle French *pistole*, a small, short firearm, in turn from the German *pistole* and the Czech *píš'tala*, a firearm, but originally a pipe or fife, akin to *pišteti*, to squeak or whistle. Nowadays, unfortunately, pistols go bang-bang instead of squeak-whistle.

plonk. This with-it term for bad-tasting wine (usually but not, alas, always low-priced) often is associated with the sound of serving it. "Surely the word 'plonk' is onomatopoeic, being the noise made when a cork is withdrawn from the bottle?" observed a writer in the London *Daily Telegraph* (11/15/67). And, indeed, the sound may have helped popularize the term. All the earliest examples of the word in print, however, suggest that *vin plonk* comes from *vin blanc*. The term seems to have arisen in Australia, perhaps deriving from the intermediate *vin blank* (1919, *OED*). The connection with white wine was made explicit as early as 1930: "Nosey and Nobby shared a bottle of plinketty plonk, as *vin blanc* was called" (H. Williamson, *Patriot's Progress*). See also SACK.

polecat. Not a feline on a *pole*, but a skunk (in the New World) or a weasellike animal, akin to a ferret (in the Old World). The *polecat* got its name from its appetite for *pol* or *poul*, Middle French for "chicken," upon which it preyed like a cat. "And eek ther was a polcat in his hawe That as he seyde his capons hadde yslawe" (Geoffrey Chaucer, *The Pardoner's Tale*, 1387–1400).

posh. The origin of this term for that which is smart, swell, elegant, fashionable, or swanky is obscure, but it almost certainly is not, as commonly stated, an acronym for *Port Out Starboard Home* (or, as has been waggishly suggested, *Port Out Sherry Home*).

P.O.S.H., so the story goes, was formerly stamped on first-class, round-trip tickets of the Peninsular and Oriental Steam Navigation Co., which carried mail and passengers between England and India, via the Suez Canal. (The initials were printed in violet ink, by one account, such details being an important ingredient in folk etymologies.) The acronym, said to date from the years prior to World War I, supposedly entitled the ticket holder to passage in one of the cooler cabins aboard ship, on the port side, facing north, on the outward bound journey, and on the starboard side, again facing north, when returning home.

Unfortunately, no one seems to have kept a ticket stub. (If you find one in your attic, you probably should talk to your local auctioneer. It might have some value—and not just to impoverished lexicographers.) Nor have searches of the records of the P.&O., which plied the route until 1970, uncovered any references to the use of *P.O.S.H.* on tickets— or, for that matter, its logical counterpart, *S.O.P.H.*, which should have been stamped on round-trip tickets purchased in India.

This still leaves a mystery. The oldest known example of *posh* in print comes from a *Punch* cartoon of September 25, 1918, where the word is explained as meaning "swish." Fifteen years before that, P. G. Wodehouse came close to *posh* with "That waistcoat . . . being quite the most push thing of the sort in Cambridge" (*Tales of St. Austin's*). No one knows, though, whether Wodehouse mistook *push* for *posh*, or if he really intended *push*, or if the *u* was a printer's error.

Best guess is that the modern meaning of *posh* evolved from the earlier use of the term to mean a dandy (from 1867) or money (from 1830). In the pecuniary sense, *posh* denoted a halfpenny or other coin of small value. The term was introduced to England by Gypsies. In Romany, *posh* means "half," as in *posh-houri*, half pence, or *posh-kooroona*, half crown. According to this interpretation, *posh* has gradually worked its way up the social ladder, from thieves' slang, to university jargon, to its present swellegant, elegant status.

posthumous. The present meaning, referring to something that arises or occurs after one's death, as a *posthumous award* or *posthumous child*, is due to a mistake by folk etymologizers well over a thousand years ago. *Posthumous* comes from the Late Latin (ca. 150–700) *postumus*, last or last-born. It is the superlative of *posterus*, coming after (which produced *posterior*), and, strictly speaking, could be applied to the last child born of a particular mother and father, without reference to death. The *h* crept into *postumus* by association with *humus*, earth, ground, perhaps with some help from *humare*, to bury, the assumption of the Late Latinists being that the *posthumus* child was born after the father's interment. Thus the modern spelling and meaning were fixed, but by mistake. The type specimen here is Posthumus Leonatus, hero of Shakespeare's *Cymbeline* (1609–10), who received this name, as the audience is informed at the start of the play, because he was born after his father died.

press gang. Army and navy commanders used to fill out their ranks by forming *press gangs*, who rounded up men and forced them into military service, e.g., from a 1739 journal note by John Wesley, "In the middle of the sermon, the press-gang came, and seized on one of the hearers." The name of the gang is the result of confusion, however—understandable enough in the context—between *press* in the sense of applying pressure and the older *prest*, as in *prest-money*, a loan—specifically, in the military, an advance against pay given to soldiers and sailors upon their enlistment. Acceptance of this sum, also known as the King's (or Queen's) Shilling, amounted to legal proof of the recruit's engagement. *Prest* derives from the Old French *prester*, to loan, and ultimately the Latin *praestāre*, to warrant, to vouch for. *Press* in the sense of to squeeze or put pressure upon comes from the Old French *presser*, to press, and the Latin *pressāre*, with the same meaning. Note that it also follows from this that *impress*, meaning to compel a person to serve in the military, and *impress*, in the sense of applying pressure or deeply influencing, as by creating a good or bad impression, are really different words.

prevaricate. Pliny and later etymologizers have traced the root sense of this roundabout word for telling a lie to Roman farmers, the theory being that *praevaicor*, I go zigzag, was applied first to men who plowed crooked furrows and then to those who gave crooked answers in court or otherwise deviated from the straight line of truth. This makes a nice parallel with *delirium*, also originally an agricultural term, from the Latin *delīrāre*, to deviate from a straight line (from *de*, away from + *lira*, a furrow).

The parallel is apparent, not real, however. *Prevaricate* actually stems from *praevāricāri*, to walk crookedly, from *prae-*, before + *vāricāre*, to straddle, in turn from *vārus*, bent, knock-kneed. The underlying idea, then, is not of plowing a crooked furrow but of walking zigzag because of the physical condition.

prick song. Not necessarily a bawdy song, but an archaic term for a song whose notes have been put into writing, as opposed to one sung by ear or from memory alone.

The musical *prick* has been dated to ca. 1325 (*OED*), but this sense of the word began to fall into disuse toward the end of the seventeenth century, except among hymn writers and others with a professional interest in music. The increase in the proportion of written to non-written works probably had something to do with this, the distinction between *prick songs* and other songs becoming less important as time went on. It seems significant, however, that the polite society's taboo on the operative term also dates from this period, e.g., from a 1671 translation, *The Colloquies or Familiar Discourses of D. Erasmus:* "One word alone hath troubled some, because the immodest maid soothing the young man, calls him her Prick. . . . He who cannot away with [abide] this, instead of 'my Prick,' let him write 'my Sweetheart.' "

primrose. The flower is not *prim*, and it is not a *rose*, either. The plant name comes from the Medieval Latin *prima rosa*, first (or earliest) flower. The line of descent of the English name is complicated. It may have come directly from the Latin or from the Old French *primerose*, in turn from the Medieval French *primerole* and the Latin *prima rosa*. In either case, the final form of the word is due to confusion with the English *rose*. Even in Latin, the flower's name is something of a misnomer, since it is not one of the very first flowers to bloom in the spring. The Latin name is consistent, however, with that for the related cowslip, *primula veris*, little firstling of spring. See also COWSLIP and ROSEMARY.

pumpernickel. The dark, heavy, sourish rye bread is distinguished for having inspired one of the more picturesque of all folk etymologies—but one that is somewhat pallid compared with its true origin.

The myth has it that the name dates to one of Napoleon's campaigns in what was to become Germany. The Emperor, so it is said, was given—or his groom was given, in another version of the story—a loaf of this bread. But Napoleon (or the groom) quickly decided that the supposed delicacy was not fit for human consumption, and gave it instead to the Emperor's favorite horse, Nicol, saying, *"C'est du pain pour Nicol,"* It is bread for Nicol (or, a variant, *"C'est bon pour Nicol,"* It is good for Nicol).

For some reason, the locals were amused by the incident, not insulted, and they proceeded in their ignorant peasant way to render *pain pour Nicol*, etc. as *pumpernickel* (*Nickel* being the German equivalent of *Nicol*). This is such a nice story that it is almost a pity to note that Napoleon was not born until 1769, while *pompernickel* has been dated to 1663 in German (as an epithet for a lout, a boob) and to 1756 (as the name for the bread) in an English account of a Continental tour.

The myth is not entirely incorrect. The last half of the bread name does come from *Nickel*. The *pumper-* part has a much lower origin, however. It derives from the German *pumpern*, a word of apparently onomatopoeic origin meaning "to break wind." The real reference, then, is to a common effect of the bread on the digestive system. Since *Nickel* (the pet form of *Niklaus*, i.e., *Nicholas*) also was the name of a goblin, *pumpernickel* actually amounts to "devil's fart." See also OLD NICK.

purloin. Deceived by appearances, John Minsheu, author of one of the first etymological dictionaries in English, *The Guide into the Tongues* (1617), explained that "*purloine*, to get privily away" arose as "a metaphor from those that picke the fat of the *loines*." In reality, it comes from the Norman French *purloigner*, to put far away, to remove, and ultimately from the Latin *pro-*, away + *longē*, far, from *longus*, long. The sense of theft seems to have been an English development of the fifteenth century. See also SIRLOIN.

Q

quadrille. This square dance does not involve any *drill*, though some practice may be required before any four couples get through the five movements without stepping on each other's toes. The name of the dance comes from the Spanish *cuadrilla*, the diminutive of *cuadro*, meaning a square formation (as of soldiers on a battlefield). The Latin root is *quadrum*, square, which is related to the number of its sides, *quattuor*, four. Before being applied to the dance (1773, *OED*), *quadrille* appeared in English as the name of a four-handed card game (from 1726) and, the immediate predecessor of the square dance, a tournament or carousel of four groups of horsemen, distinguished by different costumes or colors (from 1738).

quail. Crows crow, ducks duck, and quail quail, but in the last instance, the bird and the action are unrelated—etymologically, at least. The name of the bird comes from the Old French *quaille*, itself of uncertain origin, but most likely imitating the bird's cry, from the Medieval Latin *quaccula*, or from a Gallo-Roman or Germanic source (ancestral to the modern German *wachtel* and the Dutch *kwartel*). Thus, the bird's name is related to *cackle* and to *quack*, and the quail is one of a number of birds named for its call, e.g., the aforementioned crow, the peewee or pewit, the whooping crane, and the hoopoe. As for *quail*, the earliest example of the term in the *OED* (from ca. 1380) alludes to the bird's well-known shyness: "I stod as stylle as dased quayle." This trait led naturally to the supposition that the bird was so called because of its tendency to quail when disturbed. The verb, however, derives from the Middle Dutch *quelen*, to suffer, to be ill, and appears to be a slightly later (ca. 1450) addition to English. See also FLICKER.

Queer Street. To live on *Queer Street* is—or was, before sensitive people began avoiding *queer* altogether because of its use as a slur—to be in serious financial straits. The metaphor has been attributed to tradesmen's putting question marks in their account books next to the names of customers whose debts might not be paid. If so, *Queer Street* would appear to be a misnomer for *Query Street*.

The expression had a more general meaning, however, not involving question marks, when it first appeared on the linguistic scene. *Queer Street* can be dated to about 1800. The metaphor is not among the twenty-three entries beginning with "queer" in the 1796 edition of Captain Francis Grose's *A Classical Dictionary of the Vulgar Tongue*, but it was included by the otherwise anonymous "Member of the Whip Club," who updated Grose's dictionary and republished it as the *Lexicon Balatronicum* in 1811. The *Lexicon* defined the expression this way:

QUEER STREET. Wrong. Improper. Contrary to one's wish. It is queer street, a cant phrase to signify that it is wrong or different to our wish.

This usage is in keeping with the adjective's presumed origin, from the Low German *queer*, oblique, off center, related to the German *quer*, across, adverse, perverse. From the middle of the sixteenth century on, *queer* was a popular term among pickpockets, con men, and other low-lifes, as evidenced by the amount of space given to the term in Grose's dictionary. Among them: *queer as Dick's hatband*, out of order; *to queer*, to puzzle or confound; *queer birds*, rogues just released from prison and up to their former doings; and *queer mort*, a diseased strumpet.

The modern, financially strapped sense of *Queer Street* has been dated to 1840 by Eric Partridge in *A Dictionary of Slang and Unconventional English* (1970). The pejorative homosexual sense of the word is a much later, American innovation. The earliest example of this comes from 1922 publication of the Children's Bureau of the U.S. Department of Labor, which refers to a young man who "is probably 'queer' in sex tendency." The quote marks in the original text suggest that the usage was fairly new at that time.

quiz. A wonderful Irish story has it that this word was invented in 1791 by James Daley, a theater manager in Dublin. Mr. Daley, so it is said, won a barroom bet that he could introduce a new word into the language within twenty hours by hiring urchins to chalk *quiz* on walls all over town. And, indeed, the word was on everybody's tongue the next day, but because no one knew what it meant, it became synonymous with "a test of knowledge."

While the origin of *quiz* is not known, the fable fails on two key counts: (1) The word has been dated to before 1791, and (2) it did not refer in the beginning to a test, but to an odd or eccentric person, as in, from a note by Fanny Burney in her diary for June 24, 1782, "He's a droll quiz, and I rather like him."

The transition from the odd *quiz* to the now dominant, testing sense is not at all clear, and it may well be that the *quiz* that is a short exam actually is a different word, stemming from the traditional opening of grammar school oral exams in Latin, *Quī es?*, Who are you? This supposition might seem farfetched at first glance, but it is supported by the dialectical *quies*, as in "She com back an' *quiesed* us" (1847, *OED*). Whether or not this is so, *quies* merged with *quiz* within another twenty years, perhaps with some reinforcement from *question* and *inquisition*, e.g., "I attended the quizzes as they call them rather closely" (*Atlantic Monthly*, 10/1867).

R

racy. People often race through racy novels, but risqué books have nothing to do with speed, let alone speed-reading. The *race* that is a contest for the swift comes from the Old Norse *rās,* an act of running, rushing, a charge (as in battle); it has been dated in English to about 1300. *Racy,* meanwhile, is a much newer word (1654, *OED*), deriving from the *race* that is a distinct group or type, as in the human race. It appeared initially in connection with wines and fruits having a characteristically excellent flavor. The extended senses of liveliness and piquancy, as applied to people, animals, actions, reading material, and so on, all date from the seventeenth century. The term's ribald connotations are even newer. The *OED*'s earliest example of the use of *racy* in this manner comes from 1901 and *Vagaries of Men* by the pseudonymous but obviously perceptive "P. Bee": "Women who tell racy stories . . . can rouse a great deal of enthusiasm in a room full of men."

raft. A raft may carry a raft of people, but the words for the vessel and the quantity are unrelated. The first comes from the Old Norse *raptr,* a beam or rafter, and dates to around 1300. The second is of much more recent (1833, *OED*), but less certain origin. It probably is a variant of the older *raff,* a heap, a large amount, as in *riffraff* or, from the fourteenth century, *riff and raff,* every scrap, one and all, the rabble. The shift in spelling from *raff,* meaning a large number, to *raft,* in the same sense, may be a tribute to the carrying capacity of rafts, however. The spelling change crops up first in the United States at about the time that settlers were moving along inland waterways into the nation's interior.

rain cats and dogs. This expression for a heavy downpour has piqued the fancy of many word buffs, who have sought to explain its origin in various ways. One suggestion is that it comes from the obsolete French *catadoupe,* a waterfall or cataract. Another is that it derives from a similar-sounding Greek phrase meaning "an unlikely occurrence." Other guesses are that the thunder and lightning that accompany violent storms reminded people of cat-and-dog fights, and that the phrase stems from Norse mythology in which cats were supposed to influence the weather and Odin, the storm god, was attended by dogs and wolves. The most literal supposition is the least pretty, i.e., that heavy rainstorms washed dead animals through the streets of medieval cities.

The earliest known example of the expression comes from Jonathan Swift's *Polite Conversation* (1738), but it clearly had been around for many years previously, as Swift's satire is a compendium of clichés of his era. Almost a century earlier, Richard Brome seems to have been familiar with it, including "It shall rain dogs and polecats" in *The City Witt* (1652).

Many of the clichés cited by Swift remain in use, by the way. Thus, the opening pages of the first of the three dialogues in his satire include such golden oldies as "You can't see the wood for the trees"; "It is an ill wind that blows no body good"; "Every one as they like, as the good woman said when she kiss'd her cow"; "The sight of you is good for sore eyes"; and "Come, a penny for your thought."

rake. The rake who leads women down garden paths has been associated incorrectly with the tool for clearing leaves away from them (the paths). The dissolute, dissipated *rake* is a creature of the seventeenth century; the term itself is an abbreviation of *rake-hell* (from ca. 1550). The rake-hells were believed by all right-thinking upholders of middle-class morality to be as evil as the devils that rake the coals of hell. Originally, however, *rake-hell* doesn't appear to have had anything to do with raking coals, or garden paths, or anything else. The word actually is an alteration into more familiar terms of the Middle English *rakel* (pre-1300), hasty, rash, headstrong—all typical of rakish behavior.

ramshackle. The rickety, ramshackle house or other structure may look like a shack that has been rammed together from scraps of wood, but there is no *shack* here, let alone a *ram*. The term is a nineteenth-century (1830, *OED*) variant of the older *ranshackle* (1675), in turn from *ransackle* (1621). The root is the familiar *ransack* (from ca. 1250), in the sense of turning everything upside down in the course of a search, as soldiers were wont to do when plundering a town. The underlying idea, then, is that the *ramshackle* building looks as though it had been wrecked during looting.

Rather than helping to form *ramshackle*, the rickety *shack* may have been split off from it. It also has been suggested that *shack* is related to *ramshackle* via the dialectical *shackly*, rickety, shaky; that it comes from the Icelandic *ramskakkr*, where *ramr* = very, and *skakkr* = twisted; and, going in the opposite direction, that it derives from the Aztec *xacalli*, wooden hut, and the Mexican Spanish *jacal*, formerly written *xacal* and pronounced as though spelled *shacal*.

The last theory has the virtue of fitting in with the earliest examples of *shack*, all of which refer to living quarters in the American West. The first *OED* citation is from an 1878 report of the Commissioner of Indian Affairs: "Too much praise cannot be given to these homesteaders for . . . the erection of this building while they themselves were living in shacks." But whatever its source, *shack* certainly seems to be a newer word than *ramshackle*. See also SHANTY.

rat. If you look at Latin long enough, you probably can find a progenitor of almost any English word of otherwise unknown origin. The path may be tortuous, however. Thus, the seventeenth-century French scholar Gilles Ménage derived *rat* from the Latin *mūs*, mouse, in this way: "They must have said, first *mūs*, then *muratus*, then *ratus*, then *rat*" (A. Brachet, *An Etymological Dictionary of the French Language*, 1882). In fact, *rat* descends from the Anglo-Saxon *ræt*, which either comes from or is related to the Old Saxon *ratta* and the Old Icelandic *rottu-*.

The etymology of *rat* is difficult to trace because the animal itself did not appear in Europe until about the tenth century A.D. Whatever, the presumed Indo-European root is *rēd-/rōd-*. This also is the ancestor of the Latin *rōdēre*, to gnaw, which means that *rat*'s cousins, distant linguistically but not so far apart in action, include such modern terms as *corrode* and *erode*.

ratline. The term for the small ropes running horizontally across the shrouds of a sailing vessel, which are used as steps when going aloft, appears to be a product of folk etymology, with sailors converting a strange word into more familiar form. *Ratline* has been dated to the end of the fifteenth century in various forms: *ratling*, *raddelyne*, and *radelyng*. The word's origin is obscure. Ernest Weekley suggests in his *Etymological Dictionary* that it might be the nautical and dialectical *raddle*, to intertwine, to interlace, or *raddling*, a long, slender rod used in weaving. The *OED* speculates that *ratline* derives from a French word, ancestral to the modern *ralingue*, a rope sewn into the edge of a sail in order to keep it from tearing. In any case, all hands agree that neither rats nor lines were originally involved, though ships have always had plenty of both.

real McCoy, the. So many marvelous "explanations" of the origin of this phrase have been produced that it is difficult to determine which of them is the real thing, the genuine article, or, as the saying goes, *the real McCoy.* Collectively, they demonstrate the lengths to which people will go in order to avoid admitting that they do not know the answer to something. Among the more commonly encountered explanations:

1. The phrase comes from the *nom de guerre* of the boxer Norman Selby (1873–1940), who held the welterweight championship from 1896 to 1900. Mr. Selby billed himself as "Kid McCoy." Some say that another McCoy appeared on the boxing scene, with the result that those who follow the sweet science began to distinguish Selby as "the real McCoy." Others say that the expression stems from a barroom fight, Mr. Selby having decked a man who refused to believe he was the Kid, whereupon the doubter had to admit, "He's the real McCoy."

2. The phrase comes from Joseph G. McCoy (1837–1915), grocer, real estate agent, wrought-iron salesman, and, more to the point, the cattleman who laid out the Chisholm Trail for bringing herds from Texas to the rail head at Abilene, Kansas. (It might just as well have been called the McCoy Trail.) With the coming of the herds, Abilene blossomed from about a dozen log houses in 1867 into the cow town of Western lore, so wild that James Butler "Wild Bill" Hickok had to be hired as Marshal to keep the peace. McCoy himself served as the new city's first Mayor. By 1872, however, Abilene's moment in the sun had passed, as area farmers formed a protective association and the railway advanced further west. But McCoy's fame lasted, perhaps in part because he called himself, so it is said, "the real McCoy."

3. The term is a newer eponym, coming from a Prohibition Era (1920–33) rumrunner by the name of Bill McCoy, the idea being that McCoy's goods, brought in from Canada, were the genuine article, as opposed to illegal domestic produce from backwoods stills and urban bathtubs.

4. The phrase originated among turn-of-the-century safecrackers to designate commercial nitroglycerine from the "soup" they made from dynamite themselves. The *McCoy* in this instance supposedly came from the name of a wildcatter in the Pennsylvania oil fields who diverted nitro to the burglars, the point being that *the real McCoy* was much more reliable than the homemade stuff.

5. The expression comes from a nineteenth-century Irish ballad about a Mrs. McCoy who gave her husband a terrible thrashing, thus proving that she was *the real McCoy.*

6. The phrase is somehow—the "how" is never made very clear—related to the famous feud of the 1880s between the Hatfields of West Virginia and the McCoys of Kentucky.

7. The *McCoy* actually comes from a geographic name, *Macao*, rather than a surname. The supposition here is that drug addicts in New Orleans referred to pure heroin from this Chinese island, long a Portuguese colony, as "the real Macao."

8. Another drug-induced explanation is that the *McCoy* comes from the name of a British pharmaceutical company whose products, high in opium content, were much in demand in the United States following passage of the Harrison Narcotic Act of 1914. By extension, then, *the real McCoy* was used among dope addicts to refer to pure, commercially made drugs, as opposed to bootleg drugs.

9. The expression alludes to an ancient rivalry between two branches of the Mackay clan in Scotland, with the result that either (9a) there was a dispute as to who was the true head of the clan, that is, "the real Mackay," or (9b) the head of the northern branch, Lord Reay, was distinguished as "the Reay Mackay," with the "Reay" eventually being altered into "real" and the "Mackay" into you-know-what.

10. Finally, and most likely, though the evidence is tenuous, there is the theory that *McCoy* comes from *Mackay*, but referring in this instance to an exceptionally fine brand of Scotch whisky, distilled by A. and M. Mackay, of Glasgow. Supporting this hypothesis is an early reference to whisky as "the clear McCoy" in *A Dictionary of Americanisms on Historical Principles* (Mitford M. Mathews, 1951). This citation comes from 1908—prior to passage of the antinarcotics act and the Eighteenth Amendment, thus undermining several of the foregoing claims.

The issue remains in doubt, however, thanks to an 1883 letter by Robert Louis Stevenson in which the presumed antecedent of *the real McCoy* appears in a generic, nonliquorish sense: "For society, there isnae sae muckle; but there's myself—the auld Johnstone, ye ken—he's the real Mackay, whatever."

Possibly, some or all of the cited factors have reinforced one another—the intraclan rivalry of the Mackays, say, and the regard of the Scots for the whisky, coinciding with the name of the Kid and the nitro supplier to make the expression an enduring part of the language. But the reader shouldn't put any money on this composite explanation's being the real McCoy!

red dog. Pro football teams have used various color-coded signals over the years, but the name of the defensive maneuver in which one or more linebackers rush the quarterback comes from Don "Red" Ettinger, who played for the New York Giants during 1948–50. Regularly an offensive guard, Ettinger filled in as a linebacker during a game in 1949. At one point, when a pass play seemed certain because it was third down with long yardage to go for a first, Ettinger charged from his position and sacked the quarterback for a large loss. "Asked about the maneuver later, the red-headed Ettinger claimed he was 'just doggin' the quarterback a little.' Thus, the expression 'red dog' was born" (Tim Considine, *The Language of Sport*, 1982).

reindeer. Santa may struggle with the reins as he guides Donder, Blitzen, and the rest to rooftop landings, but the animals that pull his sleigh are not called *reindeer* because they have been domesticated and fitted with *reins*. The animal's name is Scandinavian, probably deriving from the Old Norse *hreindȳri*. The name appears in English before 1400 as *rayne-deer* in a pre-Malory version of *Le Morte d'Arthur*.

Note that in the Old Norse, *hreinn* refers to the reindeer itself, while *dȳr* is a general term for a four-footed beast. This sense of *deer* was retained in English for a couple hundred years, with Shakespeare still employing it in this manner in *King Lear* (1605–7): "But mice, rats and such small Deer Have been Tom's food for seven long year." Technically, then, Donder, Blitzen, et al. are not actually "deer." Rather, they are "reindeer-animals."

requiem shark. This alternative name for the white shark seems logical enough. It's your requiem, after all, if you have the misfortune to fall overboard when one is in the vicinity. (*Requiem* means "rest" in Latin, and it is the first word of the Mass for the repose of the souls of the dead, thus giving the service its name.) The association of the shark with the religious rite dates from the seventeenth century, e.g., "The French and Portuguez commonly call it [the shark] Requiem, that is to say Rest, haply, because he is wont to appear in fair weather" (John Davies, *The History of the Caribbee Isles*, 1666). This is another example, however, of the assimilation of a foreign word into English by its conversion into a familiar-sounding one. In this case, the name comes from the French *requin,* or the Portuguese *requieme,* both meaning "shark," and both apparently coming from a native Caribbean term for the animal, not the prayers for those it devours. See also MASS.

rewards. Half-learned literary critics have "explained" to unsophisticated readers that *rewards* in the title of Rudyard Kipling's *Rewards and Fairies* (1909) should be pronounced "roo-ards," the term actually being an antique one for elves, pixies, hobgoblins, etc. Kipling did mean *rewards* in the regular sense, however. He got the title from a line by Richard Corbet in *The Fairies Farewell* (1647), a mock lament for the departure of England's merry fairies from the realm—a flight that Corbet, a bishop as well as a poet, blamed on the rising Puritan tide.

ring around the rosy. The children's rhyme often is construed as a relic of the great plague that ravaged Britain in 1665. The rhyme has been recorded in many versions. The one that I learned as a child (about 1941 in a suburb of New York City) and heard sung by a preschooler in Southbury, Conn., in 1992, goes like this:

> Ring around the rosy,
> Pocketful of posies,
> Ashes, ashes,
> We all fall down.

Another version, played in Indiana in the 1940s, goes:

> Ring around the rosy,
> Pocketful of posy,
> Last one to stoop
> Is a dirty red nosy.

In *The Plague and the Fire* (1961), James Leasor cited this version:

> Ring a ring of rosy,
> A pocketful of posies,
> Atchoo, atchoo,
> We all fall down.

Mr. Leasor explicated the text this way:

Few people watching a group of children dancing hand-in-hand in a circle to this well-known nursery rhyme may realize that it has its origin in the plague. Rosy refers to the rosy rash of the plague, ringed to signify the tokens [blisters and buboes, the latter being swellings, typically the size of a man's fist]; the posies were herbs and spices carried to sweeten the air; sneezing was a common symptom of those close to death.

The words "all fall down" certainly referred to Londoners during that stifling August [when mortality rates rose twenty to thirty times above normal levels].

All this sounds very nice, but the available evidence weighs against the supposition that the rhyme memorializes the plague. "Ring around" is not included in the earliest known book of nursery rhymes in English, *Tom Thumb's Pretty Song Book*, published in at least two volumes in 1744. (Finding a copy of Volume I would be like winning the lottery; the British Museum has a single copy of Volume II, but no other copies of either volume are known to exist.) In fact, the rhyme is a relatively late addition to the canon, not recorded in print until 1881, more than two hundred years after the plague. And the initial version, included in an edition of *Mother Goose* famous for its illustrations by Kate Greenaway, differs from Mr. Leasor's. As reprinted in *The Annotated Mother Goose* by William S. and Ceil Baring-Gould (1962), it goes like this:

> Ring-a-ring-a-roses,
> A pocket full of posies;
> Hush! Hush! Hush! Hush!
> We've all tumbled down.

No "atchoo, atchoo" here then, an omission that led Iona and Peter Opie, the leading collectors of children's rhymes of our time, to pooh-pooh the historical connection in *The Oxford Dictionary of Nursery Rhymes* (1951) with the note: "The invariable sneezing and falling down in modern English versions has given would-be origin finders the opportunity to say that the rhyme dates back to the days of the Great Plague."

For more about the cloudy origins of nursery rhymes, see CAT AND THE FIDDLE.

rosemary. The Latin name of this plant—an aromatic evergreen shrub, not a rose—is *rōs marīnus*, sea dew. The Romans probably gave it this name because they found it growing along the Mediterranean coast. In English, however, right from the start (ca. 1440), the plant's name was rendered as *rose mary*, thanks to the influence of the familiar *rose* and the personal name *Mary*. As a result, it sometimes is associated with the Blessed Virgin, as though it were "the rose of Mary." See also PRIMROSE and TUBEROSE.

run the gauntlet. The spelling of *gauntlet* here was influenced by that of the gauntlet that is worn on one's hand or flung in the face of an enemy, but the method of punishing a person by requiring him to run between two rows of men equipped with sticks or whips has nothing to do with gloves. The operative term in the name of the punishment is a corruption of *gantlope*, which came from the Swedish *gatlopp*, gate run, in turn from *gata*, path, lane, road + *lop*, the act of running, a course (cognate to the English *leap*). The phrase is of military origin and seems to have been popularized, so to say, during the Thirty Years' War (1618–48). It has been dated in English to 1646 in the form of *run the gantelope*. Not long afterward it was extended to refer to mental as well as physical ordeals, e.g., "To print, is to run the gantlet, and to expose one self to the tongues strapado" (Joseph Glanvill, *The Vanity of Dogmatizing, or Confidence in Opinions*, 1661). Recognizing that *gauntlet* was a corruption, careful writers used the now archaic *gantlope* until well into the nineteenth century, as in "Some said he ought to be tied neck and heels; others that he deserved to run the gantlope" (Henry Fielding, *Tom Jones*, 1749). See also ELOPE.

S

sabotage. The origin of this term for destroying property or disrupting plans, especially by stealth and during time of war, generally is explained as coming from the practice of French strikers' damaging machinery by throwing *sabots,* or their wooden shoes, into the works. This makes a nice story, but there is no documentation for it and the linguistic evidence points in another direction. The French verb *saboter,* from which the English term was formed (1910, *OED*), means to work badly, to botch, to bungle. In French, *sabot* itself is used figuratively and contemptuously for any inferior article or poor worker. The pejorative senses of the word most likely derive from the clattering noise of wooden shoes, not the act of throwing them.

sack. The dry white wine was never made, as has been suggested, by being strained through a sack. Nor does it derive from the Spanish *sacar,* to draw out, referring to its importation into England from Spain and the Canaries. Still more unlikely sources of the term are *vino seco* and *vino secco,* Spanish and Italian terms for dry wine that have been presumed to exist by some English etymologists but which have not been recorded by lexicographers in the countries concerned.

The name of the sherry actually comes from the French *vin sec,* dry wine. Thus, the beverage was described from an early date (1530s) variously as *wyn seake, seck wyn,* and *wyne seck,* as well as *sakke.* The transition from *seake/seck* to *sakke/sack* may have been aided by the provincial British pronunciation of *sack* as *seck.* Hearing *seck,* sophisticated Londoners probably "corrected" it into *sack.* For more about white wines, albeit poor ones, see PLONK.

salt cellar. Salt is kept in a salt cellar, but this *cellar* is not like a *wine cellar*—or any other basement area, for that matter. The *cellar* for holding salt originally was a *saler,* as in, from the fourteenth-century romance of *Richard Coer de Leon,* "The saler on the table stood."

Saler comes from the Old French *salier* and ultimately the Latin *salaria,* pertaining to salt, equivalent to *sal,* salt—whence also the word for one's weekly wage, or *salary,* originally an allowance to soldiers for the purchase of salt. *Saler* was converted during the fifteenth and sixteenth centuries into *seller* and then *cellar* (1566, *OED*) as people confused the salt with the more familiar word for its container. (*Cellar* also is of Old French and Latin origin, from *cellārium*, storeroom, and *cella*, small room, whence also the *cells* in prisons, batteries, honeycombs, living organisms, etc., but it came into English with the Normans, probably before 1200.) Because of the confusion between the condiment and its container, asking someone "to please pass the salt cellar" is, technically speaking, a pleonasm, as it amounts to a request for the "salt salt." See also GRAIN OF SALT, WITH A.

satire. An ancient but incorrect association with the libidinous *satyr* has influenced the term for ironical or derisive writing. The original Latin *satira*, from *satur*, full, as in *satura lanx*, full dish, was a discursive composition, covering a variety of topics. In classical times, however, this literary form was confused with the Greek *satyric* dramas, so called on account of their use of a chorus of satyrs. As a result, the form of the word changed in Latin from *satura* to *satyra* to *satira*, and the meaning also was affected, with the goatish satyrs leaving the imprint of their cloven hooves upon the literary tradition. In English, the term has been dated to 1509 in the sense of a poem designed to ridicule prevailing vices or follies, and to 1675 in the general, modern sense of the employment of irony and sarcasm to ridicule someone or something.

saunter. We have it on the authority of the *New York Times* that this lovely word for a leisurely stroll is "said to be created by Thoreau" ("Around Manhattan Step by Step," 8/16/91), which is very interesting, considering that citations for it in *The Oxford English Dictionary* go back to pre-1667. Admittedly, the word's origin is obscure, and people were puzzled by it from the time that it came into use. Thus, John Ray, remembered mainly as a collector of proverbs, but who was a language buff, too, suggested in the 1691 edition of his collection of English words that the term "is derived from *Saincte terre, i.e.* The Holy Land, because of old time . . . many idle persons went from place to place, upon pretence that they . . . intended to take the Cross upon them and to go thither." Modern etymologists look askance at this picturesque story, however, preferring to derive *saunter* from the Middle English *santren*, to muse, or perhaps the fifteenth-century *saunteryng*, aimless talk, i.e., idle chatter, babbling. *Santren* and *saunteryng* may or may not represent different forms of the same word, and neither can be traced back to before about 1440. Whatever, it is clear that *saunter* was a part of the language long before the Sage of Walden was a gleam in his great-great-great-great-great-great-grandfather's eye.

scot-free. Given their reputation for canniness as well as penuriousness, it is only natural to assume that the Scots must be responsible for this term for complete escape from harm, punishment, debt, or other obligations. Therefore, it is pleasant to report that, contrary to appearance, this is not an ethnic slur. Rather, the *scot* part is a holdover from Middle English, when the word referred to a payment, a reckoning (as of a tavern bill), or a royal tax. The Old Norse root is *skattr*, tax, treasure, which shows up in other languages, e.g., the German *schoss-frei*, or scot-free, without reference to the stingy northerners who used to paint themselves blue and still wear kilts. See also HOPSCOTCH.

scrimshaw. The word for the intricate carvings of ivory and shell made by whalers with loads of time on their hands sometimes is said to honor an especially adept whittler by the name of Scrimshaw. While the origin of the term is unknown, the suggested surname seems to be an unlikely source, considering that *scrimshaw* (1864, *OED*) is antedated by the synonymous *scrimshander* (in *Moby-Dick*, 1851) and the participles *scrimshonging* (1850) and *scrimshonting* (1825–26). See also CANT and CONDOM.

scullion. A *scullion*, or kitchen helper, may work in a *scullery* (the room adjoining a kitchen in which food is prepared and utensils are washed), but the job classification is not related to the name for the place of employment.

Scullion appears to be a borrowing from the Middle French *escouillon*, a swab, a dishcloth, in turn from the diminutive of *escouve*, broom, and ultimately the Latin *scopa*, broom. Thus, the scullion is named for the tools of his trade.

As a word, *scullery* is of intrinsically higher social standing, deriving from the Middle French *escuelerie*, the office of the keeper of the dishes, in turn from the Old French *escuelle*, dish, and the Latin *scutella*, serving platter.

secretary bird. This large African raptor often is said to have gotten its name from the array of black feathers at the back of its head and neck, which, indeed, vaguely resemble the quill pens that eighteenth-century clerks stuck behind their ears. However, the naturalist A. Vosmaer, who in 1769 provided the first accurate description of the bird, was told that the *secretary* was a corruption of *Sagittarius*, the archer, which was the bird's name in southern Africa. And this name, in turn, probably is a corruption of the Arabic *sagr al-tēr* (*sagr*, hawk + *al*, the + *ter*, birds), reinforced by yet another image—this one of the long-legged bird's striding gait, resembling that of a bowman advancing into battle. The creature's scientific name is *Sagittarius serpentarius*, reflecting its taste for reptiles. (It also was called *snake eater* at the Cape of Good Hope in the eighteenth century.)

Since the 1960s, *secretary birds* also have been spotted in British offices, e.g., "Since Pinn had become what she called a 'secretary bird' she had become much smarter" (Iris Murdoch, *The Sacred and Profane Love Machine*, 1974).

sedan. The word for an enclosed automobile seating four or more people (also once called a *saloon car*) has been dated to 1912. It comes from *sedan chair*, an enclosed chair, complete with windows, a hinged door, and an opening on the roof to allow the occupant to stand. Lugged from place to place on poles by two chairmen (usually Irish, in London), this was a fashionable mode of transport from the seventeenth to nineteenth centuries. The name of the chair, in turn, often is assumed to come from that of the city on the Meuse in northeastern France.

Dr. Johnson made this conjecture, and *The Encyclopædia Britannica* (13th edition, 1926) stated flatly that the chair "took its name from the town of Sedan, in France, where it was first used, and was introduced into England by Sir S. Duncombe in 1634." Johnson, however, was better at constructing definitions than at tracking word origins (see CURMUDGEON). Meanwhile, the *Britannica*'s account is contradicted by John Evelyn, who noted in a description of his visit to Naples that the streets of that city "are full of gallants on horseback, in coaches and sedans, from hence brought first into England by Sir Sanders Duncomb" (*Diary*, 2/8/1645).

As a matter of fact, Duncombe did receive a patent for supplying "covered chairs" in 1634, and Evelyn is almost certainly right about the source, as he knew Duncombe, a physician, who had attended Evelyn's mother upon her deathbed.

Sedan probably comes from a southern Italian dialect word related to the *sede*, chair, in turn from the Latin *sēdēs*, seat, and *sēdēre*, to sit. (One wonders if Evelyn also was correct about the women of Naples, whom he describes in the same passage in his diary as "well featur'd but excessively libidinous.") See also CHEERIO, CONDOM, and DIAPER.

sexton. This church (or synagogue) official is not so called because he works six (Latin *sex*) days a week, even though the job used to be fairly demanding. Sextons maintained buildings, rang bells, and even dug graves back when cemeteries were located next to places of worship. The occupational name, however, is a doublet of the virtually synonymous *sacristan*, itself a shortened form of the Anglo-French *segerstain*, in turn from the Medieval Latin *sacristanus*, meaning the person who looks after the sacristy—the place where the holy, or *sacer*, vessels are kept. At one time, the church *sacristy* also was called a *sextry*; hence the *sexton* who had charge of it. Sometimes this position was filled by a woman, known as a *sextoness, sextrice*, or, a wonderful feminine title that merits resurrection, a *sextress*.

shamefaced. Those poor souls whose faces redden because they are bashful, shy, modest, or otherwise ashamed have been said, since the middle of the sixteenth century, to be *shamefaced* (1555, *OED*). Earlier, they were *shamfast* (or *scamfæstan* back in the ninth century). The *fast* in *shamfast* is like the *fast* in *steadfast*, meaning that the *shamfast* person was firmly fixed or fastened in shame. The change in the form and sense of the word probably was due to the blushing of those who are ashamed, the association being noted in writing from an early date, e.g., "Tho that haue that face sumwhate ruddy bene schamefaste" (*Secreta Secretorum*, 1422).

shanty. Probably because this Americanism for a ramshackle cabin, hut, or other rude dwelling is associated so closely with the *shanty Irish*, who lived in *shantytowns*, some etymologists think the term must be of Irish extraction, too. They derive it from *sean*, old + *tig*, house, which is not entirely illogical, considering that shanties tend to be old and run-down. On the other hand: (1) The word has been dated to 1820, a generation before the great potato famine of 1845–46, which led to the mass exodus of Irish from Ireland. (2) The word did not appear first along the coast, where the Irish landed, but on the frontier, the earliest citation in the *OED* being from the account of a visitor to the wilds of Ohio, who reported that the locals "lived in what is here called a shanty. This is a hovel of about 10 feet by 8, made in the form of an ordinary cow-house." (3) The word also appeared at an early date as *chanty*, e.g., "They commence by building a log cabin called a *Chanty* to shelter them from the weather, and hence another appellation they are known by, namely *Chanty Men*" (*Canadian Magazine*, III, 1824).

All this suggests that the quintessentially Irish word is not really Irish at all but French, from the French Canadian *chantier*, a log hut, a lumberjack's headquarters, in turn from *chantier*, timber yard, depot, storage place. The French word came from the Latin *cantherius*, beam, rafter, frame, and also referring to a horse or pack ass (specifically, one that is in poor condition). *Canthērius*—also the ancestor of *gantry*, the bridgelike frame that supports a traveling crane—was borrowed from the Greek *kanthēlios*, pack ass, alluding to the framework on its back for carrying a load. See also RAMSHACKLE.

shard. Entomology and etymology clash when the people who study bugs speak of the *shard* of a beetle, meaning its wing case or, another technical term, *elytron*. The entomological sense of the word is due to a misapprehension by Dr. Samuel Johnson, who wasn't quite sure what to make of Shakespeare's use of *shard-born* in *Macbeth* (1606):

> ere to black Hecate's summons,
> The shard-born beetle with his drowsy hums
> Hath rung night's yawning peal, there shall be done
> A deed of dreadful note.

Johnson thought of *shard* as a fragment of pottery—naturally enough, since the word has carried this meaning since ca. 1000. Accordingly, in his *Dictionary of the English Language* (1755), he defined *shardborn* as "Born or produced among broken stones or pots," then went on to hazard the guess that "Perhaps *shard* in Shakespeare may signify the sheaths of the wings of insects." But those who followed in the great Johnson's wake forgot his "perhaps." Thus, from a word list compiled in 1811 (*OED*): "*Shard*, the shell or hard outward covering of the tribe of insects denominated *Colcoptera*." Poets glommed on to the word, too, with Longfellow, for one, working it into a vivid passage in *Hiawatha* (1855):

> And the roof-poles of the wigwam
> Were as glittering rods of silver,
> And the roof of bark upon them
> As the shining shards of beetles.

The Johnsonian influence remains so strong that in some modern editions of Shakespeare's play, *shard-born* is rendered as *shard-borne*. For example, this is how the term appears in the text I used in college, *Shakespeare: The Complete Works,* edited by G. B. Harrison (1952). Footnoting the passage in *Macbeth,* Professor Harrison explained that *shardborne* means the beetle is "borne aloft by its horny wings."

But Shakespeare was a country boy. He was using the word in quite another sense, one that was not familiar to Johnson, whose learning came from books, not the great outdoors. By *shard,* Shakespeare meant a cow patty. And he really intended *born,* not *borne,* his true reference being to the dung beetle, or tumblebug, which lays its eggs in balls of cow manure. The origin of the *shard* that is a patch of cow dung (attested from 1545, *OED*) is obscure, but the term seems to be cognate to the older *sharn.* Thus, the dung beetle was known as a *sharnbud* back around the year 1000. The *bud* later evolved into *bug,* the beetle becoming in due course a *sharnbug.*

All of which puts a rather different complexion on Longfellow's image of the wigwam's shining roof.

Sheboygan. The name of the Wisconsin town is the subject of an ingenious folk etymology, probably devised with tongue in cheek. A Native American squaw, so the story goes, upon seeing that she had given birth to a son instead of the daughter for which she had hoped, exclaimed, "Ugh! She boy 'gain" (*American Speech,* 4/50). As it happens, the place name (and its variant, *Cheboygan,* which is how they spell it in Cheboygan, Mich.), is of Algonquian origin. It probably comes from a word for any object with holes, such as the stem of a pipe. Perhaps peace pipes were smoked at Sheboygan and Cheboygan.

shyster. Contrary to the etymologies offered in some dictionaries and collections of eponyms, this term for an unethical lawyer does not come from a particularly unscrupulous pettifogger by the name of Scheuster, said to have operated in New York City in the 1840s. Nor does it come from *Shylock,* the Shakespearean character, noted for his sharp dealings; or from the Gaelic *siostair,* barrator, meaning a person who stirs up quarrels and initiates groundless lawsuits; or from *shy,* in one of its older, slang senses of "disreputable, shady, of questionable character."

The *Scheuster* theory, proposed as far back as 1897 in a book about New York City, *The American Metropolis,* by a lawyer, Frank Moss, gained considerable popularity because all the earliest examples of the word do come from New York of the 1840s. Thus, the oldest citation in *The Oxford English Dictionary* is from a book about the city jail, *Mys-*

teries of the Tombs: "He is consulted by the magistrates on all important points of law, and the inferior shysters look upon him with a reverence approaching veneration" (G. Wilkes, 1844).

Shyster provides a fine example, however, of why *The Oxford English Dictionary* must be used with care. Although the readers who supply citations for the *OED* have, collectively, cast a very large, very fine net, the oldest citations in this great dictionary do not necessarily represent the first appearances in print of particular words and their meanings. The original *OED* readers focused on mainstream books, principally those published in Great Britain. Until publication of the modern revisions of the *OED*, starting in 1972, less-complete coverage was given to academic, technical, and underground literature, as well as to newspapers, magazines, and American works generally. As a result, there is still plenty of room in which advanced logophiles can play the game of beating the *OED* by finding earlier attestations for words than are included in it. And sometimes these early examples reveal how words actually originated.

In the case of *shyster*, Roger Mohovich, a newspaper librarian for the New-York Historical Society, found numerous pre-1844 examples of the word's use in a New York newspaper, *The Subterranean*. He relayed these to Professor Gerald L. Cohen, at the University of Missouri–Rolla, a specialist in slang origins, who had already begun work on the history of *shyster*. Professor Cohen supplemented the newspaper references with extensive research into the dozen or so hypotheses that had been proposed of *shyster*'s origin. For example, to disprove the Scheuster theory, lists of lawyers of the period were consulted without turning up any trace of a New York attorney by this name. Professor Cohen published the results of his investigations in a series of papers between 1976 and 1979 in his own valuable publication, *Comments on Etymology*, and in final form in "Origin of the Term 'Shyster'" (*Forum Anglicum*, 1982).

In the very beginning, Professor Cohen discovered, *shyster* was applied to lawyers who were incompetent but not necessarily dishonest. The meaning of the word soon was broadened, however, to refer to dishonest officials generally, as well as to the unscrupulous lawyers, many of them unlicensed, who took advantage of people incarcerated in the Tombs, charging for legal services that often were never performed.

Shyster seems to have appeared in print for the first time on July 29, 1843, in an account by Mike Walsh, editor of *The Subterranean*, of a conversation with Cornelius Terhune, himself a shyster of uncommon abilities. Terhune had approached Walsh in a bar, asking that the editor, who had been campaigning against corruption in the local courts, take care in future articles to distinguish him from run-of-the-mine pettifoggers. Terhune characterized those others with a word that was new to Walsh. When the editor asked what it meant, "The Counsellor expressed the utmost surprise at our ignorance of the true meaning of that expressive appellation 'shiseter;' after which, by special request, he gave a definition, which we would now give our readers, were it not that it would certainly subject us to a prosecution for libel and obscenity."

Walsh's initial spelling of the term (he also used *shyseter* before settling on *shyster*) and the context of the conversation point directly to the word's origin, which is not nearly as innocuous as *Scheuster, siostair, Shylock,* or *shy.* In fact, Professor Cohen has demonstrated convincingly what some others had previously suspected but not been able to prove, which is that *shyster* evolved from the use of *shiser* or *shicer* (the latter appears in British English at about this time) among criminals and their associates (lawyers, too!) to denote a worthless fellow. *Shiser,* in turn, stems from the German *scheisser,* an incompetent person— specifically, one who cannot control his bodily functions. And *scheisser,* finally, derives from *scheisse,* shit. Which is why Walsh was unable to repeat Terhune's definition without running the risk of a prosecution for libel and obscenity.

sincere. Tracers of word histories once explained with all sincerity that *sincere* derives from the Latin *sine cērā,* without wax. Roman stone-workers, according to this notion, sometimes waxed the surface of marble to make it appear smooth and shiny instead of taking the time and trouble to polish it finely. This led dealers in the right stuff to advertise their stone as *sine cērā,* which in time came to mean "without deception," "honest," or, as we say today, "sincere."

All things are possible. Someday, somewhere in the Roman world an archaeologist may excavate the ruins of a Roman stone merchant's shop and find a tablet inscribed *sine cērā.* Until that happens, however, it seems safer to adhere to modern etymological thinking, which derives *sincere* from the Latin *sincērus,* whole, pure, untainted, genuine. The Latin word may originally have meant "one growth," that is, not hybrid or mixed, from *sin-,* one + the root of *crēscere,* to grow. The Indo-European root of *crēscere* is *ker-,* as in *Cerēs,* goddess of agriculture, the *cereal* on the breakfast table, and such words as *accrue, create, crescendo,* and *increase*.

sirloin. The present spelling of the name of the cut of meat may well have been influenced by what is one of the most famous of all false etymologies. The usual form of the word in the sixteenth century was *surloyn*, from the French *surlonge* (*sur*, over, above + *longe*, loin). The English associated the *sur* with the *Sir* of knighthood from an early date, however. As far back as 1630, John Taylor (known as "the Water Poet" because he worked for a while as a boatman on the Thames) mentioned in his *Great Eater of Kent* one that "should presently enter combate with a worthy knight, called Sir Loyne of Beefe, and overthrow him." Once this story got going, the only question was which king had knighted the loin.

Thomas Fuller opted for Henry VIII: "A Sir-loyne of beef was set before Him (so knighted saith tradition by this King Henry)" (*Church-History of Britain*, 1655). Fuller even provided the kind of circumstantial detail that so often characterizes false etymologies: "Dining with Abbot of Reading, He [Henry VIII] ate so heartily of a loyne of beef that the abbot said he would give 1,000 marks for such a stomach. 'Done!' said the King, and kept the abbot a prisoner in the Tower, won the 1,000 marks, and knighted the beef."

It is hard to improve upon this, but in the next century Jonathan Swift gave it a good try. Thus, the following exchange from his *Polite Conversation* (1738):

"I vow, 'tis a noble Sir-loyn!"
"Ay, here's cut and come again."
"But, pray, why is it call'd a Sir-loyn?"
"Why you must know that our King James I, who loved good eating, being invited to Dinner by one of his Nobles, and seeing a large Loyn of Beef at his Table, he drew out his Sword, and in a frolic knighted it. Few people know the secret of this."

Yet a third king, Charles II, was fingered in *Cook's Oracle* (1822) by the well-named William Kitchiner, who reported that when the Merry Monarch was presented with an especially tasty "Loin of Beef... [he] said for its merit it should be knighted, and henceforth called it Sir-Loin."

Belief in the knighthood of the loin was so strong that it inspired

Henry Fielding's jocular reference in *Tom Jones* (1749) to Mr. Supple's desire to "pay his respects to the baronet, for so he called the sirloin," as well as *baron of beef*, meaning two sirloins, joined at the backbone, which was included by Samuel Johnson in his *Dictionary of the English Language* (1755). And Johnson was not joking. He picked the term up from an earlier dictionary, and it remains in use, chiefly in Britain.

Tastiest of the loins is the *tenderloin*, a surprisingly recent offering—semantically, at least—in butcher shops and elsewhere. The earliest example in the *OED* of *tenderloin* in its culinary sense comes from Noah Webster's *American Dictionary* of 1828. Indicative of changing fashions in table manners is the question posed in T. W. Higginson's *Army Life* (1869): "Is it customary to help to tenderloin with one's fingers?"

The extended sense of *tenderloin*, referring to the part of a city most noted for vice and, accordingly, richest in opportunities for graft, has been dated to 1887. Credit for first using the word in this manner has been given to one of New York City's finest, a police officer named Williams (*American Notes & Queries*, 10/45). Learning that he was to be transferred to the precinct west of Broadway, between Twenty-third and Forty-second streets, Williams is said to have exclaimed, "I've had nothing but chuck for a long time, but now I'm going to get me some tenderloin!" The term soon went national, as in "Portland is not a puritanic city. In fact, its tenderloin is extensive and worse than anything in San Francisco" (*San Francisco Argonaut*, 11/2/03).

See also PURLOIN.

slang. The origin of the term for "nonstandard" language is not known, but it definitely does not honor a Dutch general by the name of Slangeuburg, said to have been especially adept at chewing out his troops; nor is it of Italian origin, stemming from the negative *s-* + *lingua*, language, i.e., *slingua*, bad language.

Slang has been dated to 1756, with the *OED*'s earliest attestation coming from the cant of tramps and thieves in William Toldervy's *The History of 2 Orphans*. Because *slang* and *sling* may be cognates (and were used interchangeably in some senses in the seventeenth century, when a spit of land or a small cannon could be either a *slang* or a *sling*), it has been suggested that the term might come from the Old Icelandic *slyngva*, sling, via the Norwegian *sleng*, a peculiarity of style in speech or writing. (*Sleng* appears in such compounds as *slengord*, to taunt, to jeer, and *slengjakeften*, to abuse—literally, to sling the jaw.)

The derivation of our *slang* from *sleng* and *slyngva* is just guesswork.

But while the origin of *slang*, like that of so many slang words, is quite obscure, we at least have, courtesy of Carl Sandburg, an unusually good, practical definition of the term: "Slang is a language that rolls up its sleeves, spits on its hands, and goes to work" (*New York Times*, 2/13/59). See also CANT.

son of a gun. The standard explanation for this phrase apparently dates from *The Sailor's Wordbook* (1867), by a British admiral, William Henry Smyth, who described it as "an epithet conveying contempt in a sleight degree, and originally applied to boys born afloat, when women were permitted to accompany their husbands to sea; one admiral declared he literally was thus cradled, under the breast of a gun-carriage." Other writers have embellished this, saying that babies were delivered on a screened-off portion of the gun deck and that in cases of doubtful parentage, the child would be entered into the ship's log as "son of a gun."

It is a puzzle, however, why no girl babies were ever born on British ships of war. The earliest *son of a gun* in the *OED* comes from 1708. You would think that at least one *daughter of a gun* must have appeared in the next couple of centuries, but the record is bare. (*To kiss the gunner's daughter* was quite another thing; the sailor who did this was tied, or "married," to a gun while being flogged.) It surely is significant, too, that *son of a gun* was used at least from the early nineteenth century to mean "A soldier's bastard" ("Jon Bee," *A Dictionary of the Turf*, etc., 1823).

All in all, Admiral Smyth's explanation looks a bit too pat, like a Victorian attempt to find a polite, literal meaning for a phrase that has always been used principally in a figurative manner—as a euphemism for "son of a bitch." See also GUNSEL.

S.O.S. The international Morse code distress call sometimes is said to be an acronym. For example, during the inquiry in 1912 into the sinking of the *Titanic*, the British Attorney-General said the older signal *C.Q.D.* had been used instead of *S.O.S.*, which, he explained, meant *Save Our Souls*. Other spurious acronyms for *S.O.S.* include *Save Our Ship, Stop Other Signals, Sure Of Sinking,* and *Sink Or Swim*. In fact, the letters are meaningless. They were selected at the Radio Telegraph Conference in 1906 because they are easy to transmit in moments of stress. In Morse, the code for *S* is three dots and that for *O* is three dashes, so the distress call consists simply of the alternating series (. . . - - - . . .). The previous international signal, *C.Q.D.*, also was subject to various interpretations, e.g., *C*ome *Q*uickly *D*istress, *C*ome *Q*uickly *D*anger, and *C*ome *Q*uickly *D*arling.

sovereign. The term for a monarch, governor, or other person with supreme authority came into English around 1290 as *soverein* or *sovereyn*. The word soon began to acquire a *g*, most likely because people assumed that a *sovereign* must *reign*. The transitional *soveraigne* has been dated to 1357, and the almost modern *sovereigne* to 1377. The word derives from the Old French *soverain* and, ultimately, the Latin *super*, over.

spencer. The name for the short, close-fitting overcoat or jacket, popular with both sexes during the nineteenth century (the female model often had fur trim in lieu of collar and lapels), honors George John, the second Earl Spencer (1758–1834). But folk etymologists rarely leave well enough alone. Thus, Edward Radford's *Unusual Words* (1946) reports, without any confirming evidence, that the Earl "wagered that he could set a new fashion simply by appearing in the streets in any new kind of garment. He wore what is now called a spencer, and won his bet."

Then there is the elaborate story conveyed in *Pullen's Etymological Compendium* (revised by M. A. Thoms, 1853):

> His Lordship, when Lord-lieutenant of Ireland, being out a-hunting, had, in the act of leaping a fence, the misfortune to have one of the skirts of his coat torn off; upon which his lordship tore off the other. Observing, that to have but one left was like a pig with one ear! Some inventive genius took the hint, and having made some of these half-coats, out of compliment to his lordship, gave them the significant cognomen of *Spencer!*

But this account, too, lacking a date and referring only to the vague "some inventive genius," crumbles upon inspection. Ernest Weekley dismissed it with the comment, "This is what Pooh-bah calls 'corroborative detail intended to give artistic verisimilitude to bald and unconvincing narrative' " (*The Romance of Words*, 1912).

Whatever his reasons for cutting off the tails of his jacket, the Earl, who was First Lord of the Admiralty (1794–1801), did set a precedent for a modern commander, General Dwight D. Eisenhower, who produced the similarly abbreviated *Ike jacket*, a personal fashion that became part of the official uniform of the United States Army.

spinster. The origin of this now archaic term for an unmarried woman, usually an older one, has been attributed to a Massachusetts law of 1665 that required each household to spin yarn and weave cloth in proportion to the number of females in the family. This makes a nice story, except that the word has been dated to 1362, more than a century before Columbus "encountered" (to use the politically correct term) the New World, and some three hundred years before the Puritans enacted the law in question.

Spinster is related to *spin*, however, deriving from the Middle English *spinnen*, to spin + *stere*, one who does. Though technically neutral, the *-stere* suffix usually was employed in a feminine sense. As a result, when men began moving into the occupation, it was felt necessary to distinguish female spinsters from their male colleagues by devising *spinstress* (from 1643). In the same way, *sempster* became *sempstress*, or *seamstress*, and *songster* evolved into *songstress*. (The use of the original *-stere* suffix mainly for women also is apparent—the world being what it is—from its pejorative effect in such words as *gangster*, *punster*, *rhymester*, and *trickster*.)

Male *spinsters* were always a minority, however, and the occupational label became the legal designation for an unmarried female from the seventeenth through nineteenth centuries. The term often was appended to a person's name, as in "Constantia Neville, spinster, of no place at all" (Oliver Goldsmith, *She Stoops to Conquer*, 1773). The currently dominant sense of the word, referring to a woman who is above the usual age of marriage—that is, an old maid—has been dated to 1719.

spitting image. The "polite" explanation of this phrase for describing a person who looks exactly the same as another is that it is a corruption of "spirit and image," as in, for example, "Harry is the very spirit and image of his father." This theory assumes that the phrase arose in the American South, where people often omit their *r*'s, with the result that *spirit and* might well have evolved along the lines of *spi'it and, spi't 'en, spit'n, spitting.*

Lexical evidence suggests that the phrase is of British origin, however, and that the reference really is to saliva. Thus, *The Oxford English Dictionary* includes examples of *spit* from British sources in various forms (e.g., *spitten* and *splitten*) and with different additions (*image* and *picture*), going back to 1859, and "He would be the very spit and fetch of Queen Cleopatra" (G. A. Sala, *Gaslight and Daylight*). Before that, *spit* alone had a long history of being employed to denote an exact likeness, both as a noun, e.g., from the *Newgate Calendar* of 1825, "A daughter . . . the very spit of the old captain," and as a verb, "Twoo girles . . . the one as like an Owle, the other as like an Urchin, as if they had been spitte out of the mouthes of them" (Nicholas Breton, *Wonders Worth the Hearing*, 1602). Still further back in the mists of time, *The Oxford Dictionary of English Proverbs* traces "As like as one as if he had been spit out of his mouth" to about 1400. The *spitting image*, then, is purely physical, not spiritual, and essentially a redundancy, with *spit* and *image* both referring to exact resemblance.

spud. The slang term for a potato is of somewhat vague origin, but the suggested acronym, *S*ociety for the *P*revention of an *U*nhealthy *D*iet, can be dismissed out of hand. The word has been dated to 1845, surfacing first in E. J. Wakefield's *Adventure in New Zealand*: "Pigs and potatoes were respectively represented by '*grunters*' and '*spuds*.'" The term for the potato probably derives from the name of a narrow-bladed tool used for digging it up, i.e., "We . . . began with a spudd to lift up the ground" (Samuel Pepys, *Diary*, 10/10/1667). The name of the digging instrument, in turn, comes from the Middle English *spudde*, a short or poor knife or dagger (from ca. 1440).

stickler. The attitude of the perfectionist who pays unyielding attention to the smallest details often is associated with the straightness and rigidity of a *stick*. At first glance, early uses of the term would seem to bear this out, since a *stickler* originally (from 1538, *OED*) was the moderator or umpire at a tournament, fencing match, or other contest— and such officials did use sticks or staffs to separate opponents. The noun comes from the verb *stickle*, however, and the verb, in turn, is a variant of *stightle* (from before 1300) and the still older, Anglo-Saxon (ca. 825) *stihtan*, to set in order, arrange, place. The modern meaning of *stickler* as one who insists or contends stubbornly for a cause or principle, or who is simply fussy about adhering to time-honored procedure or ceremonies, has been dated to 1644.

stir. The *stir* that is a jail has been construed as a spin-off from the *stir* that is a movement, the idea being that prison inmates can hardly stir. (A faint reflection, perhaps, of "not a creature was stirring, not even a mouse," in Clement Clarke Moore's "A Visit from St. Nicholas," 1823.) A more learned guess is that the term derives from the Anglo-Saxon *stēor, stȳr,* discipline, punishment, penalty. Neither theory is very satisfactory, however. The first supposes that the facility's name depends on a negative quality, while the second requires a very long jump in time, from ca. 1200 to 1851, when the term was first recorded in its pent-up sense by Henry Mayhew: "I was in Brummagem, and was seven days in the new 'stir' " (*London Labour and the London Poor*).

A much more likely origin was proposed by Eric Partridge in the first edition of *A Dictionary of Slang and Unconventional English* (1937), i.e., that the term derives from the Gypsy *staripen,* a prison. As with most underworld words, the precise line of development is obscure. Possible intermediates between *staripen* and *stir* include *sturiben, stardo,* and *start.* (London's Newgate prison was known as *The Start* or *The Old Start* at least as far back as 1747.) Ultimately, as Partridge has pointed out, the Gypsy term is akin to the Latin *stare,* to stand (*Adventuring Among Words,* 1961). This makes etymological sense, considering that prisoners do more standing around than stirring in a stir. See also BRIDEWELL and CLINK.

stool pigeon. The underworld word for an informer—a *stoolie,* for short—looks as though it must certainly be related to the stool pigeon that is a decoy, tied to a stool or similar perch in order to lure other birds to their destruction. And there are reports of hunters' using pigeons in this manner, e.g., "Stool-Pigeon . . . In the former [literal signification] means the pigeon, with its eyes stitched up, fastened on a stool, which can be moved up and down by the hidden fowler" (M. Schele De Vere, *Americanisms,* 1872).

In actuality, the *stool* in *stool pigeon* is more likely to be an American variant of the much older *stale* or *stall,* both of which were used to refer to a decoy bird prior to 1500, as in "Stale, of fowlynge or byrdys takynge, *stationaira*" (*OED,* ca. 1440). Significantly, considering the apparent underworld origins of *stool pigeon* (from at least the 1830s), both *stale* and *stall* have long criminal records, referring specifically to the person who acts as a decoy for a thief or pickpocket. *Stale* also meant "prostitute" in Elizabethan times (Shakespeare used the word in this sense) because working women often set up their customers to be robbed. As for *stall* (and demonstrating that the modus operandi of pickpockets has not changed in four hundred years): "They see him drawe his purse, then spying in what place he puts it uppe, the stall or the shadowe, being with the Foist or Nip, meets the man at some straight turne and justles him" (Robert Greene, *The Art of Cony Catching,* 1591).

Thus, the *stale* and *stall* were essentially duplicitous, and *stool pigeon* really translates as "decoy-bird pigeon." See also FINK.

straitjacket. By binding the arms against the body, the garment holds a person straight, and, indeed, *straightjacket* is accepted as an alternate spelling. *Strait* and *straight* are quite different words, however. The first comes from the Latin *strictus*, past participle of *stringere*, to bind or draw tight. The second is an Anglo-Saxon term, from *streht*, past participle of *streccan*, to extend, to stretch. The same distinction applies to a narrow channel between two larger bodies of water—a strait, which may or may not be straight—as well as to *straitlaced*, sometimes spelled *straight-laced*, and to the pathway through life, known as the *straight and narrow* (also spelled *strait and narrow*), which is followed by all straight-faced, straight-thinking straight arrows.

Straitjacket has been dated to 1814. The earliest example in the *OED*, from a letter by Sir Walter Scott, gives some indication of the advances that have been made in the past two centuries in treatment of the mentally disturbed: "A madman, whom . . . he has . . . by the wholesome discipline of a bull's pizzle [the animal's penis makes a good whip] and strait-jacket, brought to . . . his senses."

surname. The word for a person's last, or family, name has been interpreted as coming from *sir-name* or *sire-name*, partly because nobles were the first to acquire these extra handles and partly because the term's initial syllable often was spelled *sir-* or *sire-* up to the start of the nineteenth century, e.g., "Two innovations devised in the eleventh and twelfth centuries: the adoption of sirnames, and of amorial bearings" (Henry Hallam, *View of the State of Europe During the Middle Ages,* 1818). The *sur-*, however, has nothing to do with knightly rank or parentage. Rather, it comes from the Middle English *sur-*, over, above, beyond, in addition. Thus, *surname*—modeled on the Norman French *surnoun*, with the same meaning—actually translates as "over name" or "above name," i.e., the name in addition to a person's Christian name. The Middle English prefix, which also shows up in such terms as *surcharge, surtax,* and *survey,* has the same Old French ancestor as the modern French *sur*, on, upon, over, above, etc. The Latin root is *super-*, above.

sycophant. On the literal level, the etymology of this term for a toady or flatterer is clear enough. It is basically Greek, *sukophántēs*, from *sukon*, fig + *phántēs*, one who shows (from *phaínein*, show, also the ancestor of such words as *fantasy, focus,* and *phantasm*). To the ancient Greeks, a *sukophántēs* was an informer. But what are the connections between the act of showing a fig, informing on someone, and engaging in abject flattery?

The traditional explanation, passed on by Plutarch, is that it was once forbidden to export figs from Attica. The sycophant, according to this interpretation, was a person who informed upon smugglers of figs. A variant of this theory is that exportation of figs wasn't actually banned, but that the smugglers were evading a tariff. In another version, the sycophant informed upon people taking figs from sacred groves. Whatever, talebearers have never been admired, and any of these explanations might account for the connection between "fig shower" and "informer," except that none of them, not even Plutarch's, has been substantiated.

Equally unproven, but much more likely, is that the fig was a metaphor from the beginning—that is, not a real fig but a fist with the thumb inserted between the first two fingers. This is a well-known obscene gesture in Mediterranean lands, where it is known as "the fig." Shakespeare and other English writers have rendered it variously as *fico, figo, fig,* and *the fig of Spain.* The hand gesture means the same as that with middle finger upraised. The allusion is to the fruit's appearance. The fig is the vulva; the thumb is the penis. In Italian, *fica* means both *fig* and *vulva*. The association is ancient: "Pick your figs. May his be large and hard. May hers be sweet" (Aristophanes, *The Peace,* 422 B.C.). According to this interpretation, then, the sycophant was so called because he made the sign of the fig when denouncing lawbreakers of all sorts, with the term eventually acquiring its modern meaning (1575, *OED*) because informers and other tattletales often slant their stories in order to ingratiate themselves with authorities.

By contrast with the hand gesture, which is supported by much circumstantial evidence, the traditional explanation of *sycophant*'s origin seems to be an imaginary figment. (That's from Latin *fingere,* to mold, to fashion, not from the fig that grows on a tree.)

T

tabby cat. The name of the feline with the striped or brindled coat often is assumed to represent the pet form of the personal name Tabitha. This is hardly surprising, considering that elderly single women frequently have cats for companions and that Tabitha ("gazelle" in Aramaic) was once such a popular female name that its diminutive, *tabby*, became generic for any elderly maiden lady, particularly a gossip, or one with a spiteful, catlike disposition.

Feline and person were joined most memorably by Beatrix Potter in the form of Tabitha Twitchet, mother of the hero of *The Tale of Tom Kitten*, published in 1904, just about the time that Tabitha began losing popularity as a given name in Great Britain. (The modest revival in the 1960s of *Tabitha*, sometimes spelled *Tabatha*, is credited in *The New American Dictionary of Baby Names*, by Leslie Dunkling and William Gosling, to the sequel to the TV series *Bewitched*, starring Tabatha, daughter of Samantha.)

The name of the cat has nothing to do with the female name, however. The animal is called a *tabby cat* because its coat looks like striped, tabby cloth. The word for the cloth, in turn, comes from the Arabic *Al-attābīya*, the quarter in Baghdad where it was manufactured. And the quarter was named for a Prince 'Attāb, not an Aunt Tabitha. See also GRIN LIKE A CHESHIRE CAT.

taffrail. The rail that runs around the stern of a vessel got its name through folk etymology. The term comes from the Dutch *tafferel*, a panel for carving or painting, and ultimately from the Latin *tabula*, table. *Tafferel* was applied initially (from 1622–23, *OED*) to the flat part of the stern, often decorated with carvings or pictures. The English soon began to associate the foreign word with *rail*, however, as indicated by the following dictionary entry: "*Tafferel*, is the uppermost Part, Frame, or Rail of a Ship abaft over the Poop" (John Harris, *Lexicon Technicum, or An Universal English Dictionary of Arts and Sciences*, 1704). And during the nineteenth century, *taffrail* supplanted *tafferel* in both spelling and meaning.

tariff. The Moorish occupants of Tarifa, a fortified seaport at the entrance of the Mediterranean (some twenty miles to the west of Gibraltar), probably taxed vessels passing through the strait. But the *tariff* that is a tax or duty on imports and exports has only a coincidental resemblance to the place name, even though both are of Arabic origin.

Tariff denoted a table or statement, such as a multiplication table, before being applied to a schedule of customs duties or a scale of charges generally, such as a hotel tariff or a railroad tariff. The English word (from 1591), like the French *tarif*, the Italian *tariffa*, and the Spanish *tarifa*, derives from the Arabic *ta'rīf*, information, notification, in turn from *'arafa*, to notify. The present name of the port (originally colonized by Romans) comes from Tarif, commander of the advance guard of the Moorish invasion of Spain in 711.

tedium. The term for boredom or wearisome monotony comes from the Latin *taedium*, itself from the verb, *taedēre*, to bore, to weary, rather than, as sometimes said, from *Te Deum*, the Latin hymn of praise, so called from its opening words, *Te Deum laudamus*, Thee God we praise. The liturgical theory presumably reflects the boredom of amateur etymologists who would rather stay at home reading dictionaries than go to church on Sundays. As explanations go, this one is on a par with the theory that the British expression *my eye* or, in full, *all my eye and Betty Martin*, derives from a prayer to St. Martin of Tours, patron saint of drunkards, that begins *O mihi, beate Martine*, Oh grant me, blessed Martin . . . which seems quite plausible, except that no such prayer is contained in the Breviary. (The true origin of the latter expression is uncertain; it may come from the name of an eighteenth-century actress whose favorite expression was "My eye" or, as the French say with the same intent, *mon oeil*.)

For more about the presumed influence of liturgical Latin on English, see HOCUS-POCUS.

ten-gallon hat. A high-crowned ten-gallon hat looks as though it might hold a lot of water, perhaps even ten gallons, but the name refers to the way the hats originally were decorated, deriving from the Mexican Spanish *sombrero galón*, hat with braids.

tenpenny nail. The three-inch nails were never priced at ten for a penny, not even in the fifteenth century, when nails and pennies were both worth a lot more than they are today. The original cost was ten cents, or pennies, per hundred nails. The term has been dated to 1426–27 as "x penynayl" in the records of a London church, St. Mary at Hill.

third degree, the. This term for a prolonged police interrogation, typically accompanied by force or the threat of it, often is assumed to be connected with the degrees in the criminal code, such as murder in the first degree, murder in the second degree, and so on. The expression comes from Freemasonry, however, in which the rank of Master Mason, traditionally the highest, or third degree, is conferred only after the candidate has undergone a long and arduous examination of his abilities and qualifications. (The first two rungs on the Mason's ladder are the Apprentice degree and the Fellow Craft degree, though finer distinctions are made in some orders; the Ancient and Accepted Scottish Rite, for example, has thirty-three degrees of masonhood.)

Third degree has been dated to 1772 in its Masonic sense and to 1880 in the sense of a severe interrogation of a non-Mason. Oddly, the earliest example of the latter in *The Oxford English Dictionary* does not come from a police report but from the more effete pages of the *Harvard Lampoon*: "He met the large and celebrated brother of one of his houries. He stopped to greet him, and was surprised at receiving a clip over the head from the brother's cane. This was followed by a personal chastisement in the third degree" (2/6/1880).

three golden balls. The traditional sign of pawnbrokers often is said to derive from the coat of arms of the Medici, whose banking house was the key to the family's domination of Florence from the fifteenth to the early eighteenth centuries. (An alternate explanation of the symbol as meaning that those who hock something have a two-to-one chance of getting it back is simply a joke that some people have taken seriously.)

The Medici never acted as pawnbrokers, however. They sometimes held crown jewels, miters, and other valuable articles as security on their loans to princes and popes, but they did not lend small sums to working people on the basis of clothing, tools, or comparable items. The family arms, moreover, featured six balls, not three, and they were red ones on a field of gold. The significance of the six balls is not known. E. Cobham Brewer suggested in his *Dictionary of Phrase and Fable* that they were supposed to represent pills, but this is very doubtful, since none of the early Medici is known to have been a *medico*—Italian for "physician."

In actuality, the three balls in the pawnbroker's sign almost certainly stand for the golden coins from Byzantium known as bezants. The coat of arms of the Arte del Cambio of Florence, the moneychangers' guild, also featured bezants. The coin was a traditional symbol for money in medieval art and heraldry, and this provides sufficient explanation for its association with pawnbrokers. See also BALL.

tinker's dam (or damn), not worth a. Both the tinker and his dam (or damn—the two are used interchangeably) have provoked more than their share of etymologizing.

The tinker was an itinerant mender of pots and pans. Like other mobile tradesmen (the scissors sharpener, the ice-cream man, etc.), he rang a bell to announce his presence in the neighborhood. Hence, it has been supposed that *tinker* derives from the *tink* or *tinkle* of his bell. (Remember *Peter Pan* and Tinkerbell?) This explanation is of some venerability, having been put forth at least as early as the fifteenth century: "tinker; and he takes his name from the sound of the trade, like the bell" (*Promptorium Parvulorum* [Young Scholar's Storeroom], ca. 1440). Dr. Johnson bought this theory, declaring in *A Dictionary of the English Language* (1755) that the occupational designation came "From *tink*, because their way of proclaiming their trade is to beat a kettle, or because in their work they make a tinkling sound." Many modern etymologists agree.

The principal difficulty with the onomatopoeic hypothesis is that *tinker* is dated in the *OED* to ca. 1265 (and before that, to 1252, as a surname, *Tynker*), well before the earliest recorded appearance of either of its presumed progenitors, *tink* and *tinkle*, both from the Wyclif translation of the Bible of 1382. This is not an insurmountable objection, partly because words often are used for many years before being committed to writing for the benefit of compilers of dictionaries, and partly because of the existence from an early date (ca. 1175) of the related *tinkler* in the sense of a worker in metal, especially a Gypsy or other itinerant repairer of pots and pans. Muddying the etymological waters still further, however, is the use of *tink* as a verb, meaning to mend a pot or pan. Though dated only to the fifteenth century, *tink* theoretically could be either the source of *tinker* or a back-formation from it.

Thus, the written record is sufficiently ambiguous to leave open the possibility that *tinker* has an entirely different origin, perhaps deriving from *tin*, via the Middle English *tinekerre*, tin worker. In this connection, the form of the word in the *OED*'s earliest example seems significant. The citation (of additional interest for showing that the profession was a liberated one from an early date) is from the tax rolls of Wallingford, in which the lowest assessment, two pence, is that of "Editha le Tynekere."

As puzzling as the etymology of *tinker* is, many trackers of word origins slide right by this issue, focusing instead on the *dam* or *damn*. The full phrase, *not worth a tinker's dam*, has been dated to 1877, when it appeared, as though from the brow of Zeus, complete with an etymology: *"Tinker's-dam*, a wall of dough raised around a place which a plumber desires to flood with a coat of solder. The material can be but once used; being consequently thrown away as worthless, it has passed into a proverb, usually involving the wrong spelling of the otherwise innocent 'dam' " (Edward H. Knight, *The Practical Dictionary of Mechanics*).

With all due respect to Mr. Knight, this explanation reeks of Victorian propriety. The *damn* form of the phrase seems to be at least a couple of generations older, with the earliest example in the *OED* coming from the journal of Henry David Thoreau: " 'Tis true they are not worth a 'tinker's damn' " (4/25/1839). Why Thoreau put *tinker's damn* within quotes is not immediately apparent. Perhaps it was his way of diffusing the power of the *damn*. Or perhaps the expression was new to him. Certainly, he is unlikely to have invented it, considering the existence of the older "not worth a damn" (Byron's diary, 1817), "not worth a curse" (*Blackwood's Magazine*, 1826), or, as a later writer, Charles Farrar Browne, a.k.a. Artemus Ward, put it: "Not keering a tinker's cuss" (*His Book*, 1865). The similar *not care a damn* and *not care a curse* have been traced back to the 1760s and the works of such distinguished men of letters as Thomas Jefferson and Oliver Goldsmith.

In sum, the damn-curse-cuss variations may have gotten some impetus from the disposable dams that tinkers built, but given the reputation of vagabonds and Gypsies generally, and tinkers particularly, for profane language, loose living, stealing, and pretending to be beggars (tinkers were prosecuted as vagrants under Elizabethan law and with some reason; see BOOZE), it seems quite likely that *tinker* is an addition—an intensifier—to the older phrase, and that the nineteenth-century *dam* is, in fact, essentially a euphemism for the original *damn*.

tip. The word for the gratuity often is said to be an acronym for *To Insure Promptness* or, a variant, *To Improve Performance*. The initials, so the story goes, originally appeared on offering boxes in eighteenth-century inns and coffeehouses. Unfortunately, no authenticated boxes of this sort have survived for resale in curio shops. Nor did Dr. Johnson or any of the other exceedingly literate gentlemen who patronized these establishments ever mention such a kitty in their voluminous writings.

The derivation is pure folk etymology, of course, on a par with the supposed acronymic origins of CABAL, COP, GORP, NEWS, and WOP.

Still, there is a minor mystery here. As a slang word, *tip*'s early history is not well recorded, leaving the field open for other theories about its origin. Among them: that it derives from *stipend* (a payment), that it comes from *tipple* (heavy tippers often being associated with heavy tippling), and that it is an alteration of *tap*, which is what patrons of bars sometimes do with coins when they wish to attract the attention of the dispenser of liquid cheer.

The last of these guesses, *tap*, probably is closest to the mark, though for the wrong reasons. *Tip* in the sense of a present of small change to a servant or employee is recorded first in George Farquhar's *The Beaux Strategem* (1706–7): "Then I, Sir, tips me the Verger with half a crown." This probably stems from the earlier cant use of the word (from 1610, *OED*) among rogues and thieves in the sense of "to give, to hand, to let one have," as in "Tip the cole to Adam Tiler," which was translated for ordinary working stiffs in Elisha Coles's *English Dictionary* (1676) as "give the (stoln) money to your (running) Comrade." And this form of *tip*, in turn, may well be a variant of *tap*, in the general sense of a light blow, a touch, but without reference to the click of a coin on a bartop.

titmouse. The name of the songbird has nothing to do with "mouse" or that other thing. The second syllable comes from the Anglo-Saxon *mase*, cognate to the German *meise*, a small bird, a titmouse. The conversion to -*mouse*, perhaps aided by the smallness and quickness of the bird as well as by the similarity in sound, has resulted in the commonly accepted but technically incorrect plural *titmice*. See also DORMOUSE.

As to the first part of the bird's name, it is of Scandinavian origin, akin to Norse *tittr*, tack, pin, appearing also in other bird names, e.g., *titlark* and *tomtit*, as well as *titbit*, which is an alternate form of *tidbit*. In bygone times, the word also applied to small horses, especially fillies, and to girls, especially hussies or other pert young things. Though usually deprecatory, the term could be used in an affectionate way, e.g., "I am sure from Lady Tavistock that she thinks the Queen [Victoria] a resolute little tit" (*A Selection from the Correspondence and Diaries of the Late Thomas Creevey a 1838*, 1903).

Still another kind of *tit* is the one that appears in *tit for tat*, but this is a variant of the older *tip for tap*, blow for blow, contrary to the sense implicit in the comeback attributed to Mark Twain:

HOSTESS. I am told you are a great wit, but tonight I shall give you tit for tat.

TWAIN. Tat, Madam.

toast. The custom of drinking toasts, originally to ladies of particular beauty or social esteem, seems to have arisen around 1700, and within a short time people began debating the origin of the term. In one way or another, it appears the lady in question was being compared to the piece of spiced toast that our ancestors formerly put in wine and other drinks, including water, to improve the taste of the beverages. Thus, Sir Richard Steele explained in *The Tatler* (6/18/1709) that *toast* was "a new Name found out by the Wits to make a Lady have the same effect as Burridge in the Glass when a Man is drinking." (If the famous essayist's prose seems a trifle dense here, burridge, or borage, is a plant whose leaves were used for flavoring, and what he meant to say was that the mere mention of the lady's name had the same effect on one's constitution as the spicy toast itself.)

The *OED* and other dictionaries, including *The American Heritage Dictionary* (1969) and *The Random House Dictionary* (2nd edition, unabridged, 1987), accept Steele's etymology. This was his second pass at explaining the word's origin, however. He initially attributed the sense of *toast* as a drink to an incident at the spa in Bath during the reign of Charles II (1660–85). Steele's first account is marginally less probable than his second one but has the advantage of being a lot more picturesque. As included in *The Tatler* of June 4, 1709:

It happened that on a public day a celebrated beauty . . . was in the Cross Bath, and one of the crowd of her admirers took a glass of water in which the fair one stood and drank her health to the company. There was in the place a gay fellow, half-fuddled, who offered to jump in, and swore, though he liked not the liquor, he would have the toast (that is, the lady herself). He was opposed in his resolution; yet his whim gave foundation to the present honour which is done to the lady we mention in our liquor, who has ever since been called a *toast*.

Other etymologists have attempted to derive this form of *toast* from *toss* or *tossed* as in *to toss a pot*, to drink, and *tosspot*, a drunkard, but these theories lack supporting evidence as well as romantic imagination.

tobacco. The noxious weed is not named after the island of Tobago, as was first suggested just a few years after Sir John Hawkins introduced the custom of smoking to England in 1565, e.g., "The proper name of it [the herb] amongest the Indians is *Piecielt*, for the name of Tobaco is geven to it of our Spaniardes by reason of an Ilande that is named Tobaco" (John Frampton, tr., *Monardes' Ioyfull Newes Out of the Newe Founde Worlde*, 1577).

This early report to the contrary, the island probably was named after the plant. (See BRAZILWOOD for a parallel example.) The real question is which hemisphere the plant name came from. Traditionally, *tobacco* is said to derive from a Spanish rendering of a Carib word for either the tube used for smoking or for a cigarlike roll of tobacco leaves. Prior to Columbus's encounter with the New World, however, Spanish *tabaco* and Italian *tabacco* were used to refer to various plants with medicinal applications. Both probably come from the Arabic *tabāq*, a euphoria-causing herb. This raises the possibility that the Europeans transferred a word they already knew to the American plant instead of picking up the Carib term for it. (See TURKEY for a parallel of his sort.)

The first Europeans to try tobacco, by the way, quickly realized something that is often not fully appreciated by smokers until they have quit the habit and ballooned in size. Thus, from an account by Hawkins of one of his voyages to the New World:

> The Floridians when they travell have a kinde of herbe dried, who with a cane and earthen cap at the end, with fire, and with the dried herbs put together, doe sucke thorow the cane the smoke therof, which smoke satisfieth their hunger, and therwith they live foure or five dayes without meat or drinke, and this all the Frenchmen used for this purpose.

train oil. The coarse oil obtained by boiling the blubber of whales and other marine animals was once used for making candles and soaps but not for lubricating the wheels or other movable parts of railroad engines and rolling stock. *Train* here comes from the Dutch *traan*, tear, dripping, oil, so the literal meaning of *train oil* (from ca. 1553, *OED*) is "oil oil."

tram. Thanks to the tropism of folk etymologists toward eponymic solutions, Benjamin Outram, owner of a quarry in Derbyshire, who experimented with carts on stone rails at the beginning of the nineteenth century, has been credited with the invention of tram cars. According to this story, popularized in an 1857 biography of George Stephenson, a pioneer locomotive builder, *tram* was formed as a contraction of "Outram way"—a derivation that the Reverend Walter W. Skeat dismissed with unusual asperity as "ridiculous; it ignores the accent and contradicts the history" (*A Concise Etymological Dictionary of the English Language*, 1910). Skeat's comment applies in spades to another presumed progenitor, General Sir James Outram, who managed to play a heroic role in putting down the Indian Mutiny of 1857 but apparently without benefit of Outram ways, let alone trams.

Tramway, meaning the track over which the vehicle progresses, did play a part in *tram*'s evolution, but the process began long before the birth of Benjamin Outram or General Outram. *Tram* surfaced first in Scottish around 1500 to refer to the shafts of a wagon or wheelbarrow. The term probably was borrowed from the Middle Flemish *tram*, beam, handle of a barrow, perhaps akin to the Middle Dutch *trame*, beam, and the Old Norse *thrōmr, thram*, with the same meaning. Often employed in connection with carts used in mining, *tram* came to be applied to the way, road, track, or rails—originally of timber or stone—on which vehicles ran, e.g., from a will of 1555: "To the amendinge of the highwaye or tram, from the west ende of Bridgegait, Barnard Castle, 20s" (in Ernest Weekley, *An Etymological Dictionary of Modern English*, 1921). *Tramroad* has been dated to 1799 (as *Dram Road*), *tramway* to 1825, and *tram*, meaning a *tram car*, or street car, to 1879. See also CANT.

troy weight. The system for measuring precious metals, gems, and drugs (of the sort sold by apothecaries) often is associated with the proverbial richness of ancient Troy, but it actually is named after the city of Troyes in northeastern France.

Troyes was a center of international commerce in medieval times, hosting two of six annual Fairs of Champagne—the great Hot Fair in July–August and the smaller Cold Fair in November–December. In the system of weights that evolved at these fairs, a pound was divided into 12 ounces, with each ounce equal to 20 pennyweight, or 480 grains. Thus, the troy pound has 5,760 grains, compared with 7,000 grains in the 16-ounce pound avoirdupois (from the Old French *aveir de peis*, property having weight), the system developed in medieval times for measuring sugar, salt, grain, wines, and other commodities, and which we now use for weighing everything except precious metals, gems, and medicines.

tuberose. A rose is a rose is a rose, but a *tuberose* is not a *tube rose*, nor is it even a *rose*. The English word for the plant is a popular corruption of its Latin name, *tuberosa*, feminine of *tūberōsus*, tuberous. Thus, the name of the plant comes from its roots, not its fragrant, creamy white, lilylike flowers. See also PRIMROSE and ROSEMARY.

turkey. The great American bird—Ben Franklin thought it should be the national emblem—is named after Turkey, the nation, but by mistake. The term was applied originally (1541, *OED*) to an African bird, the guinea fowl, known variously, depending upon sex, as the *turkeycock* or *turkey-hen*. The English apparently saddled the fowl with the wrong name because the first specimens were imported through Turkish dominions. The error then was compounded by assuming that the New World turkey, found domesticated by the Spanish when they invaded Mexico in 1518, was the same as the African bird or a species of it. The earliest example in the *OED* of an American *turkey* that should have been given a Native American name comes from 1555. (Other New World critters fared better; for example, *chipmunk, moose, raccoon,* and *skunk* all derive from Algonquian dialects.) The suitability of turkey for a meal on festive occasions was quickly realized. Thus, from 1573: "Christmas husbandrie fare . . . shred pies of the best . . . and turkey well drest" (Thomas Tusser, *Fiue Hundreth Pointes of Good Husbandrie*). See also GUINEA PIG and TOBACCO.

tweed. Scotland is famous for producing the rugged woolen cloth, and the River Tweed does form part of the border between Scotland and England, but the term for the fabric is a misnomer. *Tweed* began as a trade name, apparently coined about 1831 by the London hatter James Locke (James Lock & Co. is still in business), who misread the Scottish *tweel*, a variant of *twill*, i.e., a fabric with diagonal, parallel ribs. Probably, Mr. Locke had the name of the river in the back of his mind at the time. See also BOWLER, DIAPER, and VALANCE.

U

union suit. The undergarment, a.k.a. long johns, that combines shirt and drawers in a single piece was never worn by members of the Union Army. The association of the underwear with Federal forces probably was popularized by a turn-of-the-century joke about Robert E. Lee's showing up for the surrender at Appomattox in full dress regalia, while U. S. Grant arrived in his Union suit. The joke was based on fact: Lee did ride up to Wilmer McLean's house on April 9, 1865, wearing a new uniform and carrying a fine sword with a jewel-studded hilt, while Grant arrived in a mud-spattered uniform, looking like an ordinary soldier except for a pair of shoulder straps to indicate his rank. The contrast was due partly to the different personal styles of the commanders and partly to circumstances: Lee, pressed by Federal cavalry a few days before, had been forced to destroy all his baggage except for the clothes on his back, and so naturally had saved his newest uniform, while Grant, separated from his headquarters baggage for several days, had been unable to change clothes for the occasion.

The *union suit* that is worn next to one's skin was not popularized until the 1890s, however. The earliest example of the term in the *OED* comes from the *Ladies' Home Journal* of September 29, 1892. It has been suggested that the name refers to the type of cloth used, *union* also being the name for fabric woven from two fibers, such as cotton and linen, or silk and wool. This seems farfetched, however, considering that such fabric has many uses. The underwear almost certainly was named for its distinguishing characteristic, i.e., the way in which top and bottom are joined in a perfect union. See also B.V.D.'s.

Unready, Ethelred the. The unflattering appellation of the early English King Ethelred the Unready (ca. 968–1016) does not refer to his unreadiness or lack of preparation. *Unready* here means "without *rede*," or counsel. Ethelred often acted in a rash, ill-considered manner.

Whether or not good counsel could have saved Ethelred and his kingdom from the depredations of the Danes is an open question, but his reign certainly consisted of a series of disasters. Weak and self-indulgent, he alternated between purchasing peace from the Northmen and breaking the peace by attacking them. In 1001, he ordered that all

Danish males in the kingdom be killed, and many were, but this just precipitated another invasion from abroad. Ethelred's erratic policy encouraged the Danes to shift their goals from collecting tribute to taking over the country. His kingdom disintegrated, and the enemy was preparing to capture London when he died. Ethelred the Unready's successor was a Dane, Canute the Great. Rudyard Kipling summed it up: "If once you have paid him the Dane-geld, You never get rid of the Dane."

Technically, *Ethelred the Unready* is an oxymoron, or contradiction in terms. The king's given name is formed from *Ethel-*, noble, and *rede*, counsel, so "Ethelred the Unready" translates as "Noble-counsel Without Counsel," which probably explains why the nickname stuck. The *rede* also appears as a suffix in the more familiar *Alfred*, "elf counsel" in Anglo-Saxon, as in Ethelred's predecessor, who defeated an earlier generation of Danes, thereby becoming Alfred the Great.

upside-down. The topsy-turvy sense of the expression evolved from an ambiguous phrase in which *side* did not appear.

The expression first appears in the written record as *up so down*, e.g., in a sad passage from *The Seven Sages*, a romance of the early fourteenth century: "The cradel and the child thai found Up so doun upon the ground." The exact meaning of *so* here is not readily apparent; perhaps it was intended in the sense of "as if"—a legitimate but obsolete sense of *so*. Or perhaps the phrase began as a condensation of "upper side set so it is down." Whatever, *up so down* gradually metamorphosed into *upsadown, upsedown*, and then, as people continued to strive to make sense out of it, *upside-down*. The direct ancestor of the modern version is *yp sid doun*, dated in the *OED* to ca. 1490.

V

vagrant. Because vagrants wander around, it often is assumed that they must be related linguistically as well as actually to vagabonds with no fixed places of abode. *Vagrant*, however, stems from the Norman French *wacrant*, present participle of the Old French *walcrer*, to walk, which itself has a Germanic root, and is cognate to the modern *walk*. The spelling of *vagrant* was influenced by *vagabond* from the time of its appearance in English, however, with the *Rolls of Parliament* for 1444 including a reference to an earlier statute covering "Laborers...Vitaillers, Servauntz and Vagarauntz."

Vagabond, meanwhile, is of classical origin, deriving from the Middle French *vagabonde* and the Late Latin *vagābundus*, wandering, in turn from *vagārī*, to wander, *vagus*, wandering, rambling, undecided (hence, too, the modern *vague* and *vagary*).

In some older texts, dating mainly from the fifteenth and sixteenth centuries, *vagabond* appears as *vacabond*, as in *The Fraternite of Vacabondes* (? John Awdeley, 1561), the original title of a pioneering tract about Elizabethan lowlife. This spelling also was due to a mistake in etymology, the assumption then being that the word for idle wanderers stemmed from the Latin *vacāre*, to be idle or empty (as in the related *vacuum*).

valance. The term commonly is associated with Valence, a town on the Rhône in southeastern France. The connection has not been demonstrated conclusively, however, and another possibility is that the name of the short ornamental drape (from 1463, *OED*) descends, so to speak, from the Old French *avaler*, to go down, to descend, in turn from *à val*, go down, and ultimately the Latin *ad valley*, to the valley. If so, this would make *valance* a cousin to *avalanche*.

While the names of textile products often come from their places of manufacture—*arras* from *Arras*, *denim* from *de Nîmes*, and *jeans* from *Genoa*, for instance—such etymologies have to be examined suspiciously on a case-by-case basis. For examples of false leads, see DIAPER and TWEED.

valentine. St. Valentine gets undue credit for the sentiments expressed annually on his feast day with cards, candies, kisses, etc. Not that a

St. Valentine didn't exist. On the contrary, a number of saints bore that name, with two of them having had the misfortune to be martyred at different times in the third century but reportedly on the same day of the year, February 14. One was a priest of Rome, the other a bishop of Terni. Neither seems to have been associated especially with profane love, nor is the name significant. Valentine, or Valentinus in Latin, derives from *valēre*, to be strong. The connection between affairs of the heart and the Saint's day (or Saints' day, if one wants to be persnickety) seems to have been made on three levels.

First, Valentine's Day celebrations continued, albeit in attenuated form, the Roman festival of Lupercalia, celebrated on February 15. This was a fertility festival, intended to ensure that the land would be fruitful and that flocks would multiply during the coming year. The festival culminated with priests running around the boundary walls of the old city, whipping people with thongs cut from the skins of sacrificial animals. Women crowded forward, as it was believed that a blow from a thong prevented female sterility. The thongs were called *februa*, from *februare*, to purify; hence, our name for the second month of the year.

Second, an obvious association was made between the mating of birds, thought to begin about the time of the saint's day, and the choosing of human sweethearts. Thus, from Geoffrey Chaucer's *The Parlement of Foules* (ca. 1382):

> For this was on seynt Valentynes day,
> Whan every foul cometh ther to chese his make
> [i.e., choose his mate],

The example of the birds was much in the minds of our medieval ancestors. Among *The Paston Letters*, for example, is this note from Elizabeth Brews, encouraging John Paston in 1477 to press his suit for her daughter's hand:

> And, cousin, upon Friday is Saint Valentine's day, and every bird chuseth him a make; and if it like you to come on Thursday at night...I trust to God that ye shall speak to mine husband; and I shall pray that we shall bring the matter to a conclusion.

Third, on a purely linguistic level, and reinforcing the other two associations, St. Valentine seems to have been elected to preside over courtship activities because his name is cognate to the Old French *gal-*

210

atin, a gallant, a lover, from *galer*, to enjoy oneself. Significantly, the Saints Valentine were not the only ones to be martyred on February 14. If the linguistic associations were better, this might have become known as St. Maro's Day, and affections today might be coveyed in the from of Maro cards.

The cards, by the way, were originally lots (from ca. 1553, *OED*) that were drawn to select one's sweetheart for the coming year. The drawings often were held on St. Valentine's Eve, which thus became one of the most important dates in the year for young people. Alternatively, one's special friend for the coming year might be the first person of the opposite sex to be encountered on St. Valentine's Day. And this usually involved careful planning: "This morning came up to my wife's bedside little Will Mercer to be her Valentine. . . . But I am also this year my wife's Valentine" (Samuel Pepys, *Diary*, 2/14/1667). Given the shenanigans that have traditionally surrounded the observance of St. Valentine's Day, the dearth of churches dedicated to this otherwise popular saint should come as no surprise.

van. The *van* that drives down the highway is not the same as the *van* of an army or other group, referring to the lead division or those who are in the forefront of any movement. The vehicular *van* is a shortening of *caravan*, dating from the first part of the nineteenth century. The initial citation in the *OED* comes from an early novel by Bulwer-Lytton: "Yes, Sir, we have some luggage—came last night by the van" (*The Disowned*, 1829). The other *van* is a considerably older term, dated to 1610. It is a clipping of *vanguard*, in turn from an Old French term that yet survives in modern English for those in the advance guard, i.e., *avant-garde*.

vaudeville. Performers on the old Keith and Albee vaudeville circuits went from place to place (the troupers trooped, in effect), but the name of the entertainment has nothing to do with towns, burgs, or -villes, whether real or metaphoric. Nor does the term honor any of the villages in France that actually bear the name Vaudeville. Rather, the word is a thoroughly mixed-up compound of two French phrases, *Vau de Vire*, Valley (or Vale) of the Vire, and *voix de ville*, voices of the city.

Both French phrases involve singing. Vire, capital of Calvados in Normandy, is girded on three sides by the River Vire. The musical reference is to *chansons du Vau de Vire*, songs of the Valley of the Vire. These were drinking songs, often satirizing local personalities, attributed chiefly to Olivier Basselin (ca. 1400–50), a poet and fuller, whose mill is said to have been located in a gorge—the Vau de Vire—outside town. Other, anonymous poets were at work, too, and by 1500 songs of this sort had become popular throughout France as *vaux* (plural) *de vire*.

The next step was the muddling of *vaux de vire* with another musical form, *voix de ville*, or voices of the city, the name given to songs of courtly love. The two terms were combined at least by 1573, with *vau de ville* appearing in the title of a collection of songs published that year. The compound was then collapsed into *vaudeville*, first in French and then in English.

The extended sense of the new word, referring to theatrical sketches interspersed with songs, is an offshoot of the eighteenth-century French *comédie-vaudeville*. The entertainment and the word for it crossed the Channel in the opening decades of the nineteenth century, e.g., "I also had the honour . . . of being selected by her Royal Highness the Princess Elizabeth to write a sort of *vaudeville* farce" (Thomas John Dibdin, *Reminiscences*, 1827).

vicious circle. No one has ever been attacked by a snarling circle. This started out as a logician's term (from 1792, *OED*), deriving from the French *cercle vicieux* and the New Latin *circulous vitiosos*. The true sense of the Latin expression is closer to "faulty or defective circle." To philosophers this meant a circular argument, in which the proof of one statement depended in part on a second statement, whose proof, in turn, depended upon the correctness of the first. In English, though, *vicious* has always been associated strongly with vice (from ca. 1340) and that which is savage, dangerous, and fierce (from 1711). In view of this, it was only natural, if not entirely logical, that the technical philosophical term should acquire a more pejorative meaning as it was adopted outside the profession (from 1839). Thus, *vicious circle* refers most commonly today to a situation or process in which actions and reactions intensify each other, leading to ever greater aggravations and complications, from which there is no escape. Technically, this is not a circle at all and could be described more accurately as a *vicious spiral*.

W

waffle. When someone, typically a politician, *waffles*, he or she equivocates, uttering a lot of syrupy words, and dodging back and forth in a manner that is reminiscent of the crisscross pattern of the *waffle* one eats, also with lots of syrup.

The two words are unrelated, however. The breakfast treat and the name for it were introduced by the Dutch to the American colonies. The word comes from the Dutch *wafel*, honeycomb, which is related to *wafer*, and has been dated in American English to 1744 in the phrase *wafel frolic*, meaning a party at which waffles were served.

The vascillating *waffle* is of less-certain provenance. It became a political vogue word in the mid-1960s, but the sense of equivocation is apparent in *waffler* (1803, *OED*). Prior to that (from 1701) *waffle* was employed in a more general way as a verb to refer to a verbose, inconsequential, nonsensical manner of speaking or writing. Opinion is divided as to whether this form of *waffle* derives from the Scottish and northern English *waff* (from ca. 1440), to wave, to flutter, to be hesitant, or from yet another *waff* (from 1610), to yelp, as a dog does, especially a puppy. Either of the presumed origins fits well with twentieth-century political usage.

wallop. The term for a severe blow, a beating, or a thrashing has been explained as an eponym in one of the more elaborate folk etymologies of this sort. The hero in this instance is Sir John Wallop (ca. 1490–1551), who commanded a flotilla in the war against France in 1513–14. In reprisal for a French raid on the Sussex coast, during which Brightelmstone (now Brighton) was burned, Wallop destroyed twenty-one villages along the enemy's coast. So proud of their achievements were his men that they created the new word for a thrashing by saying that they had "Wallop-ed" the French. Or so it is said.

Unfortunately, no one seems to have written down the boasts of Wallop's men at the time. The oldest known example of *wallop* in the sense of a resounding blow or beating comes from 1823, more than three centuries after the events that supposedly gave rise to it. More likely, then, this meaning of the word echos the sound of a blow. Other possibilities are that *wallop* in the sense of a blow or beating grew out of the term's other meanings, all of which involve violent, noisy actions. These include (1) a heavy, clumsy movement of the body; (2) a bubbling action, as of boiling water; and (3) the word's oldest recorded meaning, from ca. 1350, *gallop*—a related word that superseded *wallop* to denote a horse's fastest gait.

wedlock. Even before divorces became commonplace, to be joined in Holy Wedlock was not the same as being locked into marriage—at least not etymologically. *Wedlock* is a seven-letter Anglo-Saxon word that has been dated to before 1100. It was formed from *wed*, a pledge + *-lāc*, a suffix denoting an activity. Thus, the term originally referred to the matrimonial vow, not the institution of marriage, though it also was employed in the latter sense from the early thirteenth century. Thanks to the influence of *lock*, however, the form of the word began changing. (Chaucer used both *wedlek* and *wedlok* in the fourteenth century.) As this happened, the term's original meaning began to fade, so that today we are left only with the locked-up, institutional sense.

welsh. The inhabitants of Wales look askance at the use of this word to refer to a failure to honor one's obligations, especially gambling debts. As an example of this sensitivity, Ernest Weekley cited the following communication from a Welsh contributor to a British Sunday newspaper in *Word and Names* (1932):

> Welsher, as applied on the race-course, has no reference to the Welsh, but was coined after an incident which happened many years ago on Epsom Downs, the subject of the term being one Bob Welch. Mr. Welch had 'laid the odds,' found he could not pay up, and so cleared off. His emulators have ever since been dubbed Welchers. Unfortunately, the term is invariably misspelt.

Now it is true that *welsh* in the sense of swindling or not paying debts crops up first in connection with racetrack bookmakers. It is true, too, that *welsh* and the operative noun, *welsher*, sometimes are spelled *welch* and *welcher*, as in the oldest examples of each in the *OED*, dating from 1857 and 1860, respectively.

Nevertheless—and the Welsh newspaper correspondent to the contrary—the term has the earmarks of an ethnic slur. The sense of a deadbeat or swindler accords with other disparaging uses of the term, e.g., *Welsh comb*, the thumb and fingers; *Welsh cricket*, a louse; *Welsh diamond*, a rock crystal; and, of course, *Welsh rabbit*, melted cheese on toast. Most likely, then, *welsh* originated as an ethnic insult, following the same all-too-well-worn path as *to gyp* (from *Gypsy*), *to Jew down*, and *Indian giver*.

wench. John Horne Tooke, a radical English politician as well as a philologist, derived this word for a young woman, especially a serving woman or a wanton one, from the Anglo-Saxon *wincian*, to wink, i.e., "One that is *Winked at;* and, by implication, who may be had by a nod or a wink" (*The Diversions of Purley*, 1786–1805).

Tooke may have been drawing partly on practical experience here; an ordained minister who never married, he nevertheless fathered at least three children. He also was on the right track philologically. *Wench* and *wink* are related, both descending from the same Indo-European root, *weng-*, to bend, to curve. Tooke's etymology fails, however, because it seeks to explain the origin of a ninth-century word in terms of meanings that it did not acquire until much later.

Wench's immediate ancestor is *wenchel*, originally a child of either sex (dated in the *OED* to ca. 890 in the form of *wencel*). Thus, the basic implication is not of being winked at but of youthful pliability, with a hint of learning to walk (from the kindred *wancol*, tottering). The shortened *wench* (from ca. 1290) originally referred to a female child, a girl, a young woman; the senses of a maidservant, a wanton woman, and a mistress do not begin to appear in the written record for another several generations. This is a not uncommon progression: *girl* is another word that originally applied to males and females, and that acquired its present demeaning connotations only after it was restricted to women. See also FEMALE, HARLOT, and WOMAN.

Tooke, by the way, should be remembered for more than making a bad guess about *wench*. An ardent supporter of the American colonies in their dispute with England, he signed an advertisement that asked for contributions for the relief of the relatives of Minutemen "murdered by the king's troops at Lexington and Concord." For this, he served a year in prison.

wing it. He who is unprepared and has to improvise, or *wing it*, may be flying by the seat of his pants, so to say, or in the words of the 1943 song, "Comin' In on a Wing and a Prayer," but the expression originated in the world of the theater, not that of aviation. It began as an allusion to the prompter, who stood in the wings of the stage to help actors or actresses who had not memorized their parts. Basic plot outlines might also be pinned on the wings to help unprepared performers. The oldest example in the *OED* of the expression in a theatrical context is from 1885, eighteen years before Wilbur and Orville Wright winged it over the sands of Kitty Hawk, N.C.

wiseacre. A *wiseacre* is neither *wise* nor a son of the soil, although puns were being made on the *acre* part of this term for a fatuous fool soon after its appearance as *wise-aker* in the late sixteenth century. For example, Thomas Dekker joked about "Each wise-acred Landlord" in *The Wonderful Year* (1603). In fact, the meaning of the term was reversed almost one hundred eighty degrees as it entered the language. It comes from the Middle Dutch *wijssegger*, wise sayer, i.e., a soothsayer, in turn from the Old High German *wīzzago*, prophet (the OHG *wizzi* = knowledge, intellect, wit).

While people often distort the shapes of foreign words considerably while trying to shoehorn them into English (see AGITA), the reason for the dramatic change in meaning in this case is not immediately evident. The translation from *wijs-* to *wise* can be explained by assuming that the English term was intended sarcastically, like the *wise* in the modern *wise ass*, *wise guy*, and *wisenheimer*. Meanwhile, the use of *segger* in English in the fifteenth century to denote a boaster or braggart might have led to the *-aker* ending, as well as to the change in the word's overall meaning. Or it could be that *acre* exerted a subliminal influence from the beginning, considering the many terms for rural residents that have acquired pejorative meanings parallel to *wiseacre*—boor, bumpkin, clodhopper, hick, peasant, and rube, to name just a few.

witch hazel. The liniment made from the leaves and bark of this shrub may seem to have almost magical, medicinal properties, but the name of the plant has nothing to do with the people who are reputed to ride around on brooms. *Witch* here comes from the Anglo-Saxon *wice* and the Middle English *wych*, applied generally to trees with pliant branches, such as the *witch alder* and *witch* (or *wych) elm*. Meanwhile, the broom-riding *witch* comes from the Anglo-Saxon *wicce*, the feminine form of *wicca*, sorcerer, wizard. What ordinary people thought about sorcerers is evident from the fact that *wicca* also is the ancestor of *wicked*.

wog. A holdover from the great days of the British Empire, when maps of the world were colored mainly in pinkish red, this disparaging term for an Indian (meaning a Native Indian, not a Native American), an Arab, or another Oriental has been interpreted traditionally as an acronym. Almost all amateur etymologists agree on this. The only point of dispute is the original phrase. Among the chief candidates: Westernized Oriental Gentleman, Wily Oriental Gentleman, Wonderful Oriental Gentleman, Worthy Oriental Gentleman, and Working On Government Service (or Services)—the last set of initials supposedly having been emblazoned upon the shirts of native employees of the crown at Suez and points east.

In the absence of photographic or other documentary evidence, however, *wog* appears more likely to be a clipping of *golliwogg*, the name of a black-faced male doll with frizzy hair and grotesque clothes that was popularized in Britain by a series of illustrated children's books by Bertha Upton. The first of these, *The Adventures of Two Dutch Dolls—and a 'Golliwogg'*, was published in 1895. Within a dozen years, *golliwogg* and the clipped *golliwog* were being used generically, e.g., "A clever golliwogg dance received the enthusiastic applause it deserved" (*Westminster Gazette*, 5/28/1907). Ms. Upton is credited with having coined the term, perhaps by combining *golly* with *pollywog*.

It seems but a small step from the generic *golliwogg* to *wog*, recorded first in the plural in Frank Charles Bowen's *Sea-Slang: A Dictionary of the Old-Timers' Expressions and Epithets* (1929). The term is defined in this work as referring to "lower class shipping clerks along the Indian coast." Its meaning has since been broadened somewhat. For example, in *The Goon Show*, the long-running BBC program that helped make Peter Sellers a star, a *wog* was anyone who lived more than forty miles or so outside London. See also WOP.

woman. *Woman* does not derive from *man* (let alone *woe to man*), as evidently suspected by those who have proposed such desexualized alternatives as *wobody*, *woperson*, and *wo*. Rather, the word comes from the Anglo-Saxon, or Old English, *wīfmann*, where *wīf* meant "female" and *mann* referred to a person of either sex. Thus, *wīfmann* originally equaled "female human." (And there isn't any *man* in *human*, either; the latter, from the Latin *hūmānus*, translates as "earthling," based on Latin *humus*, earth, soil.)

The manly equivalent of *wīf* in Anglo-Saxon times (ca. 800–1200) was *wer*, which still shows up as a prefix in *werewolf*, that is, a manwolf. What happened in the case of *wīfmann* was that its meaning gradually was narrowed from "female human" to "female" as males co-opted the generic *mann*, making their sex seem dominant even in such technically neutral but now dangerous-to-use constructions as "Man is a tool-making animal" (an aphorism credited to Ben Franklin by James Boswell in his *Life of Johnson*). Meanwhile, the meaning of the *wif* part of *wifmann* also narrowed, being reduced from "female" to the still smaller role of "wife." See also FEMALE, HARLOT, and WENCH.

wop. This pejorative term for an Italian, especially an immigrant or a person of Italian extraction, even unto the fourth or fifth generation, is the American counterpart of WOG, having inspired almost as many acronymic etymologies as the British slur. The principal suspects: WithOut Passport and WithOut Papers, both of which supposedly refer to the way new arrivals came to the United States, and Working On Pavement, which is what many of them did after passing through Ellis Island.

The term has been dated to 1912 in the form of *wap*, a spelling that points to its probable true origin—the Neapolitan *guappo*, a tough guy, a ruffian, a flashy dresser, a swaggerer, apparently used in much the same way as the modern *dude*, as in "He's a real dude" or "Hey, dude!" *Guappo* itself is of obscure origin, but may go back, via the Spanish *guapo*, pimp, ruffian, to the Latin *vappa*, wine that has gone flat and, hence, a no-good person.

The original *waps* or *wops* (the *o* spelling has been dated to 1914) were not so different from many modern-day dudes, as evidenced by the context in which the earliest recorded example of the term appears. Thus, from Arthur Train's *Courts and Criminals* (1912):

> . . . there is a society of criminal young men in New York City who are almost the exact counterpart of the Apaches of Paris. They are known by the euphonious name of "Waps" or "Jacks." These are young Italian-Americans who allow themselves to be supported by one or two women, almost never of their own race. These pimps affect a peculiar cut of hair, and dress with half-turned-up collar . . . and have manners and customs of their own. They frequent the lowest order of dance-halls, and are easily known by their picturesque styles of dancing. . . . They form one variety of the many "gangs" that infest the city and are as quick to flash a knife as the Apaches. . . .

wormwood. Its name to the contrary, the shrub holds no particular attraction for worms, and it is not very woody, either. The term for the plant, whose bitter leaves are an essential ingredient of absinthe, comes from the Old High German *wermuota*. This word, whose etymology is not known, is ancestral to the French *vermout*, the English *vermouth*, and the modern German *wermut*. In modern German, the *wer-* = man, while *-mut* = courage, mood. The name may reflect the folk belief in the plant's aphrodisiac effects. (Absinthe, as they say, makes the heart grow fonder.)

The English *wormwood*, meanwhile, comes from the Anglo-Saxon *weremōd* or *wermōd* (ca. 725), which then was divided incorrectly, so that the *m* became attached to the first syllable, producing *wormwode* (pre-1400) and, finally, *wormwood* (1573). The plant has been used as a treatment for worms in both man and beast, but it is an open question whether the name was partly inspired by the medicinal application or the treatment was suggested by the name.

XYZ

Xmas. People frequently look down upon this abbreviation for Christmas, thinking it is irreligious, overly commercial, or just plain improper. Modern merchandisers' motives aside, however, there is nothing wrong about it from a linguistic standpoint. X has been recognized as a standard abbreviation for *Christ* since before 1100 (*OED*). The X represents *chi*, the first letter of Christ's name when spelled in Greek (*XPICTOC*, Khristos or Christos). An X also is a cross, of course. Meantime, the first two letters of Christ's name in Greek, *XP*, or *chi-rho*, often appear on church vestments and other religious paraphernalia. The X used to appear in many related abbreviations, such as *Xp̄n*, Christian; *Xp̄enned*, Christened; and *Xp̄ian* or *Xtian*, Christianity. Yet another one, from the sketch in John Aubrey's *Brief Lives* (pre-1697) of John Milton: "He was so faire, that they called him the lady of X^ts coll." As an abbreviation for Christmas, the X has been dated to 1551 in the form of *X'temmas* and to ca. 1755 in the familiar *Xmas*. See also MASS.

Yankee. The word is bound up intimately with the history of the United States, but its origin remains something of a mystery—despite the best efforts of etymologists, scholarly and non-, who have attacked the problem with energy as well as Yankee ingenuity.

First, the high spots in the word's history, so far as they are (now) known:

Yankee has been dated to the 1680s as a nickname in connection with Dutch pirates then making waves in the West Indies. The three earliest examples—"Yankee Duch" in 1683, "Captain Yankey" in 1684, and "Captain John Williams (Yankee)" in 1687—may refer to the same individual.

The term appeared in 1725 as a personal name in an estate inventory that included a "negroe man named Yankee."

In 1758, it was used as a disparaging term for Americans in general in a letter by General James Wolfe, who did not have a high opinion of the military abilities of territorial troops.

In 1765, it was recorded as a contemptuous epithet for New Englanders in particular. *Yankee trick* has been dated to 1776, and *yankee* as a verb, meaning "to cheat," to 1801.

Dutch farmers in New York especially favored the term, applying it disparagingly to residents of Connecticut. Thus, *damn Yankee* is not, as commonly assumed, a Southern coinage of the Civil War period, but a reflection of the opinion of Dutch New Yorkers of their northern neighbors. The earliest known example of the phrase comes from an anecdote in an almanac of 1798 wherein a Dutchman complains of being fooled by a "*d——d* Yankee trick."

Early in its history, the term was linked inextricably with the song "Yankee Doodle Dandy," where neither *Yankee* nor the *Doodle* was intended originally as a compliment. (*Doodle's* meanings in the slang of the time included "dolt" and "penis.") The earliest record of the song title is from America's first comic opera, *The Disappointment* (1767), probably composed by Andrew Barton, a Philadelphia merchant. The music, most likely based on an English country air, seems to have been written about 1755, during the French and Indian War. (The original lyrics varied, tending toward bawdiness; the version now sung dates from 1776.) The tune itself quickly became popular with the British army in America. It made good marching music—and a good way of razzing the colonials.

After British soldiers tarred and feathered a Boston man in March of 1775, fifers played "Yankee Doodle" as he was paraded around town. They also played it over and over again while marching to Concord the next month, April 19, to seize munitions stored there by the Minutemen. The return trip to Boston was not such a pleasant stroll, however, as rebel marksmen pursued the redcoats all the way. Flushed with victory, the Americans adopted the British tune as their own, thus turning the taunt back upon the taunters, and changing the meaning of *Yankee* for the better—in their own minds, at least.

And right away, the rebel Americans began speculating in print about the origin of the now proudly accepted name. Thus, the *Pennsylvania Evening Post* of May 25, 1775, reported that *Yankee* came from the name of a tribe of Massachusetts Indians, the Yankoos. In their language, the name was supposed to mean "invincible ones." (Alas, no other record of this puissant tribe has been preserved.)

Also interpreting the word's origin in a favorable light was William Gordon, who in his instant history of the War of Independence (published in 1788), said that the term was popularized by Jonathan Hastings, a farmer in Cambridge, Mass. Mr. Hastings, according to this account, had been in the habit of using the word in a complimentary sense as far back as 1713, referring so often to *yankee horses, yankee cider,* and other good, *yankee* things in life that Harvard students began calling him "Yankee Jonathan" and "Yankee Hastings." (Farmer Hastings really existed but, alas, it is not clear where he picked up the word, and his reputed use of it in a positive sense does not square well with its otherwise negative meanings in this period.)

A rather different view of the term's original meaning was offered by Thomas Anburey, in his *Travels through the Interior Parts of America* (1789). As a former British officer, he may have been biased. At any rate, he asserted that *Yankee* came from a Cherokee word, *eankkle*, meaning "slave" or "coward." The term was applied to New Englanders by Virginians, according to Anburey, because the Northerners had failed to aid them in a war against the Cherokees. (Alas, students of the Cherokee language have not found any other trace of this word.)

Over the years, many other Native American origins have been proposed. Washington Irving let it be known in *Knickerbocker's History of New York* (1809) that *Yankees* came from *yanokies*, silent men, a term bestowed ironically upon white settlers by the more reserved Indians. (Irving thought he was making a joke, but some people took him seriously.)

Other etymologists have suggested that the word represented a Native American attempt to pronounce *English* or *Anglais*. Among the candidates proposed as the original Indian word are *Yanghis, Yaunghees, Yengees, Yenghis, Yenkees,* and *Yinglees*. James Fenimore Cooper was in this camp, declaring in a footnote to *The Deerslayer* (1841) that *Yankee* came from the Indian pronunciation of *English* as *Yengeese*. It has even been suggested that *Yanghis, Yaunghees,* etc. are all mutilated descendants of the same Algonquian root implying "stranger." (But, alas, the various Native American tribes had different words for the English settlers, and the term, after all, cropped up first in a different context in the West Indies in the 1680s.)

Even more exotic origins have been proposed, among them that *Yankee* comes from an English dialect word, *jank*, excrement; from a Lincolnshire word for gaiters or leggings; from either of two Scots words, *yankie*, a clever, forward woman, or the related *yanking*, active, forward, pushing; from the Swedish *enka*, a widow (supposedly applied to the English because they had left their homes in Britain); and from the Dutch *janker*, howler, yelper, whiner, or *jonkheer*, a courtesy title, similar to squire (which does seem to have produced *Yonkers*, N.Y., from people's saying they were going to "the Jonkheers'," meaning the farm of Jonkheer Adriaen van der Donck).

Finally, and most remarkably, the word has been derived from the Persian *janghe* or *jenghe*, a warlike man or swift horse. This theory, which has the effect of turning *Genghis* (or *Jenghis*) *Khan* into *Warlike Chief* or *Yankee King*, was expounded in the *Monthly Review and Boston Anthology* of 1810 in a letter that supposedly came from "the pen of N—— W————, jun., Esq."—i.e., Noah Webster. The letter was a hoax, a burlesque of the dictionary maker's writings on philology, but as in the case of Irving's *yanokie*, some people didn't get the joke. The episode demonstrates at once the strength of popular interest in the origin of *Yankee* at the time and the weakness that most of us have for associating ourselves with royalty.

Thus the field is winnowed to two theories. Both posit a Dutch ancestry for *Yankee*, and most etymologists today lean toward one or the other of them.

First, *Yankee* may come from *Jan Kees*, which is a diminutive of *Cornelius* and also a variant of *Jan Kaas*, i.e., John Cheese, a nickname (parallel to the English *John Bull*) dating from the 1650s for a Dutchman in Germany and Flanders. According to the *Jan Kees* theory, first proposed in 1929 by Dr. Henri Logeman, of the University of Ghent, the nickname came to the New World when the English applied it opprobriously to Dutch buccaneers and it was then transferred with much the same intent by the New York Dutch to residents of Connecticut and points north. A difficulty with this theory is that *Kees* is pronounced "case." On the other hand, if *Kees* was misinterpreted as a plural, as has happened with other words (e.g., *Chinee* from *Chinese*, *Portugee* from *Portuguese*, and *pea* from *pease*), the resulting *yon-kay* begins to approximate that of *Yankee*.

Second is the theory that *Yankee* comes from *Janke*, Little John, the diminutive of *Jan*, having been popularized as a slur. This was accepted by the *OED* as "perhaps the most plausible conjecture" (1921), but Professor Logeman objected on grounds that the true diminutive of *Jan* is *Jantje*. The hurdle is not insuperable, however. Anticipating the professor's argument by seventy-five years, James S. Pike, the American Minister to Holland, noted in a letter to the editor of the *Boston Advertizer* (drafted 3/14/1864) that the "expression of Jan-tje as uttered in Dutch is so near in sound to our 'Yankee,' that it might readily be mistaken, or corrupted into it. The real pronunciation, as near as I am able to define it by an English spelling, is *Yant-yeh*, giving to the last *y* a slight flavor of *k* in pronouncing it." Of course, the derisive use of diminutives of personal names is standard operating procedure in interpersonal communications, e.g., *Biddy* from *Bridget* for an Irish maid, *Heinie* from *Heinrich* for a German, *Ike* or *Ikey* from *Isaac* for a Jew, *Jack* from *John* for any man whose real name is not known, among many others. Thus, it is not terribly difficult to imagine the English using this label for the Dutch, or the Dutch pasting it onto New Englanders.

In sum, both theories take into account *Yankee*'s original disparaging associations, but neither has been proven satisfactorily. One pick probably is as good as the other. The reader can decide.

zenith. A medieval spelling error has obscured the origin of the term for the point in the sky directly above one's head—and, hence, the peak, acme, or culmination of any path or course. The word derives from the Arabic *samt*, road, as in *samt ar-ra's*, road (over) the head. This was taken into Old Spanish as *zenit*, however, some nearsighted scribe apparently mistaking the *m* for *ni*. The error was perpetuated in Old French as *cenith* and then in English, where the term appears first as *cinit* (1387, *OED*) and then, in Chaucer's *Treatise of the Astrolabe* (ca. 1391), as *cenyth*. The z spelling evolved in the sixteenth century, with *zenyth* (1549) being superseded by the modern *zenith* (1592).

The medieval scribes managed to avoid making the same mistake when transliterating the related Arabic *as-sumūt*, the ways (*-sumūt* is the plural of *samt*). As a result, we now spell the term used when measuring angular distances along the horizon as *azimuth*, not *aziniuth*.

zip. When employed by Americans in Vietnam with reference to members of the indigenous population, this term of disparagement usually was interpreted as an acronym for Zero Intelligence Potential. While the acronym may well have helped popularize the expression, this has the ring of an after-the-fact explanation. After all, the Vietnamese—also called *dinks, dips, gooks, slants, slopes*, etc.—were not thought generally to be worth anything, and *zip* is just one of several z words whose meaning amounts to nothing, e.g., *zero, zilch, zot*. American students have used *zip* to refer to a zero on a test since at least 1900, and the sense of *zero* as a demeaning term for an individual is a lot older in Great Britain, e.g., "The other gentlemen are zeros" (Maria Edgeworth, *Patronage*, 1813).

ACKNOWLEDGMENTS

IN ADDITION TO the authors of the works mentioned in the bibliography, I am indebted to other individuals in many ways. In particular, I am grateful to my wife Margaret Miner, who took time out from her own busy writing schedule to read and criticize my manuscript. Her comments led to many improvements. I also wish to thank Barbara Livesey, who has a sharp eye for offbeat books and who regularly turns up ones that she knows will interest me; Tim Beard and Betty Synnestvedt, of the Hodge Memorial Library in Roxbury, who have kindly fielded requests for hard-to-obtain publications; and the late Stuart Flexner, a leading lexicographer, who was always generous with his time and advice. Thanks also are due to Jane Jordan Browne, an editorial colleague and friend long before she became my literary agent; Dore Hollander, for an excellent job of copyediting; and Brandt Aymar, an editor whose understanding is exceeded only by his patience. All authors should be so lucky as to have such a marvelous support system.

BIBLIOGRAPHY

MOST SOURCES are cited in passing in the text. The works listed here are those that have been used most frequently. I have divided them here into three groups: (1) standard and etymological dictionaries, (2) specialized dictionaries and other books about word origins, and (3) general reference works.

STANDARD AND ETYMOLOGICAL DICTIONARIES

The first and by far the most valuable reference is *The Oxford English Dictionary*, edited by Sir James Murray, and often abbreviated *OED* in the text. I have used the compact edition, published by Oxford University Press in 1971, and the four supplements to it, edited by R. W. Burchfield, and published between 1972 and 1986. The *OED* provides the most complete record available of the development of the English language, and it is hard to imagine how such a book as *Devious Derivations* could be written without continually consulting this monumental work. Other general and etymological dictionaries that were kept close at hand:

Ayto, John. *Dictionary of Word Origins.* Arcade Publishing. New York: 1990.

Barnhart, Robert K., editor. *The Barnhart Dictionary of Etymology.* H. W. Wilson Co. New York: 1988.

Flexner, Stuart Berg, editor. *The Random House Dictionary of the English Language, Second Edition.* Random House. New York: 1987.

Landau, Sidney I., editor. *Funk & Wagnalls Standard College Dictionary.* Funk & Wagnalls. New York: 1974.

McAdam, Jr., E. L. and Milne, George. *Samuel Johnson's Dictionary: A Modern Selection.* Pantheon Books. New York: 1964.

Morris, William, editor. *The American Heritage Dictionary of the English Language.* Houghton Mifflin Co. Boston: 1969.

Palmer, Reverend A. Smythe. *Folk-Etymology: A Dictionary of Verbal Cor-*

ruptions or Words Perverted in Form or Meaning, by False Derivation or Mistaken Analogy. Johnson Reprint Corp. New York: 1969. (Reprint of 1890 edition.)

Partridge, Eric. *Origins: A Short Etymological Dictionary of Modern English.* Greenwich House. New York: 1983. (Reprint of 1956 edition.)

Room, Adrian. *A Dictionary of True Etymologies.* Routledge & Kegan Paul. London: 1986.

Skeat, Reverend Walter W. *A Concise Etymological Dictionary of the English Language.* Perigee Books. New York: 1980. (Reprint of 1910 edition.)

Shipley, Joseph T. *Dictionary of Word Origins.* Philosophical Library. New York: 1945.

Weekley, Ernest. *An Etymological Dictionary of Modern English.* Dover Publications. New York: 1967. (Reprint of 1921 edition.)

OTHER SPECIALIZED DICTIONARIES AND BOOKS ABOUT WORD ORIGINS

Ammer, Christine. *It's Raining Cats and Dogs . . . and Other Beastly Expressions.* Dell Publishing. New York: 1989.

———. *Have a Nice Day—No Problem! A Dictionary of Clichés.* Dutton. New York: 1992.

Anonymous ("A Member of the Whip Club"). *Lexicon Balatronicum. A Dictionary of Buckish Slang, University Wit, and Pickpocket Eloquence.* C. Chappel. London: 1811. (In effect, the fourth edition of Grose, listed below.)

Bartlett, John Russell. *The Dictionary of Americanisms.* Crescent Books. New York: 1989. (Reprint of 1849 edition.)

Cassidy, Frederic C., editor. *Dictionary of American Regional English, Volumes 1 and 2.* Belnap Press of Harvard University Press. Cambridge, Mass.: 1983, 1991.

Chapman, Robert L. *New Dictionary of American Slang.* Harper & Row. New York: 1986.

Ciardi, John. *A Browser's Dictionary.* Harper & Row. New York: 1980.

———. *A Second Browser's Dictionary.* Harper & Row. New York: 1983.

Claiborne, Robert. *Loose Cannons and Red Herrings: A Book of Lost Metaphors.* W. W. Norton & Co. New York: 1988.

Considine, Tim. *The Language of Sport.* World Almanac Publications. New York: 1982.

Craigie, Sir William A. and Hulbert, James R., editors. *A Dictionary of American English.* University of Chicago Press. Chicago: 1938–44.

Dunkling, Leslie and Gosling, William. *The New American Dictionary of Baby Names*. New American Library. New York: 1985.

Elting, John R.; Cragg, Dan; and Deal, Ernest. *A Dictionary of Soldier Talk*. Charles Scribner's Sons. New York: 1984.

Farmer, J. S. and Henley, W. E. *Slang and Its Analogues*. Arno Press. New York: 1970. (Reprint of 1890–1904 edition.)

Freeman, Morton S. *Hue and Cry and Humble Pie*. Plume. New York. 1992.

Funk, Charles Earle. *A Hog on Ice and Other Curious Expressions*. Harper & Row. New York: 1948.

———. *Thereby Hangs a Tale: Stories of Curious Word Origins*. Harper & Row. New York: 1950.

———. *Heavens to Betsy*. Harper & Row. New York: 1955.

———. *Horsefeathers and Other Curious Words*. Harper & Row. New York: 1958.

Funk, Wilfred. *Word Origins and Their Romantic Stories*. Grosset & Dunlap. New York: 1950.

Grose, Captain Francis. *A Classical Dictionary of the Vulgar Tongue, Third Edition*. Edited and annotated by Eric Partridge. Barnes & Noble. New York: 1963. (Reprint of 1796 edition.)

Hendrickson, Robert. *The Facts on File Encyclopedia of Word and Phrase Origins*. Facts on File Publications. New York: 1987.

Holt, Alfred H. *Phrase and Word Origins: A Study of Familiar Expressions*. Dover Publications. New York: 1961.

Matthews, Mitford M., editor. *Americanisms: A Dictionary of Selected Americanisms on Historical Principles*. University of Chicago Press. Chicago: 1966.

Morris, William and Mary. *Morris Dictionary of Word and Phrase Origins*. Harper & Row. New York: 1988.

Partridge, Eric. *A Dictionary of Slang and Unconventional English, Seventh Edition*. Macmillan Publishing Co. New York: 1970.

Potter, Stephen and Sargent, Laurens. *Pedigree: The Origins of Words from Nature*. Taplinger Publishing Co. New York: 1974.

Radford, Edwin. *Unusual Words and How They Came About*. Philosophical Library. New York: 1946.

Rawson, Hugh. *A Dictionary of Euphemisms & Other Doubletalk*. Crown Publishers. New York: 1981.

———. *Wicked Words: A Treasury of Curses, Insults, Put-downs and Other Formerly Unprintable Terms from Anglo-Saxon Times to the Present*. Crown Publishers. New York: 1989.

Rees, Nigel. *Why Do We Say . . . ? Words and Sayings and Where They Come From*. Blanford Press. London: 1987.

Rogers, James. *The Dictionary of Clichés*. Facts on File Publications. New York: 1985.

Rosten, Leo. *The Joys of Yiddish*. Washington Square Press. New York: 1970.

Spears, Richard A. *Slang and Euphemism*. Jonathan David Publishers. Middle Village, N.Y.: 1981.

Urdang, Laurence. *The Whole Ball of Wax and Other Colloquial Phrases: What They Mean and How They Started*. Perigee Books. New York: 1988.

——, editor. *Names & Nicknames of Places & Things*. New American Library. New York: 1988.

Webster's Word Histories. Frederick C. Mish, editor. Merriam-Webster. Springfield, Mass.: 1989.

Weekley, Ernest. *The Romance of Words*. John Murray. London: 1912.

——. *Words and Names*. John Murray. London: 1932.

——. *More Words Ancient and Modern*. Books for Libraries Press. Freeport, N.Y.: 1971. (Reprint of 1927 edition.)

Wentworth, Harold and Flexner, Stuart Berg. *Dictionary of American Slang*. Thomas Y. Crowell. New York: 1975.

GENERAL REFERENCE WORKS

Benét, William Rose. *The Reader's Encyclopedia, Second Edition*. Thomas Y. Crowell Co. New York: 1965.

Brewer, E. Cobham. *Brewer's Dictionary of Phrase and Fable*. Revised by Ivor H. Evans. Harper & Row. New York: 1970.

Encyclopædia Britannica, Thirteenth Edition. Encyclopædia Britannica Co. London and New York: 1926.

Flexner, Stuart Berg. *I Hear America Talking*. Van Nostrand Reinhold Co. New York: 1976.

——. *Listening to America*. Simon and Schuster. New York: 1982.

Maurer, David W. *Language of the Underworld*. Collected and edited by Allan W. Futrell and Charles B. Wordell. University Press of Kentucky. Lexington: 1981.

Mencken, H. L. *The American Language*. Alfred A. Knopf. New York: 1936. *Supplement One*, 1945. *Supplement Two*, 1948.

——. *The American Language*. Abridged, with annotations and new material, by Raven I. McDavid, Jr., with the assistance of David W. Maurer. Alfred A. Knopf. New York: 1979.

Moore, John. *You English Words.* J. B. Lippincott Co. Philadelphia and New York: 1962.

Partridge, Eric. *Adventuring Among Words.* Andre Deutsch. London: 1961.

Safire, William. *Safire's Political Dictionary.* Random House. New York: 1978.

————. *On Language.* Times Books. New York: 1980.

————. *What's the Good Word?* Times Books. New York: 1982.

————. *I Stand Corrected: More on Language.* Times Books. New York: 1984.

————. *Take My Word for It.* Times Books. New York: 1986.

INDEX

bozo, 32
brassiere, 132
brass tacks, get down to, 85
brazilwood, 32
briar pipe, 2, 8, 33
bridal, 33
bridegroom, 33
bridewell, 5, 33
Bridget, 155, 224
brush-off, 79
buck, mad as a, 135
bucket, kick the, 123
buffet, 20
bug, 185
bugaboo, 27
bugbear, 27
bullet, bite the, 21
bum, 7, 34
bumbailiff, 7, 33
bum bolster, 77
bump, 84
bumpkin, 216
bunkum, 105
bunny hop, 82
bury a Quaker, 53
butler, 34
butterscotch, 2, 110
buttery, 34
buzzard, 51
B.V.D.'s, 35
by hook or by crook, 109

cabal, 4, 36
cackle, 167
caddywampus, 124
caliwampus, 124
call girl, 36
call house, 36
Cambridge, 37
canary, 78
Canary Islands, 37
Candlemas, 138
cankywampus, 124
cant, 38
cap-a-pie, 13

caravan, 211
cardinal, 38
cardinal grosbeak, 39
carte blanche, 39
cat, tabby, 197
Cat and the Fiddle, 39
catawampit, 124
catawampus, 124
cater, 124
cats and dogs, rain, 170
cat's-cradle, 41
C.D.Q., 191
cell, 180
cellar, 3, 179, 180
cereal, 188
Ceres, 187
cesarean, 41
cesarean section, 41
chafer, 46
chance, main, 135
charlatan, 42
Chauvin, Nicolas, 49
cheap, 43
cheap Jack, 43
cheap John, 42
cheapskate, 24
Cheboygan, 185
cheerio, 43
cheers, 43
cheer up, 43
chemise, 132
Chertsey, 115
Cheshire cat, grin like a, 93
chicks, 44
chili chaser, 67
chimney-piece, 83
Chinee, 223
chipmunk, 206
chippie, 43
chippy, 43
chow, 44
Christmas, 138
claptrap, 105
clench, 45
clinch, 45

goyish, 118
grain of salt, with a, 90
grass, 15, 90, 91
grass widow, 7, 90
gravel pusher, 67
Great Caesar, 90
Great Scott, 91
green meat, 104
greyhound, 91
grid, 92
gridiron, 92
griddle, 92
gringo, 7, 92
grin like a Cheshire cat, 93
groom, 33
gross indecency, 106
ground pounder, 67
guardian angel, 12
guinea pig, 5, 94
gulp, 90
gun, son of a, 190
gung ho, 94
gun mob, 97
gun moll, 97
gunner's daughter, kiss the, 190
gunsel, 97
guzzle, 90
gyp, 215

Hackney, 115
half-seas over, 99
halt, 99
ham, 99
ham and eggs, 85
hamfatter, 100
hangnail, 100
hanky-panky, 105
Hans, 101
hare, mad as a March, 135
harlequin, 100
harlot, 3, 101
Harry, Old, 101, 153
hatter, mad as a, 135
hat trick, 102
have [one's] ass in a sling, 103

haycock, 14
haystack, 14
hazard, 136
head, 132
Heinie, 224
Heinrich, 224
helpmate, 2, 103
hen, mad as a wet, 135
hick, 216
highways and byways, 110
Hill, Fanny, 76
hillbilly, 155
hit, 84
hoax, 105
hobgoblin, 101
hocus-pocus, 104
hodgepodge, 139
hogwash, 105
hoist with one's own petard, 159
hoity-toity, 110
hoke, 105
hokey, 105
hokey-pokey, 105
hokum, 105
homosexual, 105
honeymoon, 106
honky, 107
honky-tonk, 107
hoodlum, 107
hooker, 3, 108
hookers, 109
hook or by crook, by, 109
hooligan, 107, 108
hoopoe, 80, 167
hoosegow, 45
hopscotch, 2, 110
horn, 126
Hornie, Auld, 153
horse, 71
horse latitudes, 110
hotch-potch, 105
hoyden, 102
human, 217
humble pie, eat, 2, 72
hummingbird, 80

HOLOCAUST
LANDSCAPES

HOLOCAUST LANDSCAPES

TIM COLE

B L O O M S B U R Y
LONDON · OXFORD · NEW YORK · NEW DELHI · SYDNEY

Bloomsbury Continuum
An imprint of Bloomsbury Publishing Plc

50 Bedford Square   1385 Broadway
London   New York
WC1B 3DP   NY 10018
UK   USA

www.bloomsbury.com

First published 2016

© Tim Cole, 2016

British Library Cataloguing-in-Publication Data
A catalogue record for this book is available from the British Library.

Library of Congress Cataloguing-in-Publication data has been applied for.

ISBN: HB: 9781472906885
ePDF: 9781472906908
ePub: 9781472906892

2 4 6 8 10 9 7 5 3 1

Typeset by Integra Software Services Pvt. Ltd.
Printed and bound in Great Britain by CPI Group (UK) Ltd, Croydon CR0 4YY

To find out more about our authors and books visit www.bloomsbury.com.
Here you will find extracts, author interviews, details of forthcoming events and the
option to sign up for our newsletters.

For Jonathan, Jeremy and Matthew

CONTENTS